Witkacy:
21st Century Perspectives

Stanislaw Ignacy Witkiewicz
'Witkacy'
1885 – 1939

S.I. Witkacy – *Self Portrait* 1938, Pastel 70.3 x 50.4.
This is reproduced here courtesy of Silesian Museum of Poland.

S.I. Witkacy – *Multiple Self-Portrait in Mirrors* St. Petersburg 1915 -1917,
Celluloid Negative 11.7 x 16.2.
This is reproduced here with the kind permission of Stefan Okolowicz.

Witkacy:
21st Century Perspectives

Witkacy: 21st Century Perspectives

Editors:

Kevin Anthony Hayes and Mark Rudnicki

Cover Design:
Kevin Anthony Hayes

Graphic Design
Alex C. Chater

Websites:

www.witkacy2009.com
www.witkacy2010.com
www.witkacylimited.com

Personal Website:

www.kevinanthonyhayes.com

e-mail address:

director@witkacylimited.com

The Witkacy Convention and Heritage Company Limited is a Limited Company (Coy. Reg. No. 07141458) registered at:
4th Floor,
86-90 Paul Street,
London EC2A 4NE

T: +44 (0) 208-123-6850

In Gratitude:
This collection of essays was originally published in The Polish Journal of Aesthetics through the overall editorship of Professor Leszek Sosnowski under the aegis of the Jagiellonian University of Poland. The original editorial layout and typesetting was undertaken by Marcin Lubecki and printed by LIBRON. The editors of this collection would like to express their gratitude to the primary editorial board, associated staff and original publisher.

© Copyright by; The Witkacy Convention & Heritage Company
All rights reserved
ISBN- 13: 978-0992-931-711
ISBN- 10: 0992-931-711
BISAC: Literary Collections/General

Witkacy:
21st Century Perspectives

Edited By:
Kevin Anthony Hayes and Mark Rudnicki

This Collection of essays is dedicated to the memory of Professor Daniel Charles Gerould 1927-2012, a great man of formidable intellect whose life and work was and indeed is profoundly admired by the contributors to this publication and whose presence in our world is deeply missed.

Contents

	Introduction by Kevin Anthony Hayes	13
	Acknowledgements	23

The History of the Witkacy Movement

Janusz Degler	Dedication to the Founding Mother and Fathers	29
Lech Sokół	Daniel Charles Gerould (1928–2012) In Memoriam	33
Anna Brochocka	The History of the Witkacy Collection in Słupsk	39
Beata Zgodzińska	The Witkacy Collection and Exhibition at the Museum of Middle Pomerania in Słupsk	49
Stanisław Ignacy Witkiewicz	The Rules of the Portrait-Painting Firm (trans. Beata Brodniewicz)	53

Witkacy in the Realm of the Political

Daniel Gerould	Witkacy and Conspiracy Theories	59

Witkacy and Polish Modernism

Anna Żakiewicz	Witkacy's Paintings as Frozen Drama	73
Małgorzata Vražić	Witkiewicz-Father and Son: The Double Portrait	87

The Multifacated Idea of Pure Form

Michael Goddard	Cinema, Insatiability and Impure Form: Witkacy on Film	99
John D. Barlow	Witkiewicz's Theory of Pure Form and the Music of Morton Feldman	109
Gordon Ramsay	Futurism and Witkiewicz: Variety, Separation and Coherence in a Theatre of Pure Form	121

Between: Philosophy, History and Politics

Agnieszka Marczyk	The Witkacy – Cornelius Correspondence, or How to Cure Gout with Transcendental Philosophy	137
Paweł Polit	Philosophical Marginalia by Stanisław Ignacy Witkiewicz	149
Bryce Lease	Cutting the Romantic's Throat: Witkacy's Nasty Nightmare	155
Mark Rudnicki	The Profane and the Sacred in Insatiability	167

Questions of Identity in the Work of Witkacy

Ewa Wąchocka	Identity Traps in Witkacy's Dramas	177
Dorota Niedziałkowska	Witkacy's Self-Portraits as Manifestations of the Dandy Figure	189
Christine Kiebuzińska	Witkacy and Ghelderode: Goethe's Faust Transformed into a Grotesque Cabaret	207

Witkacy in Comparative Perspective

Marta A. Skwara	What is still not known about Witkacy's Intertextuality? An Analysis of Witkacy and Słowacki	221
J. Greg Perkins	Eluding the Void: Art and Humour as Anodynes for Witkiewicz, Beckett and Faulkner	237
	Annex: Witkacy's Portraits and the Słupsk Collection	249
	About the Contributors	271

11

Introduction: Homo Sovieticus and the Evolution of a Socio-Philosophical Approach to Witkacy

By Kevin Anthony Hayes

The Beginning

I think I would not be the first person to attribute profoundly serious life decisions to the influence of a teacher. The person of whom I am thinking here was to present me with a vivid account of the tragic history of the division and separation of Poland. Later in life, whilst a student of the Social Sciences, and of Sociology in particular, I was left with many questions about the nature of communism and indeed the operation of Marxist ideology throughout Russia and eastern Europe. Furthermore, when the events of the period of Polish contemporary history known as 'Martial Law' erupted I found myself both distressed and intrigued. I was to observe the period of Martial Law with rapt attention. It was only a number of years later, following many career twists and turns, when I had taken a serious interest in acting and theatre that I was to encounter Stanisław Ignacy Witkiewicz for the first time. This took place when I was cast to play Dr. Grun in a final year undergraduate student production of The Madman and the Nun whilst studying for a pedagogical qualification at the University of Reading. What astonished me most was the freshness of the language and the vitality of the dialogue, with the added spice of references to things belonging to the socio-philosophical realm. For me, a one time devotee of the Social Sciences, I was immediately drawn in, I was hooked. This was fascinating for me because the material with which I was dealing had its origins in Poland, a country locked away behind the 'Iron Curtain.' Not only this, I was captivated by the spellbinding weirdness of everything I read by Witkacy. The College Company was later to be responsible for the U.K. premiere of The Pragmatists. I played Von Telek, in this earlier and indeed even stranger play. I was left with many questions. Later with the same group of people we created a theatre group called The Random Pact Theatre Company with which I was to stage two Mrozek pieces. After what seemed like a relatively short while later I obtained a British Council-Polish Ministry of Culture and Art Postgraduate Studentship. Over the space of two years I was thereby permitted to study both Acting and Directing at the P.W.S.T. (State Higher National Theatre School) of Warsaw and subsequently of Krakow too. As is well known these have subsequently been renamed Theatre Academies. I was therefore able to take a highly memorable journey from England to Poland by train, travelling across Europe and passing through the Berlin Wall. The main goal of the mission: to study Witkacy with the aim of promoting him in the English speaking world. The year was 1986.

What you see before you in this publication has its origins in a paper initially presented at the First International Conference devoted to Stanisław Ignacy Witkiewicz at the Actors' Centre in St. Petersburg in 1993. At this time I was asked by Professor Bohdan Michalski to present a paper at the Conference on Witkacy. When asked what I wanted to contribute I casually suggested the theme of HOMO SOVIETICUS.[1] The response of the Russian authorities led me to conclude that I had found something not so immediately apparent. I had been interested in the political elements of Witkacy's work for some time. It was a topic which had at that time only been explored in a cursory fashion in English. In the presentation and subsequent article I examined a number of Witkacy's plays using the paradigm provided by Michael Heller's provocative work, The Screw in The Machine – The Making of Soviet Man. I suggest that Witkacy's plays reflect the realities of Soviet life. More specifically, I argued that the dramas, Maciej Korbowa and Bellatrix, They, Gybul Wahazar and The Anonymous Work, The Shoemakers, are quite clearly to varying degrees concerned with the operation of Bolshevism and Totalitarianism. We are given to understand society as an all-powerful machine transforming and manipulating consciousness and truth. Parallels are also made between Witkacy's super tyrants and Lenin and Stalin. There were I felt many

---

[1] This paper was first presented in St. Petersburg at the first Russian international conference on Stanisław Ignacy Witkiewicz in 1993 and again at the conference entitled Witkacy w Polsce i na świecie (trans.) Witkacy in Poland and the World which took place in Szczecin in 1999. This essay was then published in the publication bearing the same title; Witkacy w Polsce na świecie, ed. M. Skwara, Szczecin 2001 and is reproduced here courtesy of the University of Szczecin.

more aspects of the political and philosophical aspects of Witkacy's work to be considered. Alas, it was not until 2007 that I really had chance to explore these to any great deal of depth. The conclusion of these considerations found expression in the form of Witkacy 2009 with a University of Westminster event which was framed so as to explore Witkacy as a Social & Political Visionary. I was so encouraged by both the support I received as well as the response I encountered to at once consider a subsequent conference in Washington D.C. This became Witkacy 2010, which explored Witkacy's depiction of the balance of forces between the individual and society.

The Individual and Society

Through "Homo Sovieticus" I made my way to the theoretical grounding for the present volume. I think it worthwhile and, in fact, necessary to summarize the socio-philosophical stance implicit not only in Witkacy's theoretical writings, but also in his dramatic literature. In the essay I examine Witkacy's view of the individual as a fragile malleable weak and defenceless creature destined by virtue of his own frailness to fail. According to this approach, the protagonist is by and large at odds with the social forces that surround him. The world at large is an alien domain from which it is better to retreat either temporarily or permanently. This is usually attained by a number of different means: drugs, sex in excess, maniacal work, suicide, incarceration or acceptance of execution. Alternatively, man maybe a potentate, a monster capable of the most sublime evil and possessed of the most incredible super-human powers. In some ways a little more like a deity or demi-god than a mortal. In this respect women, insofar as they feature other than as background female figures tend to be possessed of power in the sexual domain.

What then is the nature of society for Witkacy? What is the relationship between it and the individual? This, I feel, is one of Witkacy's primordial fascinations, which indeed I wished to subject to interrogation. For him social forces are of the greatest potency. I felt that his works should be viewed rather as very successful dramatisations of the operation of social forces by virtue of the fact that they seem to appear to impact so profoundly on the main characters of his plays, novels, and artworks. Along with the heroes of the works, the viewer is somehow obliged to experience a sense of hysterical powerlessness in the face of social forces. This for me, however chaotic in some of Witkacy's work seems, is entirely intentional. The key features of his work reveal him to be Anti-Utopian in his outlook with clear evidence of the influence of

Spengler. Whereas it is part of the nature of Utopian analysis to identify the major elements of society and to demonstrate how they act on one another if the best of all possible worlds are to be attained, Witkacy was rather intent on showing how the worst possible world was likely to come about. Witkacy was, dare one say, at pains to show how the most horrific social reality was to come into being. Furthermore, to paraphrase Spengler, history, steadily and objectively regarded, is seen to be without centre or ultimate point of reference. It is the story of an indefinite number of cultural configurations of which Europe is only one. It is simply another of "the flowers that grow with superb aimlessness in the field".[2] For Witkacy, there also seems to be the possibility of some kind of configuration, or organizational framework which exists to integrate all individuals. Yet for Witkacy, such a framework was rather an all-powerful machine, which would devour and destroy individuality and somehow extinguish the eternal flame of human spirituality with one puff of foul smelling breath. In general terms I think that we may safely assert that he concluded that such a state of affairs would be replaced by boredom, which would last for all eternity.

Witkacy: 21st Century Perspectives

Both the London and Washington events were designed both to celebrate and to commemorate the life and output of Stanisław Ignacy Witkiewicz, whom we clearly recognise as one of Poland's most colourful personalities. A figure who was profoundly talented and diverse; a dramatist, poet, novelist, painter, photographer, art theorist and philosopher It is argued that the life and work of Witkacy has made a fundamental contribution to the existence, meaning and self expression of generations of Polish citizens and persons of a creative and reflective inclination throughout the world. His entire life was also dedicated to the promotion of new ideas and high ideals in the intellectual and artistic realm. This, of course, being the sphere of existence that makes us aware of both who we are and where we are in the cosmos. This as we know is as essential to life as the food before us on our tables.

The events also incorporated academic conferences which included presentations made by leading Witkacy scholars. Following the two conferences we now have a collection of papers which are primarily but not exclusively designed to take a socio-philosophical approach to Witkacy's

---

[2] O. Spengler, H. Werner, A. Helps, Ch. F. Atkinson: The decline of the West, New York 1962, p. 21.

work. It is therefore hoped that within the essays presented here the reader will be afforded the opportunity to experience deeper reflection and more meaningful conjecture and a greater degree of conclusiveness, than hithertofore. All of this is really courtesy of the exertions of some of the finest Witkacologists in the world. We are therefore proud to have such a wonderful mixture of perspectives from scholars who have written extensively on Witkacy to those who are at the beginning of their scholarly careers as well as those for whom he has been a leisurely pastime.

There have been only a couple of collections of essays in English on Witkacy. In 1973, The Polish Review published a special Witkacy edition (Volume XVIII, 1973, no. 1 and 2) based on the Witkiewicz Symposium. In 1985 the Polish Philosophical Quarterly, Dialectics and Humanism, produced a special volume devoted to Witkacy, including contributions from many of the leading Witkacy scholars from Poland. Since this time, there have been individual essays and chapters devoted to this multi talented artist, but there have been no collections devoted solely to Witkacy. This present collection, therefore, certainly is timely and provides a fresh perspective on Witkacy research.

It is therefore the purpose of this collection of papers to see in what way Witkacy might be viewed as relevant in socio-philosophical terms for the contemporary world whilst turning over some of the most important questions emerging from Witkacy's work. This collection of essays should be of interest to a number of groups of individuals. Those who know absolutely nothing about Witkacy might find this work a very good introduction, albeit that it is, set at quite a high level, so to speak. I think this work could certainly prove invaluable for those directly connected with the theatre; be it as an actor, director, producer or scenographer or indeed a lighting or sound technician. All I think will derive a closer sense of what Witkacy was trying to achieve. Needless to say, since so many of our contributors are theatrologists there will be much to both discover and discuss for both professionals and students alike here. The same I think to be true for practitioners and students alike in the realm of Polish literature. The collection is so diverse, interlinked and yet unified I can see the collection being of profound interest to social scientist and indeed historian alike. The contributions which concern Witkacy's Art, which usually are presented alongside so many other aspects of his thought and ouvere, will I trust prove of great interest to students and practitioners from the realm of art as well as art history.

The publication itself is divided into multiple sections. The first section, "The History of the Witkacy Movement", provides us with a number of essays that offer a unique viewpoint by detailing the many developments that led Witkacy to become not only an eternally celebrated national figure in Poland, but also an international phenomenon. In "Dedication to the Founding Mother and Fathers" Janusz Degler offers an historical perspective on many of the developments of Witkacy scholarship. Lech Sokół's essay, "Daniel Charles Gerould (1928–2012) In Memoriam", commemorates the life and work of Daniel Gerould, who sadly passed away in 2012. In his remarks Sokół provides not only much praise for Professor Gerould, but also details his contribution to the internationalization of Witkacy's work. Anna Brochocka's informative piece, "The History of the Witkacy Collection in Słupsk", describes the activity of the Słupsk Museum in functional terms and reports on the 45-year presence of the Witkacy collection in Słuspk. Beata Zgodzińska in her article, "The Witkacy Collection and Exhibition at the Museum of Middle Pomerania in Słupsk", adopts a different perspective and describes the development of the Witkacy Collection at the Słupsk Museum. It provides an account of the original acquisitions of 1965 and the subsequent additions to the collection. All in all this section provides an historical perspective on the Witkacy movement from its nascent stages right the way through to the present time which should serve as an invaluable record for both current and future researchers.

The second section, "Witkacy in the Realm of the Political", highlights the insightful investigation of conspiracy in Witkacy's work by the late Professor Daniel Gerould who was the keynote speaker of both Witkacy 2009 and Witkacy 2010. In this article, "Witkacy and Conspiracy Theories", Gerould takes an historical overview of conspiracy theories and then examines how they have been paraded in the work of Witkacy. He also considers whether or not Witkacy actively considered them a reality for him on a personal level. The third section, "Witkacy and Polish Modernism", contains two essays which examine Witkacy's relationship with Modernism in Poland. In "Witkacy's Paintings as Frozen Drama", Anna Żakiewicz applies Tadeusz Boy-Żeleński's claim that Witkacy's paintings are "theatre frozen on canvas" by examining the many characters which seem to coexist in both his paintings and dramas. Małgorzata Vražić in her essay, "Witkiewicz-Father and Son: The Double Portrait", examines the relationship between Witkacy and his father. While noting certain differences, Vražić ultimately stresses the similarities between both Witkiewicz's because the two artists shared a common view on so many ideas and matters, e.g. the crisis of culture, the death of the Polish Universum, the ideal of a high and pure art, authenticity in personal life as well as in the field of art.

The third section, "The Multifaceted Idea of Pure Form", contains three essays which explore Witkacy's famous Theory of Pure Form as it manifests itself in various mediums. Michael Goddard in "Cinema, Insatiability and Impure Form: Witkacy on Film" discusses Cinema in relation to the work of Witkacy, in particularly its absence. He refers to Witkacy's Western contemporaries as being fascinated by this increasingly dominant 20th Century medium, which Witkacy seems to have ignored despite his interest and participation in a wide range of modern aesthetic practices including painting, photography, mass produced portraits, and theatre. Goddard also presents a very succinct account of how Witkacy's work has been transmuted into the medium of Film and Television. In "Witkiewicz's Theory of Pure Form and the Music of Morton Feldman" John Barlow examines Witkacy's idea that music is a pure art form and relates it to Witkacy's reflections on the aesthetic experience. Ultimately, Barlow applies the concept of pure form to the music of Morton Feldman. Gordon Ramsey's "Futurism and Witkiewicz: Variety, Separation and Coherence in a Theatre of Pure Form" investigates Witkacy's drama The Water Hen; he ultimately observes that the drama reveals on the one hand the interruption of narrative and linear progression, and uncertainty as to existence, identity and relationship; and on the other hand the persistent continuous underlying anxiety within the characters themselves and their sense of journey and destination.

The fourth section, "Between: Philosophy, History and Politics", examines Witkacy's philosophical work as it applies to history and politics. Agnieszka Marczyk in "The Witkacy – Cornelius Correspondence, or How to Cure Gout with Transcendental Philosophy" explores how Witkacy and Cornelius in their correspondence, discussed the body as an object of philosophical speculation and personal experience. She then briefly turns to the political elements in the personal letters, and in Cornelius' recollection of the friendship during later years. Paweł Polit also investigates lesser known textual philosophical revelations in "Philosophical Marginalia by Stanisław Ignacy Witkiewicz". Based on the exhibition Stanisław Ignacy Witkiewicz – Philosophical Margins held at the Centre for Contemporary Art at Ujazdowski Castle, Warsaw, in 2004, Polit examines Witkacy's marginal notes, which were humorous, personal, and at times artistic in nature. Polit reflects upon the connections between Witkacy's artistic concepts and his philosophical thinking. In "Cutting the Romantic's Throat: Witkacy's Nasty Nightmare" Bryce Lease tackles Witkacy's The Anonymous Work. He argues that through Plasmonick's ability to overcome his love for Rosa, Witkacy moved beyond the Romantic ideals, and in fact exposes the paradox of Romanticism: freedom and desire are exclusive; the metonymic nature of desire is always-already related directly to the subject's fundamental fantasy, that inaccessible kernel which anchors the subject to his social field. Mark Rudnicki in "The Profane and the Sacred in Insatiability"argues that Bataille's division of human time into profane and sacred time is applicable to Zip's adventures as he follows sacred/erotic passions as opposed to the world of the profane/work to encounter the mystery of existence at intense moments of transgression.

The fifth section, "Questions of Identity in the Work of Witkacy", investigates in fundamentally new ways the very important notion of identity in Witkacy's dramatic literature. In her contribution, "Identity Traps in Witkacy's Dramas", Ewa Wąchocka takes a new approach to the notion of identity in Witkacy. Instead of linking Witkacy's dramas to the modernist tradition, Wąchocka uses contemporary discourse, particularly that of Lacan, to make sense of Witkacy's oeuvre. She argues that in Witkacy's world individuals may experiment with their own sense of identity with relative freedom and with the concepts of the individual ego, derived from the realms of the Social Sciences. Dorota Niedziałkowska takes a very original approach to Witkacy's activity in the realm of the self portrait in her essay, "Witkacy's Self-Portraits as Manifestations of the Dandy Figure." She examines Witkacy's self-discrediting strategy, first noted by Grzegorz Grochowski. She critically draws attention to the way in which Witkacy assumes various roles that usually have controversial cultural connotations. These include feminine self-stylization, the role of megalomaniac, snob, or amateur. In "Witkacy and Ghelderode: Goethe's Faust Transformed into a Grotesque Cabaret" Christine Kiebuzińska offers an analysis of Witkacy's Beelzebub Sonata and Ghelderode's The Tragic Death of Doctor Faustus. Kiebuzińska explores the deformation of any traces of the Faustian myth, as each playwright situates his play in a grotesque cabaret. Ultimately, both playwrights ridicule the potential of a twentieth-century Faust figure, and they also mock Naturalism in the theatre and in Witkacy's play even the possibility of a theatre of Pure Form.

The sixth and final section, "Witkacy in Comparative Perspective", provides an interesting consideration of Witkacy in relation to other writers. Marta Skwara offers an intriguing comparative analysis in her essay, "What is still not known about Witkacy's Intertextuality? An Analysis of Witkacy and Słowacki". Skwara notes Witkacy's favourable commentary on Slowacki, yet she observes that little research has been done to explore the connection. Skwara compares Słowacki's Kordian with Witkacy's John Mathew Charles the Furious and finds profound similarities in the protagonists' dilemmas and their self-referential statements. In addition, she presents an analysis of both Słowacki's and Witkacy's treatment of the motifs of 'Violence' 'A Corpse' 'A Dream' and 'A Ghost.' Greg Perkins concludes the volume with an interesting comparison of three great 20th

Century authors in his essay, "Eluding the Void: Art and Humour as Anodynes for Witkiewicz, Beckett and Faulkner". Perkins considers the extent to which art and humour acted as anodynes in the three writers' works; there is no question concerning the importance of both in their lives. Art, or engagement in the creative process, occupied the mainstay of their intellectual lives. Moreover, humour, particularly of the black variety, is a hallmark of the trio's entire oeuvre.

We are also very happy to feature the following: "Annex: Witkacy's Portraits and the Słupsk Collection". The images here are presented in black and white within the body of the text, and we have also included colour versions of the images of the portraits within the annex. It is considered remarkably important for this publication to have had the Słupsk Museum permit us include this selection of visual images from the Witkacy Collection in this volume.

Conclusion

I should like to conclude this introduction with a number of observations and reflections of a somewhat personal nature concerning the evolution of this publication. Initially, I had put a 'straw in the wind' by undertaking a workshop; Absurdism in Polish Theatre at the Riverside Studios in 2007. I was then fortunate to gain 'support' for this project from Polish Cultural Institute in London. This took the form of being able to feature the P.C.I.. Logo on publicity material as well as be featured on the P.C.I. website. This for me was of huge symbolic significance. This support from the then Director of the P.C.I. Paweł Potoroczyn, suggested the possibility of further developments. Subsequently in September 2007 I then presented him with a one page document bearing the heading Witkacy 2009. In the form of a list I had set out everything that I thought should be included in an event which aimed to commemorate seventy years since the death of Witkacy. This initial list included performances, film viewings, an international conference, art contests, acting workshops and so on. In a sage and cautionary manner Pawel looked me directly in the eye whilst placing his hand across half the page, masking half the list as he did so, and suggested that if I were to complete even this much I would really have achieved something spectacular.

Throughout the past 25 years I have seriously endeavoured to work across cultural boundaries; I have acted, directed, produced and indeed translated and worked as a journalist in print, radio and television. Whilst bringing many things of English origin to Poland the reverse has been harder to achieve, and I have made many, attempts. I therefore saw

Witkacy 2009 as almost the last opportunity to achieve this and I felt that I was uniquely placed to effect this. In the past, the various theatre companies I had created somehow lacked the appropriate weight to develop sufficient momentum to make sufficient headway. In terms of major institutions I was certainly non-aligned so I needed a to create a formal entity that would have sufficient gravitas to achieve the desired effect. Witkacy had his Portrait Painting Firm and I would have what has now become The Witkacy Convention and Heritage Company Limited. I do not think we would be able to present this collection of essays without either this entity, the U.S.A. Interns, the Polish Volunteers, our supporting organisations and indeed our dear contributors and my fine Co-Editor Professor Mark Rudnicki.

So at last I am pleased to say that I feel that I have finally achieved what I set out to do more than 25 years ago. Strangely, many things have happened to me along the way and I have had some wonderful experiences and met some fascinating people. I have built strong relationships with leading members of the Witkacy Movement many of whom are contributors to the present volume. So in the end, it seems that I have accomplished much on that original list and perhaps much more. I am now very proud to see the result of these labours in written form in the present publication. My hope is that many more people are now familiar with the work of this fascinating thinker, writer, and artist. And so, it is with great pride I introduce such an incredible collection of essays!

Acknowledgements

At the risk of labouring a point I need to provide a context to express my gratitude to so many. Therefore, I should like to note that the contributions which are included within this inaugural volume were originally conference papers presented at Witkacy 2009 in London and Witkacy 2010 in Washington DC. There are a number of exceptions to this and in these cases it is made explicit in the body of the text itself. It must be stressed that neither the conferences nor indeed this collection of essays would have been possible without the active support of a considerable number of people and organizations. In all fairness I should like to take this opportunity to express my gratitude to them all.

Due to the fact that Witkacy 2009 was part of the Polska! Year our greatest thanks must be expressed for the support of the ultimate patrons of the Polska! Year who were; Her Majesty the Queen Elizabeth the Second and His Excellency the then President of Poland Lech Kaczyński, who, along with so many others, was tragically lost to the world in the Smolensk Air Disaster of 2010.

Furthermore, thanks are due to Paweł Potoroczyn, one time Director of the Polish Cultural Institute of London and subsequently Director of the Adam Mickiewicz Institute which co-ordinated the Polska! Year. In this context our thanks are also due to the subsequent Director of the P.C.I. Roland Chojnacki for opening Witkacy 2009 as well the then Deputy Director Anna Trych-Bromley, the Head of Literature Magda Raczyńska, Head of P.R. Karolina Kołodziej and Head of Events, Paulina Latham. In addition, gratitude should be expressed to those public figures who championed Witkacy 2009 and its broader cross cultural aims through their patronage. These are the one time M.P. and now present Shadow Lord Chancellor Baroness Angela Smith and the then Minister of Local Government and Communities the Right Honourable Sadiq Kahn M.P.

Above all there is a profound debt in particular to The University of Westminster: The Provost and Vice-Chancellor Dr. Myszka Gużkowska, her Personal Assistant Andrula 'Andy' Annis, and the Head of Marketing Sarah Carthew. I wish to extend this as well to all of the site staff in particular Vincent Gwiazda, as well as other University' facilitators including Lauren Plumb and Frances Poulton and indeed Des O' Connor, Alan Rothby, Barry Sims and John Vickery. I should also like to thank Havila

Peck the Director of the Centre for Interpreting and Translation. I greatly appreciate the use of facilities of the University which were extended on a Pro Bono basis for almost a year and subsequently for all of the events which comprised Witkacy 2009. The whole project was treated with utmost kindness and respect by the University Staff at a difficult time due to a massive renovation project and then current streamlining of the organizational structure of the University.

Thanks are also due to Poland's Minister of Foreign Affairs Radosław Sikorski and the staff of the Department of Public and Cultural Diplomacy: The Director Aleksandra Piątkowska and Deputy Director Mariusz Brymor as well as Second Secretary Anna Matysiak and other present and previous staff of the Sekretariat of the Ministry including Zbigniew Petrow and Anna Bogusz. The support of the Ministry has been and continues to be of profound importance for a project of a nature such as this.

In this context thanks are also due to Her Excellency Barbara Tuge-Erecińska then acting in her capacity as Polish Ambassador to Great Britain at the Court of St. James. Similarly I was very grateful to have received such frequent support and encouragement from Counsellor Robert Szaniewski and Marie Kato the Public Relations Specialist. I was always made to feel very welcome at the Polish Embassy and the kindness shown to me was a great source of confidence. Profound thanks are also due to the then Polish Ambassador to the United States of America in Washington D.C. His Excellency, Robert Kupiecki. None of this would have been possible without the active support of Małgorzata Szum presently Cultural Attache at the D.C. Polish Embassy. Thanks are also due to The Kościuszko Foundation, in particular the Executive Director Alex Skoroczyński and the staff past and present including the then Director of the now absorbed Polish Cultural Center of America, Patricia Hill as well as the then Washington Representative of the Kościuszko Foundation, Marta Gongora. To have been furnished with such a splendid venue and such continual and genuinely wonderful support under somewhat difficult circumstances was and indeed still is truly appreciated. The success of the London event was very much helped by Professor Jenny Plaistow of Hertfordshire University who was Deputy Director of Witkacy 2009. This formidably talented conference organiser gave so much of her experience and time to the event and left me free to direct the featured plays and undertake other administrative work. The whole project and the wider dissemination of knowledge about Witkacy owes much to her.

It should be made known that to a considerable extent Witkacy 2009 was made possible through the active involvement of a group of American Interns who were on placement with the project for a ten week period. They all had different talents and also endeavoured and indeed succeeded in making a positive input in different ways and I know that they derived a great deal from the experience and all of these received a fine certificate bearing the Witkacy 2009 design as well as a letter of commendation. The Interns were as follows; Heidi Gosen, Monique Guz, Lauren Jansen, Yelena Kart, Gina Nigrella, Samantha Smink, Agata Szymańska, Yun Chu Su ' Sue', Joey Weizenecker and Ryan Zeman. I am really very grateful to Andrea Hulme the Internships Coordinator of the Business Experience and Internships Unit for her support and assistance in this respect. The Interns were eventually succeeded by quite a number of largely Polish volunteers who worked on different aspects of the project and indeed worked without pay in a really genuine and committed way and collectively enabled the whole project come to a momentous conclusion. Some of these in particular should be singled out for a special mention because of their exceptional dedication; Sylwia Krason, in particular, Sylwia who is a really talented Arts' Administrator and Curator, worked on the project from start to finish. Further I should like to thank: Małgorzata Krzynowek, Anna Mednik, Anna Perszewska, Agnieszka Szara, Agata Szymańska, Urszula Wilk, Sylwia Włodarczyk and Andrew Wiza. All of this in turn was made possible by the staff of the Community Volunteering Unit Managed by Richard Pitts and his Administrative Assistant, San Kwan Phung. Thanks are also due to the staff & students of the Quintin Kynaston School in the London Borough of Westminster for enriching the London event by providing us with a fine 'Witkacy' Style Portrait Exhibition.

I should also like to convey a big thank you to all of those who participated in and contributed to the Witkacy 2009 performances of Witkacy's Madman and the Nun and Mrozek's Out at Sea. In particular I should like to thank John Soul for his relentless hard work as Stage Manager and support as a long standing personal friend. Thanks are also due to the Film Director & Producer Wiktor Grodecki for permission to screen his film, INSATIABILITY, at both Witkacy 2009 & Witkacy 2010.

This publication is also indebted to Paulina Rudnicka for her help with translations, and, more importantly, her overall support and encouragement throughout the Washington DC conference and subsequent development of this collection. Simon Messing and Ania Paluchowska-Messing were of great help with style edits and with translations. Profound thanks are also due to Hanna Bondarewska, the Artistic Director of the Ambassador Theater International Cultural Center in Washington D.C. (http://www.aticc.org/home/), who produced a wonderful staged reading of Witkacy's Country House (W Małym Dworku). The performance was based on Daniel Gerould's translation, and it was directed by Robert McNamara. Profound thanks are also due to Anna Juda who provided considerable help with translation work.

In relation to Design, Marketing, Promotion and Publicity I should like to mention a number of key individuals and organizations. Firstly, much of what has been achieved has been possible very much due to the world wide web. In this respect I have been really lucky to have been blessed with some remarkably good web site designers who have helped me find some really intelligent and indeed artistic solutions to quite complex questions. Chronologically these were Nicholas Milenkovic, Sam Coult and of overwhelming importance, Daniel Nugent who patiently taught me so much about website design and whose inventiveness in this realm I consider second to none. Printing was undertaken by Solopress Ltd. who always provided a really efficient and excellent service. Furthermore in this context Professor Mark Rudnicki and I were very grateful to Deseo Web Designs Studio who produced such a wonderful programme for Witkacy 2010. Likewise, thanks are due to Professor Marek Średniawa for introducing this company to the project as well as encouraging Polish side contributions to the event. All in all I must add that throughout the six years of the endeavours involved in this project I have been wonderfully supported by Alex Chater. Alex is an extremely talented Artist, Photographer and Printmaker to whom I am indebted to for his technical realisation of very many graphic design aspects of this project including both the Witkacy 2009 & Witkacy 2010 logos. In this context thanks must be expressed to Marcin Lubecki at the University Publisher for his remarkable forbearance and patience. I should also like to thank the following journalists and broadcasters for their fine reportage and publicising of the activities and the events. Here I am thinking of Jarek Sepek of Cooltura Magazine, based in London, Ela Sobolewska of Nowy Czas, Tom King of The Evening Echo, Yvonne Williams Director of Gateway Radio, George Matlock & Artur Skupieński of Radio Orla and The Third Programme of Polish Radio as well as The London Review of Books. Finally here, Dominik Ciechowski associated with the Barbican Centre of London for his kind advice in relation to such matters.

In endeavouring to promote Witkacy I sought not only the support of a number of significant individual professionals I sought also to promote important institutions and organizations. I have been very grateful to have been granted the privilege of featuring a link to many of these on the Witkacy websites as well as being featured on their websites. Those that have not already been featured include the following; the staff of the sadly discontinued Discovering Poland Magazine, Edward Robinson, Chairman of Capacity Building Solutions, Londynek Net, Director Anna Surniak at The Tatra Museum, Jonathan Rush at Jonathan Rush P.R. Consultancy, Jacek Winnicki Executive Board President and Monika Tkaczyk Executive Board Secretary, both of Poland Street, The Phoenix Club of

Acknowledgements

London, Rafał Skąpski at P.I.W. (The State Publishing House), Mieczysław Jaroszewicz Director of The Museum of Middle Pomerania in Słupsk, for his unswerving support and permitting the reproduction of so many wonderful portraits, The Centre for Contemporary Arts of Warsaw, The Polytechnic of Wrocław, the Mayor of the City Council of Słupsk, Maciej Tadeusz Kobyliński, and my professional body, The Polish Association of Theatrical Artists (Z.A.S.P.) and Dorota Buchwald of The Theatre Institute of Warsaw, Kristian Godlewski of The Bones Theatre Company, The Riverside Studios of London, The Stary Theatre of Kraków, Cricot II of Kraków, Samuel French and Diogenes of Zurich, Ivor Benjamin President of the Directors' Guild of Great Britain for his advice and support and The Writers' Guild of Great Britain.

Separately, I should also like to extend a hearty thank you to all those who have provided excellent food throughout the festivals and associated events. Here I am thinking of the Baltic Restaurant & the Knajpa both of London and the Washington D.C. caterers Danuta Konefal of Creative European Cooking.

I also extend my gratitude to many friends who have supported me including the author Phillip Gillet for advice on publishing matters. I should also like to thank the Film Director David Fairman who has always been a fine friend and a useful source of advice and information. Furthermore, I thank Terry Haynes for all his help in I.T. matters, and Jonathan Sleight for his useful remarks, as well as Gerry Taylor and his parents Mr & Mrs Taylor for all their support and kind words of encouragement. I should like to thank my old friend and vocal tutor the Opera Singer David Wilkinson. Likewise I should like to mention Rafał Walewski a former student of mine, always ready to pitch in and help out whenever required. I should also like to thank two of my sisters: Angela, as well as Susan, in particular for her spiritual support as well as my eldest brother Phillip for his business acumen and marketing advice.

There are also a number of other persons and institutions who truly deserve a really separate and special mention. One of these is Verity who has been alongside me since 2006 and has provided unrelenting moral and indeed personal support. Much the same is so true of the Co-Editor Mark Rudnicki of The George Mason University who has had to endure so much with fortitude and patience since we decided to launch Witkacy 2010. Likewise we are all very grateful to Professor Leszek Sosnowski and the Jagiellonian University for providing us all with such a wonderful opportunity to publish this very important collection of essays.

The very last words of thanks must be extended to both Barclays Bank as well as The Royal Bank of Scotland. Barclays Bank provided me with a Career Development Loan for what was initially to have been a Doctorate. The Royal Bank of Scotland must be heartily thanked for providing a Small Business Loan to Witkacy 2009 Limited, which they then effectively extended to The Witkacy Convention and Heritage Company Limited. In the case of the R.B.S., I know that these projects and this publication have received support at the highest levels of the R.B.S. Group. They should be publicly commended for this. Though operating indirectly the Banco Santander Group has also demonstrated itself to be remarkably considerate too, for which I am most grateful.

Finally, I should like to state that every effort has been made to ensure that all of the information presented here is both accurate and complete. Clearly, with so many individuals and organizations involved over such a long period of time the risk of inaccuracy or omission may have arisen. Therefore, I should like to express my apologies to anyone concerned should this have taken place in any particular cases.

Kevin Anthony Hayes

Witkacy: 21st Century Perspectives

Prof. Janusz Degler

Dedication to the Founding Mother and Fathers[1]

Dear Friends,

I am taking the liberty of greeting you all in such a manner although I don't know all of you personally. For sure, you would have been greeted in such a fashion by Anna Micińska, who sadly is no longer with us.

Indeed, it was Anna who always wanted us to be one big family connected by friendship mutual trust, and the desire to help each other.

That in fact is how it was and that is how it is now. There were never conflicts, competition, or academic egoism between us, which is so common in many circles. We are always ready to work together and share what we know and what we have. Perhaps, this is why they have called us the 'Masons' or the 'Witkacy Mafia.' Put simply, Witkacy joins us and does not separate us.

It is worthwhile to briefly say how all of this began. We have to go back to 1968 and remember a small room in the Institute of Arts of the Polish Academy of Arts and Sciences in Warsaw, where the editorial office of the Theatrical Notebook (Pamiętnik Teatralny) is located. With the occasion of the thirtieth anniversary of the death of Witkacy approaching, it was decided

---

[1] This article is based upon a pre-recorded presentation which was made in Poland and then screened at Witkacy 2010 in Washington D.C. and has been translated by Kevin Anthony Hayes.

to publish a monograph dedicated to the artist. I was assigned to prepare this monograph. I also had to prepare a history of the Formistic Theatre which Witkacy ran between 1925 and 1927. I travelled to Zakopane in order to find materials relating to this theatre in the Tatra Museum. I didn't find any documents, but I got to know 'Dunia' Micińska. Shortly thereafter, in the editorial office of 'Theatrical Notebook' I met Lech Sokół; together we were assigned the task of working on the more important biographical texts about Witkacy.

During the course of a further visit to the editorial office, I met Dan Gerould and Krzysztof Pomian and, together with Konstanty Puzyna, a firm friendship was established between us all. This is how the founding group of Witkacologists came into being. Soon, we were joined by Alain Van Crutgen, Bohdan Michalski, and Irena Jakimowicz.

From 1969 the "Theatrical Notebook" played a pivotal role in the reception of the work of Witkacy. Two texts in particular were of exceptional significance. The first of these was Philosophical Reflections, which demonstrated the close relationship between Witkacy's philosophy and his creative work. Then in a famous article, In the Valley of Nonsense, Konstanty Puzyna demonstrated the infertile and empty thought and indeed thoughtlessness seen in the staging of Witkacy up till that time and sent out the call that the theory of Pure Form must be left on the shelf. It was seen as necessary to connect with the philosophy of history and start to perform the plays as 'God ordained,' instead of repeating nonsense on the stage as if such a thing were the intention of the author. Some theatre directors listened to him and many excellent performances appeared, among these were Jerzy Jarocki's The Shoemakers and The Mother, Erwin Axers's The Mother, Maciej Prus's Jan Maciej Karol Hellcat and The Shoemaker and Krystian Lupa's Dainty Shapes and Hairy Apes and The Pragmatists.

Sometimes, I am asked how it happened that Witkacy, in such a short time achieved such a world wide career, and was translated into a dozen or so languages, such that his plays started to be performed in every European country, as well as in the United States, Australia, Brazil, Japan and Egypt.

For sure there were many factors which caused this to come about – political and social, cultural and artistic. I think, however, that without our collaboration, this career would not have been so fast and effective. I remember that I sent a dozen or so people from various countries perhaps ten examples of the 1972 second edition of The Dramas.

However, a decisive role was played by several people. The translations of Daniel Gerould paved the way for Witkacy on the stage in every Anglo--Saxon country. In the 'seventies he was one of the most frequently played authors in American university theatres. Daniel Gerould's book; Witkacy: A Study of Stanisław Ignacy Witkiewicz as an Imaginative Writer to the present day remains an excellent introduction to both Witkacy's biography and literary work. We frequently use the Polish translation of the book.

Thanks to the translations of Alain van Crugten, the plays of Witkacy can be performed in the theatres of France, Switzerland, and Belguim. At this juncture we cannot possibly omit the contribution of Vladimir Dimitrijevici's Lausanne publishing house in Switzerland, L'Age d'Homme. Through his fascination with Witkacy, he endeavoured and succeeded in publishing everything that had ever been written by him. Furthermore, from 1976 he published the journal dedicated to him called Cahiers Witkiewicz.

As a director and translator Witkacy was promoted by Giovanni Pampiglione in Italy. His work was translated into Spanish and Catalan by Josep M. de Sagaar – into Dutch by Karol Lesman, into German by Heinrich Kunstmann, into Hungarian by Gracia Kerenyi and into Croatian by Dalibor Blazina. Through some 25 years all of Witkacy's literary works have been translated and published in Russia by Andrzej Bazilewski.

An important role in the popularization of Witkiewicz has also been played by international conferences dedicated to him. The first of these took place in March of 1978 in the Cyprian Norwid Theatre in Jelenia Góra. I'm pleased to say that there is in existence even today a filmed recording of the session along with fragments of the excellent performance of Dainty Shapes and Hairy Apes directed by Krystian Lupa. In Jelenia Góra at that time the entire international Witkiewicz group met. Unfortunately, some of the members are no longer with us. Then, in February of 1980 there was a symposium in Pisa, followed by another in Brussels in November of 1981. The next was to take place in New York, but the Declaration of Martial Law in Poland made this impossible. We all met again in 1985 in Warsaw on the occasion of the Year of Witkacy promoted by U.N.E.S.C.O. Then, there was the first symposium in Słupsk in 1994 which was followed by Szczecin in 1999.

I am so sorry that I am not able to be together with you all. I wish you all inspiring debates and discussions. Support each other beautifully. This is just what Witkacy deserves!

Lech Sokół

Daniel Charles Gerould (1928–2012) In Memoriam

In Honour of his Life and Work[1]

I know exactly when I became acquainted with Daniel Gerould and I have an appropriate document to prove this. This is the first published volume of his English translation of Witkacy's plays and it contains the following dedication: "To Mr. Sokół, in appreciation and great pleasure at sharing our mutual enthusiasm for Witkacy – Daniel Gerould May 8th 1969." The book was published in 1968. When the dedication was written in this book, Daniel was 41 years old; I had not yet reached thirty and was preparing to complete a doctorate on Witkacy which I was to finish in 1973. At that time the presence in Warsaw of an American professor, translator and publisher of Witkacy in the United States was an unthinkable event and belonged almost to the realm of fantasy. This volume and subsequent translations, as well as his publications about Witkacy, at once became the decisive turning

---

[1] A longer version of this recollection was first published in Polish in Dialog 2012, no 5 (May), and was translated and edited by Kevin Anthony Hayes.

point in the reception of Witkacy's work outside Poland. It is impossible to overestimate the value and the significance of Daniel's work. I should like to say that we were connected by a relationship which I would call true friendship. It was a relationship between that of a master and a student. The student obtained much from this and remains indebted to the master. I recollect this at once because I wanted to underline the tone of my recollections: recollections of a man immeasurably dedicated to Polish culture, a person of great amiability in relation to others, endowed with a sense of humour, with immense knowledge and sensitivity in the realm of literature, theatre and art, a person of great value who played an enormous part in my life.

We met together in Daniel's office in the English department of Warsaw University in a tightly packed complex of buildings on Krakowskie Przedmieście which was where he was based at that time. The weather was beautiful and the conversation about Witkacy was conducted in English but it frequently moved to Polish which was good for both of us. Yet at that time I was pleased to talk about the apparent particular influence of Edgar Allan Poe on the early dramas of Witkacy and the inheritance of Young Poland. We very frequently returned to the presence of his poetry and prose in the work of Witkacy, in Poland, in France and in Europe. We were interested in French culture and literature, at that time in particular the symbolist art movement which also connected us both then and indeed to the end of our friendship. Fascinated by Witkacy, he at once began to learn Polish and set about work on translations.

I would argue that if Witkacy almost conquered the world, it happened to a great extent because of the translations and work of Daniel Gerould. This assertion doesn't undervalue and doesn't detract from the work of other Witkacologists who took his works to audiences and made it available in more than 30 languages. The vast majority of performances were in fact stagings of Daniel's translations or translations into different languages of his translations. In the early months of 1981 his book, Witkacy – Stanisław Ignacy Witkiewicz as an Imaginative Writer, was published. The book was also published in Polish by the State Publishing House (P.I.W.) in November of 1981. The publications were in effect prepared in parallel using a Xerox copy of the manuscript sent both to the American publisher and to the Polish publisher and translator. The creative work of Daniel Gerould was extremely diverse as it embraced not only Witkacy and academic work. He was also the author of several plays; one of them was translated into Polish by Grzegorz Sinko and published in Dialog. Witkacy belongs nonetheless to one of the most important authors which interested him through a very long period of time. After all it was he who brought about the international revolution in Witkacology and introduced the work of the author of The Shoemakers into the wider cultural space of the English speaking world. Daniel Gerould created a research programme of an interdisciplinary character which he developed and continued to the end of his life. There are many remaining tasks for the programme and there is still much to be done. As opposed to us so suffering internally from the Polish inferiority complex, Daniel had a natural way of seeing the universal in Witkacy and the culture of so called Central Eastern Europe. In relation to Witkacy he took a point of view that which would be difficult for us to embrace and maybe not even to achieve. He perceived things and matters unimaginable for us. Like every foreigner he taught us native Poles something new. He was an original thinker and was possessed of great imagination: this is something which ranks very highly in my system of values. Regardless of many fundamental issues he had introduced our consciousness to, he woke up the imagination of his readers and provoked them to think. His books about Witkacy and his numerous excellent studies and articles maintain that strength even up until his last text about Witkacy which was presented at the conference in Washington in May of 2010. I have this article in my computer and of course I've read it and it bears the impressive title: Witkacy and Conspiracy Theories and it addresses themes which have only been touched upon superficially and occasionally by researchers. To conclude a complicated matter succinctly, I would like to state the obvious: to write about Witkacy without mentioning the accomplishments of Daniel Gerould is totally impossible: such Witkacology would be markedly deficient.

It is essential to mention, albeit briefly, his other literary output. This of course cannot be an exhaustive list. I have had some of his work with me for many years and I have learnt a great deal from it. This is true above all from the work which I recollect. Among his literary output Daniel had much editorial work of great worth. Usually, his work took the form of an ingenious translation, commentary and authors introduction to such work. Through 25 years he was the publisher and author of the journal Slavic and East European Performance. The last official letter that he sent to subscribers was dated December 2011 and it was signed from 'The Director of Publications and Academic Affairs.'

It is also necessary to mention another book alongside those concerned with Witkacy which Daniel Gerould had published in Polish, which unfortunately met with little response. In English it bore the title: The Guillotine – Its Legend and Lore, 1992. It is the author's excursion into the field of cultural history. The history of the guillotine has intertwined itself and its reflection in literature and art, from the serious to the popular. I was a chance witness of the birth of his interest in the theme of the book. In 1989 I was in New York for three months on scholarship provided by the

Kościuszko Foundation and we went together to an exhibition dedicated to the French Revolution of 1789, in which the main exhibit along with the documents of the epoch was the original guillotine. At that time Daniel already had a considerable knowledge concerning this terrible invention.

It is not possible to understand Daniel without his wife Jadwiga Kosicka, translator of Polish literature into English and the author of interesting dissertations, commentaries and introductions to translated texts of literary experts and many other personal manifestations. When I think of Daniel I normally see them together, although I became acquainted with Jadwiga rather one or two years after I had met Daniel. To complete their particular type of partnership was the excellent cat Tomek; this is a wonderful example of the extent to which the presence of a cat becomes nature's true reflection of people's true dignity. All three should really be shown against the backdrop of their own specific scenery. In order to know Daniel more closely it was necessary to meet him in his own backwoods, or rather both in New York City as well as in the town of Woodstock in the State of New York about two and half hours away by car. In the late 1980's Daniel spent normally half a week in Woodstock and Jadwiga was there for a longer time period and remained in their houses which were about 6 km from the town. The houses there were set out quite a long distance apart from each other, hidden in the woods, and normally invisible behind the greenery. The forest allotments were quite extensive and protected from noise and intrusion. Animals and birds were not fenced in and felt safe. On their land it was possible to see various birds and animals and I managed to almost befriend a family of wild turkeys. For me, to see them indolently take off was such an exotic sight.

Next to the house, arranged in levels slowly rising up the hill, Jadwiga's 'Polish' garden could be found: tomatoes, carrots, parsley, and flowers arranged in an irregular semicircles bordered by stones. In a very comfortable and well planned library, computers and a music centre could be found. Guests had a separate little house for themselves. Here once again there was an enormous quantity of books in several languages, and comfortable sleeping accommodation. The books interfered with sleep because there were so many and they were so unusual. All around there was wonderful and endless peace. In the morning, though not too early, Jadwiga would call me for breakfast from the doorway. To be a guest in such a household was extraordinarily pleasant. Their hospitality was excellent but – which also bears witness to their excellence – immeasurably discreet caring and feeling without the least pressure or, as we might say today, domination. They always had enormous empathy, delicacy and sensitivity. We made some very memorable visits to the town centre when Daniel was free. My one and only short stay in Woodstock belongs to the most marvelous American memory; of all my enjoyable stays in the United States it was extraordinarily enjoyable and successful. For sure it is not easy to give a full picture of these recollections and although to some degree I managed to repay the debt of hospitality. In Woodstock, their extraordinary relationship with people was made apparent. It revealed discretion, goodwill, and warmth and willingness to help in whatever need. I am grateful for his inspiration which introduced me to the spirit of American culture, and indeed both New York and at the same time European culture too. I know that they helped many others too; including Konstanty Puzyna, a brilliant theatre critic and Witkacy specialist, who was able to go to New York to work on his doctorate. He also helped my son who undertook his doctoral studies there and now works at the New School for Social Research in New York City. The list of the grateful is very long.

The 1990's did not really help our personal contact. Through almost 6 years I lived and worked in Norway and I didn't participate in any Witkacy conferences and I couldn't meet with Daniel and Jadwiga during their stays in Poland. However, I met her two or three times in Warsaw. I saw Daniel only after a gap of many years during a memorable stay in Chicago in 1998. Several times we planned a meeting, but it never came about.

During the winter of 2011–2012 Daniel had taken ill several times, but then recovered and felt much better, and it seemed as if the difficult times had passed. He passed away in the night between the 12th and 13th of February in 2012 in New York. We were going to meet in June of 2012, of course, in New York...

Anna Brochocka

The History of the Witkacy Collection in Słupsk[1]

This text is an endeavour to report on the 45-year presence of the Witkacy Collection in Słupsk. This presence is shrouded in a series of events, which developed into a coherent whole and is indeed intertwined with the history of the town. This has taken place with such strength that at present Witkacy is associated with Słupsk in the same way that he is associated with Kraków, Warsaw and Zakopane. Słupsk, a city which he never visited, has now become his second home and, most importantly, an important research centre devoted to his work.

It is also important to highlight that this text is written from the standpoint of an individual whose relationship with Witkacy is somewhat perfunctory. As an assistant to the curator of the collection there is little involvement in substantive work; however, there is involvement in the popularization of the collection as well as educational and administrative work. Hence, much of what is presented here, based upon observations from a distance so to speak, provides the opportunity to evaluate and to summarize many activities.

---

[1] This article was originally presented in summary form at Witkacy 2010 in Washington D.C. and has been revised and translated by Kevin Anthony Hayes.

The bringing of the first 110 works of art, which belonged to the collection of Birula-Białynicki, to Słupsk in 1965 was an attempt to build a Polish identity in the "New Poland." Following the Second World War, one of the aims of political propaganda was the popularization of culture in the territories which returned to the 'motherland.' It was a time when numerous initiatives were implemented in Słupsk in order to instill a new tradition in the territories which had been subject to Prussian or German influence for a number of years. This tradition was, of course, not foreign to people who lived in these territories after 1945.

In a short period of time, the collection of work by Stanisław Ignacy Witkiewicz became the primary exhibition at the Słupsk museum. Interest in it eclipsed other collections – those of contemporary and ancient art as well as ethnographic and archival collections. Because of its popularity, the Słupsk Museum is often mistakenly called the Witkacy Museum in Słupsk.

Since 1982, the Słupsk Museum has a permanent exhibition of Witkiewicz's work. It is so far the only monographic exhibition of the artist. The present exhibition, which was established in 1988, has at any one time more than 125 works of art on display, which is more than in all of the other Witkacy collections in Polish museums combined. Annually, some of the works on display are replaced with others. This is mainly due to the requirements of conservation and the need to vary the exhibition.

The presence of the collection in the city was more successful than expected. Above all, the proximity of Ustka – the local resort - meant that the exhibition is seen by a decidedly wider audience than just those living in Słupsk or in nearby towns and villages. The audience now includes people from all over Poland as well as tourists from other countries. This also led to the artist attracting broad interest outside the museum. The subject of Witkacy has been taken up by other institutions – the cultural centres as well two leading theatres in Słupsk. For several years, the Słupsk City Council features the Witkacy collection in its promotional strategy. Therefore, the Witkacy Collection's functions can be divided into three areas: it is an exhibition which popularizes the activities of the museum, it supports the cultural and educational activities of other institutions, and it plays a role in promotional activities of the City of Słupsk.

The Museum's Activities

Witkacy's presence in Słupsk has meant that in addition to basic operations, such as organizing, compilation, and display, the museum has had to manage with considerable public interest which the collection attracted. Guided tours and access to the collection have adopted a special form, the aim of which is to prepare the audience for the proper reception of the artworks. According to the curators, Witkacy's artworks, which are highly complex, can be received only through an appropriate lens and by comprehending the thoughts that guided the artist. At the very outset the Museum rejected an unreflective approach and to the present day every effort is made to educate the visitors. This teaches both the young as well as adults how to appreciate art. For many years, the work at the Museum has been substantive and not based on contemporary approaches to advertising and profit-making which is consistent with the law governing museums.

Within the framework of the educational activities, museum classes and lectures are organised and conducted at the exhibition. Such meetings are taken up mainly by schools from Słupsk and across Poland. Meetings are also organized for other groups – the University of the Third Age, the Society of Friends of the Central Pomeranian Museum in Słupsk, and the Polish Tourist Country-Lovers' Society. Every few months meetings open to the public are also organized. On such occasions, lectures are frequently enriched by a slide show, presenting works from other collections.

Substantive tasks are also realised through publication and ongoing development of the collection. The fundamental publication is the museum's catalogue of collections. The first of these, authored by Anna Krzyżanowska-Hajdukiewicz, was published in 1987. The next one, prepared by Beata Zgodzińska-Wojciechowska and Anna Żakiewicz, was released in 1996. Up to the present this catalogue covers a majority of the collection, and any new acquisitions are accounted for in additional publications. For example, The Leszczyński Bequest, comprising 14 portraits and archival documents, are discussed in the 17th issue of the newsletter "Słupia," which is published by the Society of Friends of the Museum. Additional information was also published through the album released by Parma Press in 2006 as well as the publication concerning the Portrait Painting Company issued by the Słupsk City Council in 2010.

Important elements of the popularization of the collections are the dozens of agreements for reproduction which the Museum issues annually. Currently, almost all publications on the artist, especially Polish, but also foreign, are illustrated with works from our collection. Thanks to the collection of portraits of important people from inter-war Poland, the Słupsk artworks are used as illustrations in books, biographies, scientific publications and journals, among others.

The Museum also organizes exhibitions of Witkacy's work in Poland and abroad. It is open to co-operation with other museums and cultural institutions. The following is a summary of events between 1965 and 2009. There were more than 40 temporary exhibitions displaying Witkacy's artworks exclusively from the Museum's collection, including 28 outside Słupsk. Witkacy's artworks were also shown in more than 70 different temporary exhibitions. The Słupsk collection has been shown mainly in Poland, but also in Germany, Holland, Italy, France, Bulgaria and England. In general, considering the 45 year presence of the Witkacy Collection in Słupsk, these numbers are not particularly high, but due to the requirements of conservation, touring the work is limited. Most of the works in Słupsk are delicate pastels.

The Museum is also a patron of numerous cultural undertakings. It supports artists pursuing projects based on the work of Witkacy. It also collaborates with theatrical projects as well as offers patronage of cultural undertakings.

An example would include co-operation with the artist Piotr Szwabe, who proposed the painting of murals inspired by Witkacy's art in Słupsk. This artist had been already famed for several similar projects – including a monumental portrait of Lech Wałęsa in Gdańsk. Although the idea was well received by the curators, and the Director Mr. Jaroszewicz supported him, the Słupsk City Council rejected the proposal.

In earlier years the most significant co-operation took place with Waldemar Świerzy, one of Poland's most renowned poster artists. Because of his individual style and high profile, in 1985 the museum commissioned him to undertake a poster project: Paintings and Drawings from the Collections of the Museum of Central Pomerania in Słupsk: On the 100th anniversary of the artist's birth. A further example of such activity was the joint venture with Ewa Olszewska-Borys, a Polish sculptor known for her numerous projects of medals and coins. In the same year (1985) through a commission from the Słupsk museum, she designed a commemorative medal bearing the image of Stanisław Ignacy Witkiewicz. In 1995, the Słupsk artist Mieczysław Łaźny designed a commemorative envelope.

One of the few situations in which the museum refused to co-operate was the most recent film by Jacek Koprowicz, The Hoax. The film, which tells the story about the alleged life of Witkacy after World War II, aroused too much controversy and portrayed the artist in a bad light. Therefore, the museum refused to support the authors and did not consent to the creation of copies of the artworks from its collections. Nevertheless, these artworks ended up being used in the film.

Nonetheless, the museum's most important activity are the international conferences devoted to the life and creative work of Witkacy, which take place every five years. They are typically academic and serve to generate a deeper understanding of the artist. Those who participate are both known Witkacologists and those who are taking their first steps in this field. Presented themes encompass the current state of research on Witkacy's work. For many years, the audiences have included people from Słupsk and those coming from afar. The first session took place in 1994, and the fourth, most recent, in 2009. Every conference leaves us with materials comprising all the papers which were presented during the conference. Throughout the long history of the conferences, only a few of the papers presented were not published. At the time of writing the present article, the papers from the fourth conference are being edited by Professor Janusz Degler. Previous editors have included Janusz Degler (conference 1994, published 1996), Anna Żakiewicz (conference 1999, published 2000) and Józef Tarnowski (conference 2004, published 2006). It is worth noting that last year's session and three temporary exhibitions, including an exhibition of the entire Słupsk Collection, have been acknowledged by the judges of the 'Pomeranian Arts Award' and Beata Zgodzińska received a nomination in the category of "creations" for organizing the session, for serving as an exhibition curator, and for authoring two catalogues.

Recently, the museum has striven to prepare an assortment of souvenirs and items, which are designed to promote the collection and the museum. Visitors to the museum frequently pointed out that following a visit it was not possible to buy a souvenir or a simple object associated with the collection. For many years, the museum reacted to this kind of criticism by investing in both large and small publications. The first idea to meet the demands of tourists was to publish postcards, which happened successively in 1994, 2002 and 2005. Reproductions of artworks also appeared in the 1996 calendar. While preparing these items great care is always taken to frame each image precisely in order to retain the important elements of the composition and its notations. Even promotional items should fully adhere to the principles of professionally prepared reproduction. For the past two years, the Museum offers T-shirts adorned with the work of Witkacy and linen bags bearing his photograph.

The Activities of Other Institutions

Thanks to the popularization and educational activities of the museum, Witkacy has become the leading figure of the cultural life of the town. One of the fields to take full advantage of his legacy is the theatre. The Słupsk

Theatre Centre Rondo is famous for a number of dramas and performances which have been produced since 1973 and are based on compilations of texts drawn from famous plays. This has been the case with both small-cast plays as well as monodramas. Among the first of these were: Juvenilia, New Deliverance, Cocaine Séance, Dinner with Beelzebub, The Water Hen or Damn, PULPWITKAC, Bite (based on themes from The Mother), 'Das Küchendrama,' Speed – Witkac Dangerous, Rage Theatre, DissONaNce, The Madman and the Nun. Among the monodramas that deserve attention are: Kalamarapaksa (performed by Caryl Swift), Leon (based on The Mother) with Krzysztof Protasewicz, Hygiene (derived from Narcotics and Unwashed Souls) played by Daniel Kalinowski. The latter was also presented in the museum on several occasions.

The Rondo Theatre also organizes celebrations to commemorate the anniversaries of the birth and death of the artist. In February, Quirky Nights takes place, during which performances and concerts dedicated to the memory of the artist are presented. However, their main aim is to bring together the enthusiasts of Stanisław Ignacy Witkiewicz. In contrast, a festival aimed at the young, Witkacy under Thatched Roofs, takes place in September. During the festival, secondary schools present wide-ranging creative projects inspired by the artist. Up till now, they have presented small and quasi-theatrical dramas, as well as attempts at photography, painting, music and dance. Annually, there are more than a dozen presentations which are judged by a panel of artists, actors, and Witkacy scholars.

The Dramatic Theatre in Słupsk also had Witkacy's works in its repertoire. The first performance was Jan Maciej Karol Hellcat in 1969. Further realizations included: Lecture on Witkacy in the program New Deliverance of Stanisław Ignacy Witkiewicz, The Madman and the Nun, and Beast of the Theatre of Stanisław Ignacy Witkiewicz in 1989. The Dramatic Theatre in Słupsk ceased to exist following an official decision taken in the 1990s. The New Theatre in Słupsk, established in 2004, inherited the repertoire. The inaugural play was a production of The Crazy Locomotive, directed by Jan Peszek. Coincidentally, in 2005 the museum purchased the typed manuscript of this play from the Leszczyński Collection. In 2009, on the 70th anniversary of the artist's death, the theatre took the name, The Witkacy New Theatre. This new assignation of patronage was accompanied by the premiere of Witkacy – It is 20 to X (i.e. Witkacy – it is Twenty to Ten), directed by Andrzej Maria Marczewski. This theatrical realisation was combined with a series of lectures concerning the literary, dramatic and theatrical work of Witkacy prepared by the director for secondary schools. An important event accompanying the implementation of the performance was a trip to the Great Lakes in Ukraine, which was attended by representatives of the theater and museum. The expedition was accompanied by a TV crew which produced a documentary film about the place of Witkacy's passing. The film was directed by Maria Mrozińska.

Two books which were published in 2009 summarized the theatrical activity in Słupsk: 23 Theatrical Incidents by Wioleta Komar and Theatrical Traditions of Słupsk 1945–2008 by Anna Sobiecka. The first book concerns the history of monodrama on the boards of the Theatre Centre Rondo; the other is about the history of theatre in Słupsk after 1945. Importantly, both books discuss how the figure of Stanisław Ignacy Witkiewicz has functioned in the theatrical culture of Słupsk.

It is worth mentioning that for the past two years an art competition called 'Witkacy and I' has taken place. This project was devised by Wioletta Miś, a teacher, and is organised in collaboration with the Słupsk Museum, the Teacher's Advisory Centre, and secondary schools. Its purpose is to promote Witkacy's plastic arts among the youth. The first instalment of this competition included art works, and in 2010 photography was added. Despite its short history, the contest is very popular; in fact, the organizers are now planning to expand it across the voivodship.

Promotional Activities of the Town Council

As a result of Witkiewicz's omnipresence in the culture of Słupsk, the interest in the artist became a means of attracting more tourists to the town. Widespread publicity and information sharing have become important elements of the realisation of this goal. Reproductions of artworks appear on posters promoting the city at the international expos, as well as on leaflets and advertising materials.

Information about the museum, and in particular about the Witkacy Collection, is also available on the town's website. For several years, the main entrances to the town have been marked with welcome signs advertising the art collection of the Słupsk Museum.

In addition, the City Council funds the production of souvenirs which are distributed free of charge or used as prizes in contests. Among these is a calendar containing 12 large-format reproductions, produced in 2008. There is also a silk scarf imprinted with the Portrait of Irmina Bajer-Nowowiejska. However, the most important initiative was the 2010 edition of the book Witkacy in Słupsk: The Portrait Company of S. I. Witkiewicz by Beata Zgodzińska. The publication was prepared on the occasion of the 700th anniversary of the city. In principle, it is not intended for sale; instead, it is distributed free of charge.

In 2008 another form of promotion entailed the issuing of a special commemorative coin – a ducat with the nominal face value based on a currency inspired by the river Słupia on which the city of Słupsk sits. The obverse face of the coin carries an image of Witkacy. In principle, the coin served to advance the idea of the twin towns of Słupsk–Ustka, but it was also used to display the connection with culture.

The City Council also supports the expansion of the collection. The most spectacular example of this was the co-financed purchase of 14 portraits and archival items which belonged to Jan Leszczyński. This was done jointly with the Ministry of Culture in Warsaw and the Office of the Marshal in Gdańsk in 2005.

Conclusion

Work on the popularization of Witkacy is extraordinarily difficult. This is not an easy artist to embrace, so the 'struggle' for an audience can take place only through publishing and education. Currently, the consumption of culture, set for a quick profit coupled with minimal intellectual effort, does not coincide with the concept of cultural institutions, especially museums. In order to maintain an adequate status, the museum avoids participating in activities related to advertising and promotion. For many of today's observers, this is completely incomprehensible – especially in the context of potential profits. Hence, the accusation, which frequently appears in the local media, that the Museum does not appropriately use the vibrant potential of the collection. However, for the Słupsk museum, the most satisfying achievements include the following; instilling in the city's inhabitants a sense of awareness of Stanisław Ignacy Witkiewicz's art collection and serving all those who already know Witkacy and want to explore him in greater depth.

Abstract

This account describes the activity of the Museum in functional terms and reports on the 45-year presence in Słupsk of the Witkacy collection. The presence of Witkacy's work in Słupsk was instigated by an initial acquisition of 110 works which were brought to Słupsk in 1965. This was part of a post-war endeavour aimed at countering the influence of Germanic traditions then present in the region. In a short space of time the collection of works by Stanisław Ignacy Witkiewicz became the primary museum collection of Słupsk, eclipsing all other collections including. The museum now works with the City Council in a three-fold way: through exhibition, educational outreach, and as part of broader promotional activity of the City of Słupsk. However, perhaps the Museum's most important measure of success is the international scholastic conferences dedicated to the life and work of Witkiewicz.

Anna Brochocka
Assistant Curator Museum of Central Pomerania in Słupsk

Beata Zgodzińska

The Witkacy Collection and Exhibition at the Museum of Middle Pomerania in Słupsk[1]

The Collection[2]

In effect the Witkacy Art Collection at the Słupsk Museum came into being in 1965 when the Museum purchased 110 works consisting of 109 portraits and 1 composition executed in pastel from Michał Białynicki-Birula (pic. 1), who was the son of Theodore and Helena (pic. 2). Dr. Theodore Białynicki, a doctor and a painter, was in attendance and 'scientifically' observing whilst Witkacy undertook his famous 'experiments' with various stimulants. Today, it may seem unbelievable, but in the mid-sixties a Witkacy portrait could be purchased for the equivalent of one month's salary of either a newly quali-

---

[1] This article was originally presented in summary form at Witkacy 2010 in Washington D.C. and has been revised and translated by Kevin Anthony Hayes.

[2] All of the 38 images used in this article are also to be found in the Annex. The editors and publishers wish to express their profound gratitude to the Director of The Museum of Central Pomerania in Słupsk, Mieczysław Jaroszewicz and the Curator of the Witkacy Collection Beata Zgodzińska for their continued support and extension of permission to reproduce the images to which this article refers.

fied teacher or a junior museum assistant; however, it should be added that this was a very small amount in post-war Poland. In 1973 the collection grew by 14 in number; these were received from the collection of Józef Jan Głogowski (pic. 3). He was an engineer and an amateur photographer, who was also responsible for a series of photographs of Witkiewicz. In the following year the museum bought an additional 40 items from Witkacy's dentist, Włodzimierz Nawrocki (pic. 4). According to their agreement, Nawrocki provided dental treatment in exchange for portraits depicting Nawrocki and various members of his family. Subsequently, a further 14 portraits were acquired in the form of a bequest made by Jan Leszczyński (pic. 5). Leszczyński was a philosopher and one of the first editors of Witkiewicz's work. This group of portraits also includes items from the collection of Modesta Zwolińska, who was the sister of one of Witkacy's favourite models, Nena Stachurska (pic. 6–8). Presently, the Słupsk collection consists of 254 works by Witkacy. The earliest of these is an oil painting entitled Italian Landscape (pic. 9) completed in 1904, and the latest completed work is a pastel entitled Portrait of Jadwiga Netzel, which was finalised on August 15th in 1939 (pic. 10). All phases of the artist's work are represented at the Museum: the Youthful Period (pic. 11), the Russian Period (1914–1918) (pic. 12), the Formist Period (1918–1924) (pic. 13) as well as the period of work at The "S. I. Witkiewicz" Portrait Painting Firm (Firma Portretowa "S. I. Witkiewicz") (1925–1939).

The core of the collection consists of more than 210 portraits from the era of the Portrait Painting Firm. All the basic types of portraits are represented in the collection. These include the following: A (pic. 14), B (pic. 15), B + d (pic. 16), C (pic. 17), D (pic. 18), E (pic. 19), and B + E (pic. 20). All of these are defined in the Rules of the Portrait Painting Firm first published in 1928 and again in 1932; the Rules were also featured in many other publications following the 'war. There are also various combinations of types, for example, E + B +d or B + D. Among the people portrayed are some very well-known figures from the world of art and culture from inter-war Poland. These include: the writer Irena Krzywicka (pic. 21), the writer Michał Choromański (pic. 22), the translator Kazimiera Żuławska (pic. 23), the painter and writer Rafał Malczewski (pic. 24), and the writer and translator, Tadeusz Boy-Żeleński (pic. 25). Additionally, numerous figures from the military sphere are featured. These include portraits of high ranking officers: General Janusz de Beaurain (pic. 26) and General Kazimierz Sosnkowski (pic. 27), Colonel Ludwik de Laveaux (pic. 28) and Father Col. Jan Humpola (pic. 29), who served as Chaplain to the last pre-war Polish President, Ignacy Mościcki.

The collection also includes 19 drawings, which were primarily completed in the 'twenties and 'thirties (pic. 30–31). Originally, these drawings were not intended for public display. Among the charcoal drawings, the portrait of actress Irena Solska is most noteworthy (pic. 32). Irena Solska was one of Witkacy's first amours, and she became the prototype of Mrs. Acne – the main character of Witkacy's youthful novel, The 622 Downfalls of Bungo or The Demonic Woman. This was published for the first time in 1972.

The collection is complemented by six oil paintings, which includes Witkacy's earliest known self-portrait from 1906 (pic. 33). There are also some interesting early landscapes (pic. 34). Especially noteworthy are three pastel compositions, which include Lady Macbeth of 1933 (pic. 35), and the Australian Landscape of 1918 (pic. 36), which recollects the 1914 expedition undertaken with Bronisław Malinowski. In 1914, Witkacy accompanied Malinowski to the Congress of the British Association for the Advancement of Science which was held in Adelaide, Australia. This entailed a two week stay in Ceylon as well as an exploration of Western Australia. Witkacy was commissioned as draftsman and photographer for the duration of the expedition. Interestingly, there are also four menus designed by Witkacy for a well-known ball in Zakopane (pic. 37–38).

Exhibition

In addition to paintings and drawings by S. I. Witkiewicz, the museum also has a collection of archival material. This includes post-cards written to friends, single letters, pre-war photographs as well as manuscripts and typescripts. Of particular interest here are the archives of first edition books complete with handwritten dedications. This collection also includes photographs relating to performances and set designs for Witkacy's plays. These have been regularly exhibited in Poland since 1956.

The exhibition is set out in two halls located on the second floor of the Pomeranian Dukes' Castle, which is the headquarters of the Museum of Central Pomerania. The first permanent exhibition opened in May 1982, and the present one opened in September 1988. Approximately, 125–130 works of art are permanently on display. The exhibition is partially changed every twelve months or so.

The exhibition reflects the character of the collection; it is, therefore, dominated by portraits completed in pastels on coloured paper. Almost all of the portraits are notated. The notations can be broken down as follows: the artist's signature, the type of portrait and the date of execution. This information is accompanied by defining abbreviations including what influences he was either under or not under. The majority of these abbreviations have been decoded. Some portraits are completed with certain comments, such as "The Colonel became awkward" or "Dishonest sketch."

Oil paintings, pastel compositions, and two charcoal portraits, as well as other drawings and portraits and compositions are all on display. An archive of selected works, including letters, postcards, editions of books from before the war, supplement the collection. The work is displayed in chronological order from the Youthful, Russian period to the Formist period; those from the Portrait Painting Firm Period, on the other hand, are exhibited according to type.

Recently, an added element to the collection is the enlarged photographs of locomotives from Witkacy's film negatives taken sometime between 1899 and 1900 and enlarged photographs of Pulling faces from Jan Józef Głogowski film negatives from the 'thirties.

The exhibition also includes a relatively brief commentary in five languages: English, French, German, Italian and Polish. These provide basic information about the biography of Witkiewicz, the history of the collection, the characteristics of the permanent exhibition, and an explanation of the abbreviations.

Abstract

This article describes the development of the Witkacy Collection in the Słupsk Museum. It details the original acquisitions in 1965 and the subsequent additions to the collection. While most of the exhibit consists of portraits, the author explains that other artistic works have been added to the collection, including drawings and oil paintings. In addition to the art works, the museum also maintains archival documents including postcards, letters, manuscripts, typescripts, and first editions.

Beata Zgodzińska
Curator of the Witkacy Collection Museum of the 'Słupsk Museum

Stanisław Ignacy Witkiewicz

Rules of the S. I. Witkiewicz Portrait-Painting Firm[1]

> The customer must be satisfied.
> Misunderstandings are ruled out.

The rules are published so as to spare the firm the necessity of repeating the same thing over and over again.

§ 1

The firm produces portraits of the following types:

1. Type A – Relatively the most 'spruced up' type. Rather more suitable for women's faces than men's faces. 'Slick' execution, with a certain loss of character in the interests of beautification, or accentuation of 'prettiness.'

---

[1] This version of The Rules of the "S. I. Witkiewicz" Portrait Painting Firm was originally published in Witkacy in Słupsk. The "S. I. Witkiewicz" Portrait Painting Firm, pub. Słupsk 2010. The City Hall in Słupsk (ed.) Beata Zgodzińska & translated by Beata Brodniewicz. We are able to reproduce this extract here thanks to the kind permission of Maciej Kobyliński The Mayor of Słupsk. The text presented here appeared in print in Polish in 1932 and was published by "UNIVERSUM" Printing House, 9 Oboźna Street, Warsaw.

2. Type B – More emphasis on character but without any trace of caricature. The technique is more dab-like than in type A, with a certain touch of character traits, which does not preclude 'prettiness' in women's portraits. Objective attitude to the model.

3. Type B + d – Intensification of character, bordering on the caricatural. The head larger than actual size. The possibility of preserving 'prettiness' in women's portraits, and even of intensifying it in the direction of the 'demonic.'

4. Type C, C + Co, Et, C + H, C + Co + Et, etc. – These types, executed with the aid of C_2H_5OH and narcotics of a superior grade, are at present ruled out. Subjective characterization of the model, caricatural intensification both formal and psychological are not ruled out. Approaches abstract composition, otherwise known as 'Pure Form.'

5. Type D – The same results without recourse to any artificial means.

6. Type E – and its combinations with the preceding types. Spontaneous psychological interpretation at the discretion of the Firm. The achieved effect may be the exact equivalent of that produced by types A and B – the manner by which it is attained is different, as is the method of execution, which may take various forms but never exceeds the limits of (d) A combination of E + d is likewise available on request.

Type E is not always possible to execute.

7. Children's type – (B + E) – Because children can never be still, the purer type B is in most instances impossible - the execution rather takes the form of a sketch.

In general, the firm does not pay much attention to the rendering of clothing and accessories. The question of the background concerns only the firm – demands in this regard are not considered. Depending on the disposition of the firm and the difficulties of rendering a particular face, the portrait may be executed in one, two, three, and even up to five sittings. For large portraits showing the upper body or full figure, the number of sittings may even reach twenty.

The number of sittings does not determine the excellence of the product.

§ 2

The basic novelty offered by the Firm as compared to the usual practice is the customer's option of rejecting a portrait if unsatisfied with its execution or resemblance. In such cases the customer pays one-third price, and the portrait becomes the property of the firm. The customer does not have the right to demand that the portrait be destroyed. This clause, obviously applies only to the pure types: A, B, and E, without supplement d – that is, without any supplement of exaggerated characteristics, or in other words the types that appear in series. This clause has been introduced because it is never certain who will be satisfied with what. An exact agreement is desirable, based upon a definite decision by the model as to the type requested. An album of samples (but by no means 'of no value') is available for inspection at the premises of the Firm. The customer receives a guarantee in that the Firm in its own self-interest will not issue work that could damage its trademark. There may be cases in which the artist himself will not authorize his work.

§ 3

Any sort of criticism on the part of the customer is absolutely ruled out. The customer may not like the portrait, but the firm cannot permit even the most discreet comments without giving its special authorization. If the firm had allowed itself the luxury of listening to customers' opinions, it would have long ago gone crazy. We place special emphasis on this rule, since the most difficult thing is to refrain the customer from making remarks that are entirely uncalled for. The portrait is either accepted or rejected – yes or no, without any explanations whatsoever as to why. Inadmissible criticism likewise includes remarks about whether or not it is a good likeness, observations concerning the background, covering part of the face in the portrait with one hand so as to imply that this part really isn't the way it should be, comments such as, 'I am too pretty,' 'Do I really look that sad?,' 'That's not me,' and all opinions of that sort, whether favourable or unfavourable. After due consideration, and possibly consultation with third parties, the customer says yes (or no) and that's all there is to it – then the customer goes (or does not go) up to what is called the 'cashier's window,' that is, and simply hands over the agreed-upon sum to the Firm. Given the incredible difficulty of the profession, the Firm's nerves must be spared.

§ 4

Asking the firm for its opinion of a finished portrait is not permissible, nor is any discussion about a work in progress.

§ 5

The firm reserves the right to paint without any witnesses, to the extent possible.

§ 6

Portraits of women with bare necks and shoulders cost one-third more. Each arm costs one third of the total price. For portraits showing the upper body or full figure, special agreements must be drawn up.

§ 7

The portrait may not be viewed until finished.

§ 8

The technique used is a combination of charcoal, crayon, pencil and pastel. All remarks with regard to technical matters are ruled out, as are the requests for touch ups.

§ 9

The Firm undertakes the painting of portraits outside the Firm's premises only in exceptional circumstances (sickness, advanced age, etc.) in which case the firm must be guaranteed a secret receptacle in which the unfinished work may be kept under lock and key.

§ 10

Customers are obliged to appear punctually for sittings, since waiting has a bad effect on the Firm's mood and may have an adverse effect on the execution of the product.

§ 11

The Firm offers advice on framing and packing of portraits but does not provide these services. further discussion about types of frames is ruled out.

§ 12

The firm allows total freedom as to the model's clothing and quite definitely does not voice any opinion in this regard whatsoever.

§ 13

The firm encourages a careful perusal of the rules. Lacking any powers of enforcement, the firm counts on the tact and good will of its customers to meet the terms. Reading through and concurring with the rules shall be deemed synonymous with concluding an agreement. Discussion about the rules is inadmissible.

§ 14

Paying by instalments or billing may be possible. Considering the already low prices the Firm charges, requests for discounts are not advisable. Before the portrait is begun, the customer pays one third of the price as a down payment.

§ 15

A customer who acts as 'an agent of the Firm' and refers others to the Firm for jobs in the amount of 100 zlotys or more, shall obtain a premium of the customer's own portrait or that of any person the customer wishes in the type of the customer's choice.

§ 16

Notices sent by the firm to former customers announcing its presence at a given location are not intended to force them to have new portraits painted, but rather to assist friends of these customers in placing orders, since having seen the Firm's work they may wish something similar themselves.

§ 17

It is recommended that customers not unpack portraits after they have have been wrappped by the packaging department of the Firm, but have them framed immediately in order to avoid the kind of destruction that has occurred many times.

The 'S. I. WITKIEWICZ' Firm

Price List

Type A = 350
Type B = 250
Type B + d = 150
Type E = 150–250
Type C = priceless
Type D = 100
Children's Type = 150–250

Daniel Gerould

Witkacy and Conspiracy Theories

Introduction

In Witkacy's plays and novels, as well as in his philosophical writings and his paintings, drawings, and photographs, the lonely protagonist – a vulnerable and embattled individual – is confronted by encroaching worlds of otherness, concentric circles of constraint and encroachment, in the form of the cosmos, political and social order, family, and self (where malevolent doubles lurk).

At the heart of Witkacy's work, at the very centre of those concentric circles, lies the quest for identity on the part of a creative personality in the face of entropic and mendacious social orders that thwart the individual's attempts at self-definition and authenticity.

The individual's troubled relation to society is the centre-piece of Witkacy's analysis of the predicament of modern man. At one end of the scale is the individual's position within the cosmos, at the other the individual's relation to the hostile and alien forces that lie within. Humankind's existential status at these extremes occupies much of Witkacy's attention – here are the sources of our feelings of the metaphysical strangeness of existence.

But at the centre are found the individual's connections to society – in the form of social institutions such as the family, the tribe or community, and the state. And it is this aspect of Witkacy's work that has attracted the most attention during the years that Poland was part of the Soviet bloc. From 1956 to 1989 it seemed that his plays and novels were above all anti-communist. But the anti-utopian, anti-ideological fears expressed by Witkacy's protagonists are directed toward all manifestations of mass regimes, whether liberal democratic, collectivist communist, or fascist corporate.

What in fact renders Witkacy's portrayal of the familiar romantic opposition between the individual and society innovative and contemporary in sensibility is the pervasive ambiguity with which society in his plays and novels is perceived. Society as experienced by the Witkacian protagonist is no longer a fixed knowable entity. Above all in its institutional manifestations as the state, society as portrayed by Witkacy is a many-layered fraudulent hoax constantly undergoing duplicitous and unfathomable metamorphoses. Oppression by and resistance to the state is no clear-cut ideological battle, but an enigma and a "rather nasty nightmare."

Witkacy is a pioneer in the theatrical and fictional use of what has become known in the late twentieth century as conspiracy theory and dietrology, "the science of what lies hidden behind the event." Humankind can no longer be sure who is actually running the show. Here is the foundational premise of the conspiratorial view of the world, which profoundly colours Witkacy's dramatic and fictional universe.

In a social order in which there is an inherent discrepancy between appearance and what lies beneath, disbelief in objective truth is bound to prevail. Where does the real power reside? In their search for identity in themselves and in their worlds, the heroes of Witkacy's plays and novels confront masked power structures and develop paranoiac fears of secret societies, buried plots, and disguised tyrannies.

In such a duplicitous world, the individual lives in constant dread of hidden power structures whose real identity and operation are unknowable, given the manipulation of appearances by sinister and mysterious conspiracies. Anxiety, mistrust, and suspicion about government give rise to ingenious theories.

Before looking more closely at Witkacy's dramatizations of conspiratorial thinking, I wish to consider briefly the nature and history of CONSPIRACY THEORY.

Conspiracy Theory

CONSPIRACY THEORIES utilized to explain historical events have existed since ancient times, and they have flourished at times of crisis, social change and upheaval, during wars and revolutions, invasions, and foreign occupations when nations, social groups, and individuals have felt threatened and overwhelmed by inexplicable disasters and perils. No longer certain of providential guidance, suspicious of the state, and mistrustful of official interpretations of history given by the authorities, entire nations or groups within nations have found in hidden plots logical and satisfying explanations for the distressing and incomprehensible collective experiences confronting them. Individuals too may engage in private conspiratorial thinking to explain why they are singled out and persecuted. Conspiratorial thinking detects labyrinthine plots and finds individuals or, more often, groups that can be held responsible for menacing social changes.

The Romans suspected the early cave-dwelling Christians of hatching plots to overthrow the established order. Once installed themselves as the ruling power, the Christians accused Jews of kidnapping and killing their children as part of a religious ritual – the so-called blood libel. In the fourteenth century lepers were accused of seeking to seize power by poisoning the water supply; later this suspicion was extended to Jews and to sorcerers.

Political extremists, members of the lowest social classes, and racial minorities and pariahs, have traditionally been singled out as members of cults or secret societies seeking to seize power by covert means. But also powerful individuals – princes, monarchs, and dictators – and elites, sheltered branches of government, and the state itself have also been viewed as conspirators by those out of power who feel oppressed and wish to challenge the insidious ruling clique.

At the present time it is often as a form of collective thinking on the part of fringe groups of the right or left that conspiracy theory gains notoriety and comes to occupy a visible position both in popular culture and in journalistic analysis of radical political movements.

Conspiratorial thinking reduces all complex historical events to the consequence of hidden plotting. It pits different groups, races, and classes against one another. Through conspiratorial lenses, the masses of people are seen as easily misled by sequestered elites or subterranean gangs who manipulate appearances in order to seize and secretly wield political power.

Conspiracy came to the forefront of political philosophy in the Renaissance, when its master theoretician, Machiavelli, anatomizes the subject in

The Prince and Discourses, without making clear if he is providing the prince with strategies to use against the people, or if he is rather forewarning the people against the prince's devious maneuvers. In his analysis of conspiracy, Machiavelli remains ambiguously conspiratorial.

In volume II of The Open Society and Its Enemies the Austrian philosopher Karl Popper dismisses conspiracy theories as ineffectual. While admitting that conspiracies may in fact exist, he argues that they usually fail because they are based on the false assumption that all actions are the results of deliberate plans that produce predictable results, whereas in Popper's view nothing works out as planned and the consequences of actions are not predictable. Conspiracy theory is therefore a simplistic view of historical causation. However, this reductionism is precisely the reason why it has such a tenacious hold on the popular imagination. No matter how false conspiracy theory may be, it has proved influential on the masses and useful to dictators and demagogues.

Conspiratorial theories may be perpetuated by the regime or power-wielding ruling establishment to defend the status quo, or they may be originated by out-of-power minorities to challenge the legitimacy of the de facto order. The most devious and tenacious have been those accusations of conspiracy invented by secret plotters and attributed to "suspect" others, such as Jews, communists, capitalists, Bolsheviks, Mensheviks, Catholics, and masons.

Conspiratorial thinking becomes a stimulus for the imagination of the masses, for whom it offers the gratifications of myth. Lying outside officially sanctioned sources of information, conspiracy theory is an alternative way of understanding and interpreting history that makes the world more vivid and interesting.

It has been suggested that conspiratorial thinking is central to post-modern sensibility, and that we can expect a proliferation of paranoiac conspiracy narratives in an age marked by the disappearance of grand explanations. Conspiracy theory thrives not only under tyrannies, but also under liberal democracies. The decline of traditional societies and their age-old institutions giving a sense of consensus creates a breeding ground for cognitive relativism, distrust of official channels of communication and of any unified belief system, and fragmentation into subcultures, producing conspiratorial thinking as rabid as under totalitarian regimes and now granted the freedom to expand unhindered by censorship.

Modern conspiratorial thinking begins after 1789. A seemingly spontaneous popular movement such as the French revolution is revealed, on the contrary, to be actually the covert seizure of power by a secret society or organization. Nothing can be what it seems to be or happen by accident; everything is the result of a hidden plan whereby the most disparate events are interconnected in a covert fashion.

By the end of the nineteenth century, with the rise of international Zionism, Jewish conspiracies for world-wide domination were seen everywhere. Jews made responsible for the Dreyfus affair, the Bolshevik Revolution, and the economic crash of 1929.

But at the turn of the century a menacing invasion of races from the East moved into the sight-lines of European conspiracy theory and rivaled the Jews as a sinister threat to Western civilization. Believers in the yellow peril, as it was called, which was given imaginative immediacy in many works of fantastic fiction, religious polemics, and political caricature, found convincing historical evidence in Japan's rise as a world power, the Sino-Japanese War of 1894–1895, the overwhelming defeat of Russia in the Russo-Japanese War of 1904–1905, and then in the violent anti-colonial Boxer Rebellion of 1908.

In his poem Pan-Mongolism (1884) the Russian poet and religious thinker Vladimir Solovev forewarned of a new Mongol horde gathering strength in the East, ready to sweep over Russia and bring an end to Western civilization. In Stories of the Anti-Christ of 1900, he predicted Japan's uniting the peoples of Asia who would then conquer the world and usher in the reign of the Antichrist.

Under the influence of Solovev, the modernist Andre Bely wrote two apocalyptic novels, The Silver Dove and Petersburg, in which sinister conspiracies emanating from the East spread nightmare and terror: "The yellow hordes of Asians [...] will encrimson the fields of Europe in oceans of blood."[1] Alexander Blok's poem The Scythians continued to develop the idea of an Armageddon between Asia and Europe.

In the West, the British novelist M. P. Shiel – a pioneer in science fiction – had already written his Yellow Danger in 1898. But it was G. G. Rupert who first used the phrase "yellow peril" (purportedly coined by Kaiser Wilhelm II) as the title for his The Yellow Peril, or Orient versus Occident. The symbolist playwright Maurice Maeterlinck voiced his fear that Oriental countries would end up dominating the world because their political philosophy included psychic partnership among the dead, the living, and those on the brink of the grave.

---

[1] A. Bely: Petersburg, trans. R. A. Maguire and J. E. Malmstad, Indiana University Press, Bloomington 1978, p. 65.

The yellow peril, as well as having a highbrow literary vogue, became a popular motif in the pulp novels, science fiction, and horror genres of the early twentieth century. Fear of Asiatic culture engulfing the world was shared by many writers including H.P. Lovecraft and Jack London, whose Unparalleled Invasion tells of a take-over of the West by the Orient. In Philip Francis Nowlan's novella Amageddon 2419 A.D., America is occupied by cruel invaders from China.

Russia, the Soviet Union, and its satellites were prime breeding ground for conspiracy theory. Conspiratorial thinking has for centuries flourished in Russia and Russian dominated countries. Closed, secretive tyrannies rely on conspiracy as a means of governance, masking their own machinations while accusing others of being anti-state conspirators. At the same time, such regimes create feelings of fear and mistrust of all social institutions in their citizens, thereby fostering conspiratorial thinking. Distrusting their own rulers, those living under Fascism, Communism, and right-wing authoritarian regimes, are suspicious of all official explanations. Because egregious manipulation of public information in totalitarian societies destroys belief in the regime's honesty, whispered suspicion of social institutions and need for conspiracy theories become ubiquitous.

Paranoia and perception of pandemic cheating prevail. Poland, having recently recovered its national identity, feared conspiracies could undermine it.

Witkacy's Dramatization of Conspiracy Theory

Witkacy's first play, Maciej Korbowa and Bellatrix, written in November 1918 a few months after the ex-tsarist officer's return from Russia, takes as its subject the activities of a secret society dedicated to resisting the growing mechanization of life taking place in the larger surrounding society, which is heading toward revolution, mirroring the February and October uprisings that bring first the Provisional Government and then the Bolsheviks to power.

But in Witkacy's drama nothing proves to be what it at first seems. The leader of the secret society, Maciej Korbowa (known to his disciples as the Master), is revealed at the last moment to be Comrade Mangle, a double agent working conspiratorially with the Revolutionary Sailors of Death, seemingly his ideologically enemies, but actually his allies in the seizure of power from the defeated Centralists. As the play ends, at Comrade Mangle's bidding the Revolutionary Sailors of Death slaughter all of Korbowa's former disciples. The clandestine betrayal has achieved its goal.

Witkacy's second play, The Pragmatists, is an intimate chamber work, where the five characters seem to be players in a private game. The theatrical impresario (and former drug czar) Franz von Telek appears to wield the ultimate power and literally to run the show in which his friends Plasfodor and Mammalia are to appear as cabaret artists. But in The Pragmatists, as in all Witkacy's dramas even the least political, "society is masked," and nothing is what it seems. The social institutions that von Telek represents are bizarrely concocted frauds. By the end of the play, the Chinese Mummy is revealed to be the strongest of all, able to control both the living and the dead. Here Witkacy offers a passing glimpse at the "yellow peril" conspiracy theory that he will develop fully ten years later in his novel Insatiability.

In The New Deliverance, Richard III is a borrowed character from Shakespeare's history play, now held captive by two Murderers in a gothic chamber that occupies half the stage. One of Witkacy's Shakespearean favorites, Richard III is alluded to as a feudal lord in several of his works of drama and fiction. Above all, Witkacy remembers Richard as a master practitioner of conspiracy, who, claiming he could "set the murderous Machiavel to school,"[2] seizes power by means of theatrical plots and counter-plots, while at the same time accusing his opponents of conspiring against him, for which they are ruthlessly exterminated. Despite his unbroken record of perjuries and betrayals, in The New Deliverance the aristocratic Richard, however, cannot tolerate the present-day breed of conspirators who are bringing about a new tyranny of mass society over the individual; the disgusted monarch stalks offstage as the dictatorship of the proletariat is inaugurated.

...

At the very end of The New Deliverance, the UNKNOWN SOMEONE enters with SIX THUGS, dressed as workers and carrying tools doubling as instruments of torture. While the curtain falls, the UNKNOWN SOMEONE, masked as had been the MURDERERS, starts torturing FLORESTAN with pincers and a blow-torch, as though it were a Grand-Guignol horror play. The guilt-ridden bourgeois weakling FLORESTAN screams in pain, while the brutal new totalitarian era has come to power by assuming the trappings of a working class movement.

---

[2] W. Shakespeare: Henry VI, Part 3, III.ii.193.

Continuing to dramatize governance as a masquerade, Witkacy makes conspiracy the principal theme of his next work. The title of his seventh play, completed in 1920, is ONI, or THEY, the third person plural pronoun written all in emphatic capital letters. Whispered with unease or uttered questioningly in dismay, the word THEY refers to a crazy band of imposters, a secret government within the government that has hijacked the state, taken over its police functions, and turned political repression into a flamboyant theatrical event, whose aim is to destroys art and suppress individuality. Ubiquitous and protean, THEY are the real power-holders, lurking behind those who only seem to be in control.

Reality has become entirely problematic. A group of madmen are revealed to be running the entire show, which takes the form of a farce dell'arte and is a theatrical ruse put on to discredit the theatre. The idea of government as a masquerade (an image that Witkacy could have found in Schopenhauer's World as Will and as Idea) gives THEY its brightly coloured hyperactivity as well as its unsettling tone of ambiguity and menace.[3]

. . .

A bizarre gang of fanatics, adventurers, and playboys, led by Seraskier Banga Tefuan, Chairman of the League of Absolute Automation, THEY are a ludicrous yet sinister conspiratorial organization that plans to take over the government during a staged performance. In order to enforce conformity and order, THEY will reduce the social institution of theatre to absurdity.

On the other hand, their program for the total annihilation of art leads them to destroy the precious collection of modern masterpieces in the hero's private gallery, including his Picassos. Art, as the expression of human creativity that affirms the uniqueness of each individual, can no longer be tolerated in the automated regime of the future.

The hero renounces his previous artistic goals and confesses to a crime that he has not committed in order to go to the dungeons of the secret government, whose spies and agents are ubiquitous. Unable to escape from plurality into unity, he is divided against himself. A secret government of irrational forces and subconscious desires rules his own psyche.

Gyubal Wahazar, written in 1921, is Witkacy's most complex study of the modern totalitarian state and its inherently conspiratorial nature. In Act III

---

[3] In Wole Soyinka's Opera Wonyosi "the government is itself a conspiratorial secret society, a cartel created for mass exploitation and terrorization, implemented always by 'unknown soldiers.'" D. Wright: Wole Soyinka Revisited, New York 1993, p. 110.

of Gyubal Wahazar, while his victims languish in jail, WAHAZAR himself is shoved "by someone from above"[4] through the huge, iron prison door and then rolls down the stairs to the prison floor. Across the different levels of conspiracy, where each layer of being grinds down the one beneath, there is an ascending hierarchy of oppression, rising from the personal through the social to the cosmic. Above even the topmost kicker, ready to kick him in turn, the presence of someone still higher can always be felt – whether it be the mysterious THEY who rule the world by secret conspiracy, or the still more enigmatic HE, the superkicker of the universe. The ending of the play, in which Gyubal's glands are cut out and transplanted into Father Unguenty mixes Grand Guignol medical experimentation and fantastic Sci Fi in a grotesque apotheosis parodying the eating of the king in Frazer's Golden Bough.

The anonymity of conspiracy found in governance by masquerade finds full expression in The Anonymous Work, which, in the form of a spy thriller, contains double revolution, the second within the first, causing the faceless masses to rise up and seize power from the leaders of a secret society – a strange political sect – who have deceptively manipulated them.

In Dainty Shapes and Hairy Apes the alienated conspiratorial group lurking in the background is a seething Jewish mob which ultimately seizes power by devouring the reigning queen and providing a male to breed the future race. Fear of the procreative power of Jewish sexuality, which is regarded as more potent and fertile, has relegated this mass to a marginal status. This is a conspiracy of the id. The anonymous 40 Mandelbaums are a lumpenproletarian embodiment of libido, with an ironic nod to Freud. They are vertical barbarians from the lower depths of the psyche, fighting to gain access to the privileged regions from which they have been excluded.

...

As a young man Witkacy experienced this paranoia in his family's reactions to his close association with Jews as friends and lovers. In 1903 the elder Witkiewicz wrote to his sister: "Stasiek is surrounded by Jews. He's immersed in Zionism, he's almost growing a side-curl."[5] In 1912 when Witkacy became engaged to a sixteen year-old Jewish girl, Anna Oderfeld, his father

---

[4] S. I. Witkiewicz: Gyubal Wahazar, [in:] idem: Tropical Madness: Four Plays, trans. by D. and E. Gerould, New York 1972, p. 149.

[5] S. Witkiewicz: Listy do syna, eds. B. Danek-Wojnowska i A. Micińska, Warszawa 1969, p. 695. Also quoted and translated in D. Gerould: Witkacy: Stanisław Ignacy Witkiewicz as an Imaginative Writer, University of Washington Press, Seattle and London 1981, p. 204.

voiced his serious reservations. Witkacy gave ironic expression in his charcoal drawing, "Consequences of Marriage with a Jewess," which shows an emaciated young man towered over by his fertile Jewish wife and surrounded by Jewish babies and relatives.

In The Madman and the Nun, none of the characters is exactly sure just who is in control of their lives. The Madman Walpurg organizes a conspiracy by which he overthrows the psychoanalytic regime that has incarcerated him.

One of Witkacy's most impenetrable plays, Janulka, Daughter of Fizdejko puts forward for consideration different theories of history, which are both discussed and enacted by the characters. Among these theories conspiracy occupies a prominent place, and the play itself seems deeply conspiratorial.

In Janulka, we witness the machinations of the princess and hangers-on at the court of Lithuania in what may be the fourteenth or the twenty-third century. Everyone appears to be manipulating appearances and plotting the overthrow of the government. The Jews are once again a subject of conspiratorial discussions.

THE MASTER OF SEANCES, who is a major theoretician of conspiracy, explains his position about the role of the Jews: "The entire anti-Semitic campaign will have to be launched in a covert manner. But anyhow, we don't have to fear the Jews, nor hate them either, just use them so that they don't even know they're being used." But PRINCESS AMALIA warns him: "You might get used yourself, and yet be convinced that you were the one running the show." To which VON PLASEWITZ adds: "You won't be able to get along without the Semites. They – or actually we – are the indispensable frame for every picture of the future."[6]

The conspiratorial Boyars troop in and out are paired off and kill one another on orders from the Master. They repeat these obsessional actions, which start up all over again, as though they were on a treadmill.

At the end of JANULKA, the twelve Lithuanian BOYARS rush onstage brandishing axes with which they massacre Elsa, Fizdejko, de la Trefouille, Der Zipfel, and the Master.

Joel Kranz, a transcendental Zionist, (whose name first occurs in Witkacy's notations in 1912 as a character for a dramatic version of his novel Bungo), appears from behind the bush in a purple coat with a crown on his head, accompanied by Princess Amalia. Having seized power and ready to found a new dynasty, Kranz and Amelia smile at the massacre. They are the breeders-to-be of a new race.

---

[6] S. I. Witkiewicz: Janulka, Daughter of Fizdejko, [in:] The Witkiewicz Reader, trans. D. Gerould, Northwestern University Press, Illinois 1992, p. 170.

Witkacy's surprising denouements are coup de théâtre that occur as coup d'état. Often, at the end of Witacy's dramas, an upstart conspirator comes forward with a triumphal laugh. The reins of power are suddenly seized by someone unexpected emerging from the shadows, the undergrowth, or the underground. Sometimes it is someone who has not even appeared on stage previously, as is the case at the very last moment of Tumor Brainiowicz with Arthur Persville who delivers a speech of some fifty words. Power rapidly shifts hands, new alliances are formed, and offspring are promised from such cross-breeding. The last-minute take-over results from some ultimate double-cross. Once the hidden structures are unmasked, and the conspirators come out into the open, we perceive that conspiracy has been a sure route to a successful power grab. The worst paranoia seems fully vindicated.

In Witkacy's novel Insatiability, conspiratorial thinking is given its fullest expression in the shape of the menace from the east, the yellow peril, called "the mobile yellow wall" – a line of Chinese troops "flawless, fearless machines" with its countless invisible feet marching relentlessly west. It is a successful plot to take over first Poland, the bulwark, and then the entire world through a mysterious drug, the Murti-Bing pill, that produces a state of euphoria that destroys the will to resist.[7] Those who take the pill are soon relieved of the anguish and torment of the individual personality; they quickly become lulled into mindless happiness. The populace succumbs to the collectivist ideology of the Chinese despite the heroic attempts of the Polish general to defy the oncoming juggernaught. "As a dangerous individualist belonging to a bygone era," he is executed in ceremonial decapitation.[8]

What now remains to be determined is the legitimacy of Witkacy's use of conspiracy theory.

Is Witkacy a Proponent of Conspiracy Theory?

Having established that conspiracy theory is central to Witkacy's prophetic dramatization of the collective anxieties of his age, I must ask what are the risks and consequences of entering into the conspiratorial mind and cultivating its sensibility? Is Witkacy endorsing the inflammatory views that his characters adopt?

---

[7] Idem: Insatiability, translated by L. Iribane, Northwestern University Press, Illinois 1996, p. 91.

[8] Ibidem, p. 515.

What are we to make of Witkacy's exploitation of conspiracy theory? Is Witkacy a purveyor or a parodist of paranoia?

If in the charcoal drawing Results of a Jewish Marriage, we have a parody of his father's fears of Jewish procreativity, in the plays do we have a similar parodistic rendering of the phobias and paranoias relating to Jewish, Chinese, and Bolshevik threats and perils?

In unmasking the prevailing view of things, in showing that the power structure is not what it seems to be, in revealing that true power lies elsewhere, does Witkacy foster irrational fears and phobias, or does he simply show a world that is a prey to the fears and phobias of conspiracy theories?

Is Witkacy actively preying on the anti-Bolshevik, anti-Semitic, anti-Chinese fears and paranoias of the period, or is he simply playing with them and parodying them, thereby rendering them as ridiculous caricatures?

Does Witkacy feed the fires of the bias and prejudice, which he adopts? Does he further and advance conspiracy theories, or does he explore the state of mind that produces them?

Does Witkacy believe in these conspiracy theories or does he simply use them as the subject matter or content?

Witkacy himself denied the importance of ideology in his work. Using Ludwig Wittgenstein's formularization, I should say that the plays convey philosophy not as a body of doctrine, but as an activity. The role of ideas in Witkacy's plays is as dramatic activity – thought as action.

We should remember what Witkacy says in his "Theoretical Preface" (1921) that we should not take seriously the content:

> These fantasies are only pretexts for certain formal combinations. [...] What we are now attempting is to impart to certain masses of events in time a kind of 'dynamic tension.' This is the formal significance of the so-called 'content' of poems and plays. Please note that we do not attribute any objective significance to the "opinions" expressed by the characters in these plays.[9]

Conclusion

In the final analysis, Witkacy believes in the theory of pure form that can encompass the most diverse social and political theories. This is the ultimate conspiracy theory that Witkacy believes in – the theory of pure form that dominates and controls all else.

---

[9] Idem: Theoretical Preface, [in:] idem: Seven Plays, translated by D. Gerould, M. E. Segal Theatre Center Publishing, New York 2004, p. 4.

Abstract

In this article the author takes an historical overview of conspiracy theories and how they have been paraded in the work of Witkacy. They have been with us at least since the time of Ancient Rome, connected both with the Christians and Jews. The author argues that they have been used to explain historical events, especially at times of crisis, social change and upheaval, when nations, social groups, and individuals have felt threatened by inexplicable disasters and perils. Conspiratorial thinking detects labyrinthine plots and finds individuals or groups that can be held responsible for menacing social changes. They have clearly influenced Witkacy's work. It is argued that the lonely protagonist is confronted by encroaching realms of otherness, 'concentric circles of constraint and encroachment' in the form of the cosmos, political and social order, family, and even the self.

Prof. Daniel Gerould
City University of New York

Anna Żakiewicz

Witkacy's Paintings as Frozen Drama

In an enthusiastic article about Witkacy's drama published in 1928 in the French-language journal Pologne Littéraire, Tadeusz Boy-Żeleński observed that Witkacy's "painting and theatre become a unity. The paintings of Witkacy are theatre frozen on canvas, theatre of life so intense that the artist must externalize his excess energy through the lungs of an actor, transposing them to the human voice; at the same time he repeatedly transforms his theatre into a series of motionless pictures, which amazingly recreate the dream of life."[1]

Unfortunately, Boy said nothing more to enlighten us as to how exactly Witkacy's "motionless painting" was "theatre frozen on canvas" or how the artist "recreated the dream of life." Yet it seems that there is nothing to stop us comparing Witkacy's oil paintings and pastel compositions with his dramas written, during the years 1918–1925 (with the exception of The Shoemakers). As we can find many characters and situations that co-exist in Witkacy's dramas and in his paintings, we can safely assume Boy-Żeleński's quote as being plausible.

The best example of such a phenomena is in Fantasy-Fairytale (pic. 1), a large oil painting executed between 1920 and 1921 depicting the first scene with Edgar Walpor from The Water Hen (Witkacy's drama from 1921) on the left of the canvas and four monsters who play important roles in Janulka, Daughter of Fizdejko (a drama from 1923) on the right.

---

[1] T. Boy-Żeleński: La Théâtre de Stanisław Ignacy Witkiewicz, "La Pologne Littéraire" 1928, nr 18.

In the stage directions in The Water Hen it reads: "HE stands to the left, dressed in the style of the three bound men in the illustrated edition of Robinson Crusoe. Three cornered hat, boots with very wide tops turned down (eighteenth-century style). He's holding a double-barrelled shot gun of the worst make [...] To the left, a red sunset."[2]

Similarly in Fantasy-Fairytale, we have a man dressed as was described above, with the simple difference of having a sword at his side, rather than a gun. Additionally, the sunset is on the right side of the canvas. Here we can also see four bizarre creatures with birds' heads and animals' legs, two of which have peculiar pink and blue crinolines covering the lower parts of their bodies. These details reflect a further drama by Witkacy – Janulka, Daughter of Fizdejko written in 1923. And indeed on the list of the dramatis personae we find: "Two Characters Without Legs –on stands which stretch as though made of flabby guts. Bird faces with short, hooked beaks like bullfinches. Covered with variegated plumage (red, green and violet colors). One without a right arm, the other without a left."[3] In Act III of the drama these creatures discard their crinoline skirts and change into two-legged men.

Another example can be taken from a pastel composition from 1920 (pic. 2) depicting two men – one of them digging a grave, and the other observing. Analogously, the opening scene of the Witkacy's 1921 drama The Anonymous Work, takes place in: "An almost entirely flat field on the outskirts of the capital of Centuria. Day begins to break. In the background the glow of the distant city. [...] The field is covered by bushes with dark-green leaves and fluffy, light-blue flowers. In addition, high greenish-yellow grass with bronze tufts is growing everywhere. There are no trees. In places the earth shows through, cherry red in color. [...] To the right, we can see TWO GRAVEDIGGERS in gray-blue blouses and trousers of the same color are working, waist-deep in a freshly dug grave. [...] In the middle of the stage, near one of the rocks, stands MANFRED COUNT GIERS. He has long hair, and quite a long beard and mustache. No hat. He is wearing the same kind of blouse as the GRAVEDIGGERS, fastened around the waist by a black belt with a large gold buckle. Wide crimson pants. [...] Black patent-leather shoes with violet pompons. His face is turned toward the audience. He is leaning on a tall black cane with a gold knob."[4]

---

[2] S. I. Witkiewicz: The Madman and the Nun and Other Plays, translated and edited by D. C. Gerould and C. S. Durer with a Foreword by J. Kott, University of Washington Press, Seattle and London 1968, p. 45.

[3] The Witkiewicz Reader, edited, translated and with an introduction by D. Gerould, Northwestern University Press, Evanston, Illinois 1992, p. 156.

[4] S. I. Witkiewicz: Seven Plays, translated and edited by D. Gerould, M. E. Segal Theatre Center Publications, New York 2004, p. 175.

Such a similarity between two works of the same artist cannot possibly be accidental. Too many of the details are the same: the colours of the ground, the flowers and the clothing, the brightness of the distant city, the appearance of the central character in the scene.

It is important to note that both the compositions that I have described were executed either during the same period or somewhat earlier than when the related dramas were written: Fantasy Fairytale was painted in 1921–1922, while Water Hen dates from 1921 and Janulka dates from 1923; the pastel composition was however completed one year before The Anonymous Work was written.

It can be concluded thus, that the marked similarities between the paintings and the dramas suggest that Witkacy, as a painter, first imagined the scenes and characters and painted them; only subsequently did he invent the roles and actions and put pen to paper to create the dramas.

So far I have presented the most evident examples from the mature period of Witkacy's oeuvre, but the beginnings of the whole process are of equal interest. Before the First World War Witkacy executed many bizarre charcoal compositions called "monsters" by his father, Stanisław Witkiewicz, because of their ugliness, darkness and the rough style of drawing. The direct inspiration for the name came from the title of Francisco Goya's engraving, The Sleep of Reason Produces Monsters (pic. 3).

Most of Witkacy's "monsters" are lost; we know them mainly from photographs[5] but some of them fortunately survived. I discovered a 1906 work in a private collection in Krakow in the late 1980s while preparing a large Witkacy's exhibition at the National Museum in Warsaw. The Demonic Composition (1906) (pic. 4) depicts a mysterious scene – a man and a woman looking at a bizarre figure just visible through a slot between curtains. Importantly, the figure is carrying a torch. Professor Daniel Gerould suggested once that the composition may be connected with the play Deliverance by Stanisław Wyspiański produced in the Słowacki Theatre in Krakow precisely in 1906. I compared the charcoal by Witkacy to the scene from Wyspiański's drama where two characters, Konrad and the Muse, discuss the roles in the drama and identify the figure with a torch as Contemporary Poland. Not only was the similarity striking, but it seemed to suggest a very exciting idea of what the origins of Witkacy the dramatist could have been. The scene from Deliverance must have impressed the young 21-year-old

---

[5] The photographs were published in: W. Sztaba: Stanisław Ignacy Witkiewicz. Zaginione obrazy i rysunki sprzed roku 1914: według oryginalnych fotografii ze zbiorów Konstantego Puzyny (The Lost Paintings and Drawings from the Period before 1914 from the Collection of Konstanty Puzyny), Oficyna Wydawnicza Auriga, Warszawa 1985.

Witkacy so much that he not only depicted it in his own artistic composition drawn in charcoal, but he may well have also discovered inspiration in the theatre.

The next inspiration was Shakespeare's Hamlet. In 1907 Witkacy painted a garden scene Gravedigger's Monologue (1916) (pic. 5) with Hamlet dressed in a white shirt and black pants and Ophelia in a long pink robe with a flower in her hair. This most likely depicts the scene of Ophelia's madness. The composition is in a private collection, probably in Krakow. Nine years later, in 1916 (perhaps because of the 400th anniversary of the Shakespeare's death), Witkacy returned to the drama depicting Hamlet's famous soliloquy in the cemetery [V, i]. Correspondingly, a pastel composition in the National Museum in Krakow presents a man in the centre with two gravediggers on each side, skulls and shinbones at his feet and a spectral figure in a black dress rising up behind him – evidently Ophelia's ghost.

The similarity between this composition and the later one also depicting two gravediggers suggests that the scene of Hamlet's monologue could have been an inspiration for Witkacy's The Anonymous Work.

In the same year, 1916, Witkacy also completed another pastel composition, "freezing" another stage scene – not from the theatre this time, but from the ballet. Composition with Swans (from the Castle Museum in Lublin) is evidently connected to Swan Lake by Piotr Tchaikovsky. We should remember that in 1916 Witkacy was in St. Petersburg so it would not be strange that the famous ballet inspired him at that time.

Returning to comparisons to Witkacy's own dramas, in 1911 he painted an exotic landscape Landscape Scene (pic. 6) depicting a bay with blue sea and a house. A lemon tree is on the shore as well as a couple with a cat between them. The woman is giving the cat something to eat. The scene may easily be taken at face value, but when we read The Water Hen we come across one of its characters, the Father who says: "Don't you remember when the three of us lived in the little house on the other side of the bay at Stockfish Beach? Remember her mania for feeding lemons to my ginger cat?"[6] It is quite obvious that the landscape depicts the idea used by Witkacy 10 years later in the drama.

The mixing of characters and situations in his paintings and his dramas was a regular occurence for the artist. The best example of a wonderful mixture of paintings, dramas and reality is a lost portrait of Eugenia Dunin-Borkowska from 1912, which presents a character sitting on a sofa with strange scenes depicted on the wall behind her. Until earlier compositions,

---

[6] S. I. Witkiewicz: The Madman and the Nun and Other Plays, op. cit., p. 52.

Scene in a Garden (1906) (pic. 7) Hamlet and Ophelia in the Garden, and The Landscape with the Red Cat, were discovered in private collections in Krakow and Warsaw it was assumed that Witkacy had deliberately created a strange background to make the portrait more bizarre; while in fact he had simply put two of his own paintings on the wall above the sofa in Borkowska's living room. I think that both interpretations are in fact correct. Witkacy did create his own new reality by using elements taken equally from real life and from the reality of art. What is more, the sitter for the portrait was an actress, so perhaps his depiction of her with two paintings in the background presenting important scenes with great female roles in brilliant dramas could have additional significance and could be said to create a quite new reality.

Witkacy also mixed real life with art – he depicted it in his paintings and in his novels as well, the best example of which could be an oil composition from 1922 Composition with a Woman (Jadwiga Janczewska's Suicide) (pic. 8). The painting depicts the suicide of Witkacy's fiancee, who went to the Tatra mountains and shot herself in February 1914. An analogous scene can be found in his novel Farewell to the Autumn (written in 1925 and first published in 1927), where the wife of the protagonist, commits suicide in a very similar way.

All of this introduces us directly to the world of Witkacy's characteristic imagination, where everything seems to be fluid, but in fact is highly organized. His ideas penetrate one another, supplementing and complementing the others. Daniel Gerould, in his book Witkacy as an Imaginative Writer, invented a very useful term: "a unified world of imagination," for describing the situation in which various characters appear in various literary works by Witkacy (mainly in the dramas but also in the novels). The phenomena could also be extended to Witkacy's paintings where characters and situations from his own and other authors' works meet and create a great frozen theatre of art and life.

It is an interesting supposition, that if he were living now, Witkacy would likely be a great filmmaker, similar perhaps to David Lynch, whose films Mullholand Drive or Inland Empire, are, in my opinion, incredibly "Witkacian" given their rapidly changing characters and loopy plots.

To conclude, I would like to close with an anecdote. A while ago I had a dream... One morning I arrived at the National Museum in Warsaw where I was working, and I looked at Witkacy's Fantasy Fairytale hanging on the wall. I reached out to the painting and touched it. First the left side – where the figure of a man is depicted. The painting at once came to life – Edgar Walpor moved and shot the Water Hen. Then I touched the right side – now alive, the monsters began to move and change into men, as in Witkacy's drama. But what next? What would happen if all his characters really met? I'm afraid that only Witkacy could answer that question.

I would like to thank The National Museum of Warsaw, The British Museum in London, The National Museum in Krakow and a number of Private Collectors for Permitting the Reproduction of the images included in this Essay.

Abstract

In this article the author applies Tadeusz Boy-Żeleński's claim that Witkacy's paintings are "theatre frozen on canvas" by examining the many characters who coexist in both his paintings and dramas. This is evident not only in the content of his later drawings and paintings when he was most productive with his dramatic literary output, but also in the subject matter of earlier art pieces before he even began the fruitful period of his dramatic works. Moreover, some of the images in his artwork reflect his own real life experiences. The author borrowing a phrase from Daniel Gerould claims that Witkacy creates a "unified world of imagination" in which various characters appear in multiple literary and art works.

Dr. Anna Żakiewicz
National Museum of Warsaw

S. I. Witkiewicz: *Fantasy-Fairytale*, 1921, oil, 74.5 x 150 cm
National Museum in Warsaw

S. I. Witkiewicz: *Composition with Gravediggers*, 1920, pastel, 48.8 x 60.5 cm
National Museum in Warsaw

Francisco de Goya y Lucientes (Spanish, 1746–1828):
The Sleep of Reason Produces Monsters, 1799 etching,
aquatint, drypoint, and burin, 21.5 x 15 cm
© Trustees of the British Museum

S. I. Witkiewicz: *Demonic Composition*, 1906, charcoal, 32.4 x 40 cm
private collection

S. I. Witkiewicz: Gravedigger's Monologue, 1916, pastel, 51 x 65 cm
National Museum in Krakow

S. I. Witkiewicz: *Landscape Scene*, 1911, guache, 49 x 68 cm
private collection

S. I. Witkiewicz: *Scene in a Garden*, 1906, guache, 48.2 x 66.2 cm
private collection

S. I. Witkiewicz: Composition with a Woman (Jadwiga Janczewska's suicide), 1920
oil, 58 x 78.5 cm, private collection

Małgorzata Vražić

Witkiewicz-Father and Son: The Double Portrait

For professional literary researchers and admirers of Witkacy's works, the artist's relationship with his father, Stanisław Witkiewicz, artist, art critic, man of ideas and thinker, is a compelling issue. Although extensive research has been carried out in the main on both private family relations and between father and son, little has been done to find common ground in the realm of their thoughts and concepts. The significance of Stanisław Witkiewicz's original pedagogical system in relation to his son has however been covered, particularly with the publication of The Letters to a Son,[1] which reveals the inner history of the father-son relationship and reveals Stanisław Witkiewicz's desire to see his son confirm his own artistic theses. The letters constitute an extremely intriguing document of the period; they are, so to speak, a transcript of a turbulent debate on fundamental artistic, literary and philosophical issues, suffused with original concepts on art and life and a reflection of Stanisław Witkiewicz's pedagogy.

Witkacy has always been and indeed will surely remain a focal character in Polish art, with new critical studies and analyses of his works appearing regularly. Stanisław Witkiewicz, his father, however, appears to be a forgotten figure, mistaken for or identified with Witkacy, who both outshone his father and also rejected his authority. This notwithstanding, during his own life-time Stanisław Witkiewicz had been considered a leader of

---

[1] S. Witkiewicz: Listy do syna (The Letters to the Son), Warsaw 1969.

the art world, considered by some to be a spiritual guru or even a prophet. Nonetheless, contemporary studies of Witkiewicz are rare. Indeed, the most recent monograph, entitled The Strange Man, was published in 1984.

Therefore, I would argue that studies of the memoirs of family members and friends have led to a rather one-sided impression of the matter of the Witkiewiczes', which on the whole emphasize the striking differences in their attitudes and theories. However, it can also be claimed that neither the family nor their groups of friends could objectively evaluate the psychological, characterological and artistic points of intersection and overlap of these two personalities. As such, it is necessary to seek out a fresh and more extensive treatment of their relationship. It is felt that a singularly contrastive approach should be abandoned albeit that, despite the obvious differences, the Witkiewiczes' standpoints may well in fact be reduced to a common denominator. Rather than concentrating only on discrepancies between the two artists, if we would care to approach their relationship from the point of view of similarities, we may be able to form the conclusion that Witkacy shaped his art not so much 'in opposition to his father' but rather 'in relation to his father.' Granted, at the early stage of his artistic development, Witkacy tried to depart from Witkiewicz's theses as far as possible. It would seem that it was during this period that Wikiewicz senior was reduced to the role of antagonist. I would posit that, ultimately, Witkacy did in fact follow Witkiewicz's path.

The Witkiewiczes' intellectual discoveries and strategies dovetailed at many points, and as such, this article will primarily concern the similarities rather than the differences in the works of both artists. Moreover, literature and art historians have usually sought analogy in the area of formal concepts, seeking to trace affinities between Witkacy's Theory of Pure Form and Stanisław Witkiewicz's aesthetic assumptions, in which he emphasized the significance of colour, light and composition. Such conclusions are naturally of a restrictive nature, since the relations between the Witkiewiczes are not merely a question of aesthetics. For example, both Witkiewiczes questioned cultural norms, and the common kernel of their ideas is the assertion of the crisis of culture, understood as the fall of a particular system of values, such as national unity, the notion of high art, and the readability of signs of culture. It is true however that they claimed there to be differing causal reasons for such a crisis, such as on the issue of evaluating our national characteristics. Despite such apparent discrepancies as these their work would seem to be united by several common fundamental features. Here examples could include: the cult of authenticity in the act of creation, of aesthetic sensations and of authenticity in the field of social communication;

the necessity to search for a deeper meaning of reality and human existence; the need for a continuity of culture; faith in the role of artistic and intellectual elites as well as antipathy to certain phenomena, contemporarily termed 'popular culture.' Undoubtedly, the Witkiewiczes shared the common conviction, albeit arising out of divergent origins, that Poles had become a quasi nation, incapable of functioning correctly and creating a culture which would not only confirm its strength and vitality but would also enrich European cultural output. They observed the disintegration of what one might call 'the form of the Polish character,' the Polish universum,[2] since in the field of the life of national society 'the non-form' was no alternative for form for either of the Witkiewiczes.

Their pessimistic diagnoses of the crisis of culture also provoked the Witkiewiczes into taking an active stance. In the text of Art and Critique Here, Alexander Gierymski, Vallenrodism or Debasement?, Stanisław Witkiewicz observed the signs of torpor and unmasked the decline hiding behind the economic prosperity and the progress of civilization which, according to his analysis, surfaced after the unsuccessful uprising of 1864. He saw this decline as tantamount to subjugation, thralldom and the devaluation of art as a significant element of social life. Specifying the spheres of life in crisis, Witkiewicz simultaneously created a list of damage to be repaired, losses that were experienced after the defeat of the uprising. He never took the length of the list as a reason to be discouraged. His concept of culture was predicated upon an attempt to break a paradigm and the awareness that the basic component of the Polish national ego is a tendency towards auto--destruction and dwelling upon loss along with the cult of death. After 1864, Polish society was in a critical situation again – the decline of values, of the sense of unity and national uniqueness, pessimism, the lack of faith in the future – but paradoxically, it was on the road to revival and the recovery of its inner energy. Following Nietzsche's philosophy, Witkiewicz wished to see new forces born out of pain, and not just the continuation of frustration, which should rather be seen as the outcome of decline. For Stanisław Witkiewicz, the sense of culture lay in the continual development and enrichment of traditional elements, in the continuous evolution and remodelling of the paradigm.

Whilst not limiting himself to the suggested characteristics of the crisis, Witkiewicz prepared a concept of the revival of culture, attempting to re-

---

[2] See Anna Micińska: Na marginesie „Narkotyków" i „Niemytych dusz" Stanisława Ignacego Witkiewicza, [in:] S. I. Witkiewicz: Narkotyki. Niemyte dusze (Narcoticks. Uncwashed Souls), Warsaw 1975 and J. Degler: Witkacy – wychowawca narodu (Witkacy as an Educator of the Nation), „Odra" 1976, nr 10.

define the notion of being Polish – an idea which was neither nationalist nor loyalist by nature, but an idea of a moral understanding of the Polish character in the Romantic sense.[3] He viewed Polishness as being similar to a lost text, which he looked for among the people of the Podhale region. He found manifestations of the Polish character in the literary works of Henryk Sienkiewicz as well as in the paintings of Juliusz Kossak, both of whom he considered typical Polish artists and whose works he employed to serve his purpose. In his project, an education based on Nietzsche's philosophy played a crucial role and his ultimate goal was to rear a New Man and to metamorphose humanity spiritually. Such a man would be an artist, a philosopher and a lay saint, concerned with contemporary issues. Architecture and the Zakopane style, presented by Witkiewicz as the national style, constituted the crux of the entire concept, since architecture and art were universal systems of communication and convenient means of influencing the social imagination. Witkiewicz treated Polish culture as a space to manage under the slogan ONE STYLE – ONE NATION. The Zakopane style was utopian by nature, but utopianism was one of the languages of the era.

Stanisław Witkiewicz's diagnoses were a central, although not the sole, point of reference for his son's assertions, who, like his father, attempted to create an aesthetic-cultural system. One of the differences between the Witkiewiczes' culture-oriented assertions lies in the accepted perspective. Witkiewicz senior focused mainly on the Polish issue, rarely mentioning the broader context, whereas his son represented a more global standpoint, writing on the crisis of culture as such. For Witkacy, the situation in Poland was a prefiguration of the fall of Europe, which can be seen as proof that he managed to liberate himself from the 'cursed' Polish issues, for example, the national issue, messianism, the need for protection of all that is 'genuinely' Polish, the Romantic heritage, utopian thinking. He was, therefore, able to view culture in a more universal way, something which would be possible only in a free Poland.

Clearly Witkacy's vision of history was based on the triad of birth, development and the inevitable fall. Such an approach, however, did not exclude attempts to defeat the danger of the decline of culture, as it might always be tempting to try once more. Thus, the issue arises concerning the way Witkacy functioned within catastrophe as well as the relationship between his works and the sphere of his diagnoses.

---

[3] M. Janion: Życie pośmiertne Konrada Wallenroda (The Posthumous Life of Conrad Vallenrod), Warsaw 1990, p. 605.

The theme of the manifestations of decline grew in Witkacy's works to the rank of a mission, since once you cannot be the guardian of the Mystery of Being, you can only become transfigured into a bard of destruction. Witkacy expressed his cultural abeyance between the 'expectation and experience' of catastrophe in many theoretical articles as well as in literary texts, writing other decline-infected quasi novels under the auspices of Thanatos through the creation of character, the means of creating and the shaping of literary space, the image of the state, language and style, and the form of a 'badly' written novel. Witkacy saw the cause of crisis in, among others things, the democratizing processes of society, and understood them as absolutely irreversible. Since their ultimate outcome was unpredictable, in his New Forms in Painting Witkacy proposed a program which could be called one of conscious democratization. The awareness of participation in the evolution or remodeling of the paradigm of culture remained a primary theme, to which Witkacy returned in his works: Narcotics – Unwashed Souls. This may be interpreted as a rescue strategy, integrally inscribed in Witkacy's catastrophic concept. Narcotics – Unwashed Souls is Witkacy's most important text, the handbook which he employed to conduct a specific therapeutic action and through which he teased his readers, playing with his own biography as well as forms of popular culture. This was the crux of his concept of culture. Narcotics – Unwashed Souls indicates the direction in which Stanisław Ignacy Witkiewicz's views evolved and it is precisely at this point where both of the Witkiewiczes converge again. By the end of his life, Witkacy assumed a role similar to that of his father's – the role of a social activist and a spiritual leader. He became 'socially-oriented' and, striking a moralizing tone, encouraged and preached to the people, all of which he did however in accordance with his own original standards and principles. Only in such a form, when humour is an element introduced consciously, resulting from the assumption that intellectual work also has its humorous angle, did Witkacy intend "[...] to do something tangibly useful"[4] for society. Witkacy can hardly be called an educator of the nation, at least not in the classic meaning of the notion; however, he did also reflect on the condition of the national soul of the Poles, and Narcotics – Unwashed Souls is an interesting and original study of the issue.

The question of Witkacy's catastrophism also arises, as his entire cultural strategy was based upon a continuous swinging – between despondency and further attempts to open a dialogue, between the conviction that art, phi-

---

[4] S. I. Witkiewicz: Narkotyki. Niemyte dusze (Narcoticks – Unwashed Souls), op. cit., p. 53.

losophy and religion were non-existent and a game played with their contemporary forms. Thus, the game undertaken in his avant-garde plays and novels has, by and large, a quality justifying Witkacy's writing. This was a man who once officially declared the death of art and refused to treat the novel as a work of art. His games also have a cognitive purpose and help to embrace and understand the area of the new in culture. A game is only possible when its elements, themes, structures and principles are comprehensible.

The same mechanism governed the Witkiewiczes' culture strategies – a sense of danger pushed them to produce explicit or even provocative actions. Neither of them looked for a haven in dwelling upon pain. Neither contented himself with the ascertainment of crisis.

Both Witkiewicz's and Witkacy's fears for the future and the form of culture are typical for modernity. According to Anthony Giddens, high levels of fear are not a distinguishing factor of modern times, but each era has had its fears and concerns. What changes is the form and content of the fears, as it is they that distinguish modernity from other epochs.[5] Jerzy Jedlicki adds that ascertaining crisis is inherent in experiencing modernity but, paradoxically, all these crisis related diagnoses and emotions constitute a positive factor:

> The crisis of culture, regardless of its definition, is its standard, not unique quality and there is no, and might never be, any charm, [...] or philosophers' stone which will bring release. That's good, as every progress is born out of misery, horror and rebellion. [...] The sense of crisis of values results in willingness to defend them and this will only become dangerous when it aims at perfection.[6]

The essence of Witkacy's catastrophism, which is not so much total or constant as perverse, may just lie in this. Once Witkacy's games with the novel, literature, art or even philosophy become an approved fact, why should he be denied the right to play games with his own culture-oriented diagnoses? It is obviously a situation in which the discovery of the decline, treated quite seriously and experienced profoundly, is accompanied by the conviction that pondering over crises is of a cognitive, existential and preserving value. It should be remembered that the observation went in the name of dying values which, by nature, are ephemeral and require protection and careful handling.

---

[5] See: A. Giddens: Modernity and Self-Identity: Self and Society in the Late Modern Age, Warsaw 2001, p. 47.

[6] J. Jedlicki: Świat zwyrodniały. Lęki i wyroki krytyków nowoczesności (The Degenerated World. Fears and Judgments of the Critics of Modernity), Warsaw 2000, p. 60–61.

Many other 'points of convergence' of the Witkiewiczes' thoughts, actions and strategies are evident in their works. Witkacy is well known to have been using the strategy of scandal, but in truth Witkiewicz senior was scandalous in a comparable degree for his own time. It is noteworthy that he dared to engage in a turbulent argument with the respectable and renowned art critic, Henryk Struve, practically mocking his critical methods. He considered Struve's texts the epitome of incompetence, dilettantism and stupidity. Witkiewicz also defied the unquestionable authority of Jan Matejko, the greatest historical painter of the time, pointing out the flaws in his technique and accusing him of excessive exploitation of themes related to Polish history. This act of defiance marked his forceful entry into the area of national taboo and unleashed an enormous wave of criticism. The list of various scandals, on Witkiewicz's instigation or with his participation, is quite long, but even these few examples show that Witkacy's primacy in the field of scandal seems gravely undermined.

An authoritative tone, uncompromising arguments and theses and radical opinions approving of no critique are features which can be applied to both of the Witkiewiczes. Witkiewicz senior's method of formulating thoughts and objections are worth noting. In 1905, he wrote: "The so called monumental structures of society are wretched, stinky, filthy and vile, full of dark nooks which breed crime. This must be fought ruthlessly!" This notion bears a striking resemblance to Witkacy's words from Narcotics – Unwashed Souls: "We must begin to bash the mugs, wash the slovenly muzzles and shake the heads, forcefully bang the mucky noggins against walls of some pigsty [...]"[7]

The radicalism of the Witkiewiczes' texts, although unquestionable, did in fact differ in approach. Witkiewicz, in striking a militant, bellicose tone, practically never violated the typical forms of communication. He disturbed neither the stylistic principles, orthography nor linguistic ettiquette, and yet, his texts evoked violent reactions from his readers, fans and adversaries. He expressed the meaning of his own intellectual discoveries and appealed to people within general standards. Witkacy, on the other hand, did not only cause a stir and 'bang the table', but also resorted to verbal abuse, grotesque jokes and invectives while addressing his readers and enemies, betraying profound affinity for the dramatic potential of language. Neither of the Witkiewiczes abandoned their attempts to establish a relationship with their recipients. Even Witkacy did not forget to reinforce his influence over his

---

[7] See: A. Micińska: Istnienie poszczególne. Stanisław Ignacy Witkiewicz (The Particular Being: Stanisław Ignacy Witkiewicz), elaborated by J. Degler, Wrocław 2003, p. 214.

audience in his games with popular culture and literature. Witkiewicz senior chose a more serious format which made the reception of his texts more palatable, whereas Witkacy employed palimpsest-based texts, constructed grotesquely, which greatly impedes communication.

The presence of Thanatos, of sickness and death, manifesting itself in both Witkiewicz's and Witkacy's works is clearly detectable. The broadly understood decline is unusually distinct not simply as a motif in Witkacy's works. Approached comprehensively, it can be perceived as a consistent study into decline or atrophy. Metaphors of dying, of diseases or of crumbling buildings had already become quite frequent in Stanisław Witkiewicz's texts.[8] He described the ever more powerful social-national atrophy after the unsuccessful uprising of 1863 with corporal references and comparisons. The decline develops like a disease of the body which is shrinking, vanishing, dying: 'life is suffocating, passing away.' He mentions the disintegration of 'the crux of the soul' and 'a crumbled structure/edifice of the spirit.' Certainly, the presence of the metaphors of dying and disease did not result in the vision of the total annihilation of the fundamental values of culture. The metaphors described the situation of crisis, depicted meanings of the intellectual discoveries of the Polish thinker, remaining subject to his revivalistic concepts. Even a superficial analysis of Witkacy's works leads to different conclusions. The primacy of Thanatos in diverse configurations and schemes is undeniable and inalienable. Its painful, tangible existence can be treated as a figure of Witkacy's catastrophic thought. Witkacy employed the same 'metaphor of dying' more distinctly than his father. "Our blushes are not the blushes of health, but hectic colours, our gleam in the eyes is not a healthy flame, but a feverish gloss, our impetuous movements and agitation are not the sign of excessive strength, these are convulsions, the spasms."[9]

The motif of the body played a more forefrontal role in Witkacy's works; however, the corporal sphere and the distortions in this sphere can still be associated with the recognition of the fall of culture and the expanding decline. The discrepancy in the approach to the body as well as in the treatment of personal corporality of both of the Witkiewiczes, manifests itself in their epistolography, Witkiewicz's The Letters to a Son and Witkacy's The Letters to a Wife.

In his theory of art, Stanisław Witkiewicz conducted a revalorisation of ugliness in the name of aesthetic and formal values. He justified and rationalised the presence of ugliness in a painting or a novel with a mastery of tech-

---

[8] E.g. S. Witkiewicz: Vallenrodism or Debasement?

[9] S. I. Witkiewicz: Nowe formy w malarstwie (New Forms in Painting), Warsaw 2002, p. 160.

nique which was not equal to a simple reproduction of nature. Witkiewicz validated themes which were not approved of by idealist aesthetics, such as poverty, the gloom of existence, the ugliness of the body, and immorality. A naturalist himself, he did not want 'a re-mastered, sickeningly sweet image of the world', but was convinced of the fusion of beauty and ugliness, of sumptuousness and asceticism in real life. He thus wanted to transpose this complex interdependence into the field of art, which according to the thesis of naturalism, should reflect the truth of life and incorporate all areas of existence. The arrival of ugliness, deformity and the grotesque in Witkacy's works should be viewed from three angles: the wish to reject realistic tendencies in art, a catastrophic vision of the fall of art and the attempts to evoke aesthetic shock. Witkacy argued that the blasé and empty modern audience, in the widest sense of the meaning, needs shock and an adrenaline rush, and thus should not be influenced by harmonious beauty which evokes pleasant associations. He used ugliness as one of the strongest stimuli, serving the purpose of a kind of aesthetic shock therapy. In both Witkiewicz's and Witkacy's theories, the revalorization of ugliness intended aimed to alter the perception of the role of art.

Abandoning the role is thought to be the Witkiewiczes' key specialty. It came to be ascribed mainly to Witkacy, who took on many different roles and put on various masks. However, Stanisław Witkiewicz's personality was also dynamic: a painter by profession, he became a writer, journalist and critic. Later, however, he abandoned the role of leading Polish art critic and iconoclast, responsible for causing a stir in the field of idealistic aesthetics. Witkiewicz eventually decided on a more monumental role for himself, resulting from the conditions of his era, still wrapped up and burdened with Polish problems of the past and identity. He became a teacher, a profound sage, a prophet of the Zakopane style.

Such choices resulted from a different concept of becoming mature and the perception of its meanings. The pedagogical system created by Witkiewicz aimed at educating artists who would produce a work of art in the future, who would become the epitome of a perfect creator and transmute into a masterpiece incarnate. In directing the process of his son's education, Stanisław Witkiewicz wrote to Wikacy: 'be yourself,' 'impose yourself,' 'define yourself,' predicting such maturity, the unity of the self, the ease and directness in articulating one's own self in art marks the end of the process of growing up. Witkacy's discoveries led in a different direction as he grew up in a climate of an era which questioned identity in a disparate way and the main interests of which lay in youth and unreadiness.[10] He took on various pseudonyms, each of which corresponded to a slightly different identity. It was the strategy of a player who experienced the fragmentary nature of reality, who recognized its lack of cohesion and who did not treat life as unified. Such is the point of convergence between Witkacy and contemporary philosophers of culture such as Zygmunt Bauman.

The Witkiewiczes were bound by a postulate of authenticity. They both searched for its sources in the artist's work and in the art-recipient relationship. For Witkiewicz, authenticity was a prerequisite for realism. The modern fear of non-authenticity manifested itself in his multiple dictates of authenticity in personal and artistic life as well as enthusiastic postulates of uniqueness, addressed to his son in his letters. In both Stanisław Witkiewicz's and Stanisław Ignacy Witkiewicz's theories, the artist and his worlds constitutes an ultimate resort and instance of authenticity – he shoulders responsibility. Granting the artist this particular type of power, Witkiewicz felt that development prospects opened up for art. For Witkacy, the responsibility an artist was obliged to shoulder, the awareness of what art should be, is dearly paid for in the currency of despair, as mysterious, metaphysical worlds are going to irretrievably pass away. Therefore, the artist raves, tossed between the sense of mission, the awareness of his own uniqueness and the sense of danger. He is a dying species, not protected by the institutions of the culture of the new era, and who nevertheless does not relinquish his uncompromising stance on acts of creation and art overall. In Witkiewicz's texts, the artist pays for his choices – he is doomed to incomprehension, oblivion, social ostracism and suffering, like the painter Aleksander Gierymski. In Witkacy's texts, the artist's tragedy occurs at a circus arena or in the lunatic asylum, since the ultimate price for authenticity is nothing else but madness and death.

Despite his idealistic perception of the culture of the Podhale region, Stanisław Witkiewicz observed a certain intrusion of mass culture into folk culture. He was aware that the highlanders were sucked into the crucible of the commercial demands of tourists and were keen to accept the new situation quite quickly. They easily parted from the traditional lifestyle and conduct as well as from original models of folk art. The highlander's wooden house, which Witkiewicz almost worshipped practically ceased to be the home of the highlander and became a product for sale, a regional attraction, not a sign of culture or symbol of Polishness.

---

[10] See: E. Paczoska: Dojrzewanie, dojrzałość, niedojrzałość (Maturation, Maturity, Immaturity), Warsaw 2004, p. 5.

A problem with Stanisław Witkiewicz's texts consists in their glaring 19th century stylistics and sentimental-romantic mannerisms which overshadow the novelty of some of his discoveries and conclusions. However, it is noteworthy that the artist did not renounce old-fashioned stylistics. Stanisław Witkiewicz wrote and acted as he did, despite his full knowledge of the world. The choice of such a strategy is particular to a utopian way of thinking and Witkiewicz's texts can undoubtedly be classified in the literary trend which builds a utopian image of society and creates a vision of a new man, and may in consequence, indeed be set alongside the works of John Ruskin, William Morris, and many others. It would probably be difficult to prove that building a utopia must be unconditionally connected with the lack of basic knowledge of the bank of ideas contemporary to Witkiewicz.

With all his distaste for popular culture and mass literature, Witkacy was not only aware of what such a form of culture was and could decipher its main principles and unmask its traps, he was also able to use it to his advantage. He constructed an educational situation consisting of the application of patterns of popular literature in conveying his own outlook on life.[11] Witkacy employed such patterns not only in his novels but in his palimpsest-based Narcotics – Unwashed Souls, which he formed as a quasi (psychological) handbook, thus using the potential of popular literature. His conclusions about culture anticipate the discoveries of contemporary philosophers, sociologists and psychologists, concerning the presence of narcissism in the 20th century.

The case of Witkiewicz the father and the son transgresses the traditional struggle of generations who stand on opposite sides of the barricade of family and social life, since there is such a significant point of convergence for both artists in the sphere of modernity and Polish Modernism. The Witkiewiczes' artistic and literary works, as well as public commitments, fall into different phases of Modernism; however, they reflect its complex, variable character, the logic of development and the dynamics of transformations. Both of the Witkiewiczes were 'boundary' figures, existing at the pass between the generation of the so-called positivists and modernists. Their strategies and conclusions entered into the realm of complicated dialogue of paradigms, not only just between their own concepts. In attempting to understand their own contemporary times, both of them anticipated the questions posed by subsequent generations of artists on art, literature and culture. Witkiewicz was profoundly interested in the achievements of mod-

---

[11] See: M. Kochanowski: Powieści Witkacego wobec schematów literatury popularnej (Witkacy's Novels Towards to the Patterns of the Popular Novel), Białystok 2007.

ernists and supported their work; he visited the studios of young painters and wanted to meet futurists and cubists. Witkacy's philosophy met half-way with the aesthetic and philosophical achievements of the 21st century, which allows us to analyze his works in the context of the language of the new media or cyberart. The parallel treatment of the reflections of both Witkiewiczes creates an opportunity to present the various faces of Polish Modernism as a dynamic space to form models of Polish cultural identity.

Abstract

In this essay, I describe the relationship between Stanisław Witkiewicz and his son, Stanisław Ignacy Witkiewicz (Witkacy) as a relationship between two artists in the broadest sense of the word. That is both were painters, writers, and thinkers. Initially, I perceived the Witkiewicz's as 'challengers' in the realm of culture issues. I ultimately turn my attention to stress the similarities between both Witkiewicz's rather than the differences because the two artists shared a common view on many ideas, e.g. the crisis of culture, the death of the Polish Universum, the ideal of a high and pure art, authenticity in personal life as well as in the field of art. Their artistic works reflect different stages of Modernism, but at the same time they show how complex Modernism was. This comparative work shows Modernism as a 'space' for the formation of Polish culture identity.

Dr. Małgorzata Vražić
Warsaw University

Michael Goddard

Cinema, Insatiability and Impure Form: Witkacy on Film

Introduction: The Absence of Cinema in Witkacy's Work

Cinema in the work of Witkacy is notable principally by its absence. Whereas many of Witkacy's Western contemporaries were fascinated by the emergence of this increasingly dominant 20th Century medium, Witkacy seems to have more or less ignored it altogether despite his interest and participation in a wide range of modern aesthetic practices including painting, photography, and mass produced portraits and theatre not to mention cultural criticism and philosophy. Whereas many of the artists associated with Dada or Surrealism including Dali, Duchamp, Man Ray and Leger all tried their hand at cinematic works, and even figures from the avant-garde theatre such as Brecht and Artaud both had their 'cinematic episodes' even if these were subsequently rejected, nothing of the kind seems to be the case with Witkacy. Part of the explanation for this must lie in the relative underdevelopment of cinema in Poland prior to World War II; most of the local cinema produced was in the form of highly conventional romances, with an avant-garde cinema only developing towards the end of Witkacy's life, that is to say in the late 30's. This avant-garde cinema was far removed from Witkacy's own aesthetics, being comprised of both a purely constructivist artistic cinema (Krystyna Kobro or the Themerson's) or social realism (the START group) and there is no evidence that Witkacy was aware of or interested in these tendencies. Nevertheless, it is highly unlikely that Witkacy would not have been aware of earlier forms of artistic cinema such as German Expressionist films, Soviet Constructivism or at the very least the films of Charlie Chaplin which had such an effect on Surrealist artists and critical theorists like Walter Benjamin. Even Witkacy's contemporaries such as Witold Gombrowicz show in their work more traces of a productive encounter with cinema, for example, in the references to Chaplin in Gombrowicz's Ferdydurke.

One of the few places where there is a reference to cinema, if a negative one, is in Witkacy's manifesto, New Forms in Painting and Misunderstandings Arising Therefrom (1919). In the section that considers the decline of art in response to the already analysed onslaught of modernity and its destructive and equalising tendencies that Witkacy saw as fatal for European art and culture, the cinema is mentioned precisely when Witkacy is considering the decline of the role of the theatre in modernity, in a passage that is worth quoting at length:

> For people nowadays, the forms of Art of the past are too placid, they do not excite their deadened nerves to the point of vibration. They need something that will rapidly and powerfully shock their blase nervous system and act as a stimulating shower after long hours of stupefying mechanical work [...] Today's theatre cannot satisfy the average spectator; only the dying breed of theatrical gourmets appreciate the revived delicacies, whereas Cabaret on the one hand and cinema on the other are taking away most of the audience from the theatre [...] Cinema can do absolutely everything that the human spirit might desire, and so if we can have such frantic action and striking images instead, isn't it well worth giving up useless chatter on the stage which nobody needs anymore anyhow; is it worth taking the trouble to produce something as infernally difficult as a truly theatrical play when confronted by such a threatening rival as the all-powerful cinema.[1]

It is worth considering this evaluation of cinema as a 'threatening rival' to the theatre fully as it is no mere simple condemnation of mass culture in the name of high art. Considering that this piece was written in 1919 and in Poland, when the cinema was considered a highly degraded form of popular entertainment and yet to attain the global economic dominance and artistic respectability it would acquire over the course of the 1920's, it was rather

---

[1] S. I. Witkiewicz: New Forms in Painting and Misunderstandings Arising Therefrom, [in:] The Witkiewicz Reader, ed. and trans. D. Gerould, Northwestern University Press, Evanston 1992, p. 115.

prescient for Witkacy to ascribe to cinema the power to 'do everything the human spirit might desire.' This would imply a view of cinema not based on its current achievements but on what it was capable of but yet to realise. This ascendancy is only ascribed in part to the wave of modernisation and mechanisation which Witkacy clearly saw the cinema as a symptom of. Equally to blame was the decadence of the theatre itself, whose retreat into psychological realism in the wake of Ibsen and others had more or less sounded its death-knell; for Witkacy, the power of theatre, as of other aesthetic practices lay in its proximity to the powers of ritual, to provoke the kind of metaphysical experience that Witkacy referred to in terms of Pure Form.

The question remains as to why Witkacy saw the cinema as a rival rather than an ally in the artistic creation of Pure Form. Apart from the relative impoverishment of cinematic means of expression at this time, for Witkacy it seems that cinema, as the industrial art form par excellence was far too contaminated with the forces of modernity and modernisation to contribute to the kind of artistic insurrection he saw as being the role of 'those artists who would be absolutely incapable of living without creating' among whom he numbered himself. It is interesting to note in this respect that when Witkacy came to write his manifesto, 'Pure Form in the Theatre' there is no direct consideration of cinema at all, while nevertheless many of the terms Witkacy employs to describe Pure Form are paradoxically highly cinematic. For example, Witkacy refers to the work of art as an autonomous construction made of plastic and sonic components, utterances and actions, rather than deriving from any principle of psychology, representation or realism. While this might not in fact account for the dominant tendencies of narrative cinema then or now, it is highly resonant with what the cinematic apparatus makes possible in the cutting out of blocs of space-time composed of aesthetically recombined fragments detached from any prior context; this is the abstraction intrinsic to cinema that is not dissimilar than the formal abstraction called for by Witkacy in relation to the theatre. Furthermore, Witkacy's elaboration of the means for producing experiences of Pure Form via the mechanisms of shock is even more resonant with contemporaneous accounts of cinema such as by Eisenstein or Artaud that saw cinema's power to shock the nervous system directly as essential to its functioning, an approach later taken up by Walter Benjamin in his Work of Art essay. Why then if Witkacy's description of Pure Form in the theatre is so close to the radical potentials of cinematic experience does he refrain from even mentioning cinema in this manifesto? This cannot be answered definitively but I suspect that it would have something to do with the association of cinema with both modernity and Insatiability, the concept that is both a pre-condition for the experience of Pure Form and its antithesis. For Witkacy, modernity is essentially a narcotic experience, filled with all kinds of obsessions and distractions that cover over its essential emptiness. This state of addictive insatiability applies as much to contemporary forms of philosophy such as pragmatism or materialism as popular entertainments like the cinema as well as the obsession with the occult and mysticism and literal narcotics themselves, the charms of which Witkacy was hardly immune from. These various 'petty mysteries' serve to foreclose any genuine metaphysical experience, while at the same time expressing the insatiable desire for this experience; one can only suppose that, for Witkacy, Cinema, in a similar manner to the way he viewed the modern novel was too contaminated with both reality and modernity to be capable of Pure Form, even if it was an exemplary expression of the modern experience of insatiability; like the modern novel, the cinema would then be a formless 'bag in which one could put anything' rather than a medium capable of expressing Pure Form; however, this has not stopped several Polish filmmakers from attempting to give Witkacy's aesthetics and life a cinematic form, and it is to these attempts I will turn in the second part of this essay.

Tadeusz Kantor's Cricot 2 Theatre and The Dead Class

If there was a key post-war successor to Witkacy in Polish theatre it was clearly Tadeusz Kantor. Not only did he combine an engagement with contemporary art and artistic theatre but he saw his theatre as so indebted to the legacy of Witkacy that he named it the Cricot 2, after the pre-war Cricot theatre that was one of the few to present any plays by Witkacy and which met with the approval of Witkacy himself as being not an experimental but a truly artistic theatre. It is therefore unsurprising that six of the early productions of the Cricot 2 theatre were Witkacy adaptations. The Dead Class can be seen as a crucial turning point in Kantor's Theatre between these Witkacian beginnings and fully expressing his own vision of theatrical performance which would take on many subsequent forms while always retaining a commitment to an avant-garde performative practice for which Witkacy remained a key inspiration. The Dead Class was in fact a kind of integration of the works of the key pre-war writers Witkacy, Schulz and Gombrowicz, drawing on specific works by all three yet combining them into a single space of a re-animated classroom directly evoking the lost reality of pre-

-WWII Poland. Kantor's innovation was to double the figures appearing in the play with mannequins, an idea perhaps adapted from Schulz yet given a new level of intensity and monstrosity in Kantor's unique combination of plastic and theatrical art. Also in The Dead Class, Kantor challenged the usual idea of the naturalness of theatrical performance by appearing onstage himself as a deranged conductor or puppet-master, manipulating and provoking his theatrical creations, again echoing the descriptions of Jacob's mad father in Schulz's short stories. Yet despite the onstage presence of Kantor, The Dead Class is very much a performance of absence, the resurrection of a range of pre-war figures who do not realise that they are dead and therefore keep performing the same repetitive gestures that characterised them in their former lives, now transformed into monstrous and perverse imitations of their former selves, heightened by their accompaniment by hideous prostheses. There is something highly cinematic in this conception of theatre; in distinction to Kantor's contemporary Grotowski, for whom theatre should aim towards its origins in ritual by dissolving the boundaries between the stage, the performers and the audience and instead bringing out the living human essence of both performers and spectators, for Kantor, theatre is by definition the demarcation of an uncrossable line between the two, the act of producing an alien, virtual space, the space of the dead and of memory that tears reality in two rather than unites. In distinction to Witkacy's prophetic catstrophism, however, in Kantor's theatre, the catastrophe, directly associated with WWII and the holocuast has always already taken place and it is the role of theatre to bear witness to and evoke this past catastrophe from which we are yet to emerge and for which everyday forgetfulness is no solution. In this, he not only demonstrated his affinity with Witkacy's theories of Pure Form that are also based on the production of artificial, virtual, other spaces but also with cinema; as Metz and other theorists of the cinematic apparatus have noted, what defines cinematic perception is precisely the presence of an absence, of figures that were once present before a lens but are now absent from the bloc of space-time being presented to an audience in the form of 'imaginary signifiers' of an unbridgeable absence. Whether this cinematic dimension of Kantor's work is what drew Wajda to adapt The Dead Class or not, few commentators on this adaptation, including Wajda himself, saw it as an artistic success as a film. Perhaps the direct involvement of Kantor in the production prevented Wajda from realising his own vision of the work as he had done with Wsypiański's The Wedding; nevertheless, the resulting made for TV film is at the very least an invaluable document of Kantor's work and thereby the theatrical legacy of Witkacy himself.

Filming the Witkacy Legend: In a Country House and Farewell to Autumn

In one of the most perceptive treatments of cinematic adaptations of Witkacy's work, Katarzyna Taras's essay Witkacy's Film Counterfeits from 2001 treats a number of film adaptations of Witkacy's work, leading up to Treliński's Farewell to Autumn (which had recently appeared at the time the article was written). For Taras, all of these films take place under the sign of a double legend exerted by Witkacy's life and work. For Taras this double legend can be summarised as the legend of Witkacian catastrophism and the legend of Witkacy's own life. However, as the account of Witkacy's suicide on the eve of WWII which begins Taras's essay implies, these two legends are intertwined and inseparable, since Witkacy's life was intimately bound up with his aesthetics and in a sense he took the catastrophe of European modernity on himself, particularly in this final desperate performative self-annihilation.

The effect of these legends on cinematic adaptations of his work is to render them as something more than mere transpositions of theatrical works or novels into a cinematic form, since they also inevitably take on bio-historical qualities to greater and lesser extents. This is particularly the case with In a Country House or The Independence of Triangles in the version directed by Andrzej Kotkowski in 1985; rather than simply being an adaptation of the plays mentioned in the title, this film refers to a large number of Witkacy's plays including The Water Hen, Mother and The Cobblers amongst others. The structure of the film is perhaps most informed by The Water-Hen, based as it is on the killing of the heroine who nevertheless keeps reappearing in a perfectly corporeal form. However, Kotkowski was not content to simply combine several of Witkacy's theatrical works but also drew inspiration for his visual works, particularly his photographic self-portraits such as his famous self-portrait in a mirror that multiplied his own image in a play of reflections. He was also very interested in Witkacy's commerical portraits for the S. I. Witkiewicz portrait painting firm, especially for the way they represented female figures: the appearance of Beata Tyszkiewicz in the film was directly modelled on some of these portraits from the 20's and 30's. The end result of all these elements of the film was a film that was as much about Witkacy himself as the presentation of his works and many elements of Witkacy's biography found their way into the film. More than this, the incorporation of many of the visual elements of Witkacy's work attempted to reconstruct not just his world but his way of perceiving it, a tendency that would be repeated in subsequent Witkacy-based films.

Mariusz Treliński's adaptation of Farewell to Autumn took place in the very different context of post-communism and was the work of a director no less idiosyncratic than Kotkowski. Like Kotkowski, Treliński has only directed a few films of which the most well known is the more recent The Egoists (2000) a damning indictment of life in post-communist Warsaw that is not without a certain Witkacian catastrophism, shock and cruelty. Treliński for the rest of his career has devoted himself to theatre and especially opera and his films also share an operatic sensibility. Treliński's film begins in a no less biographical manner with a description of Witkacy's suicide in 1939, accompanied by the photographic self portrait 'the last cigarette of the condemned man' from 1924 and then a photograph of Witkacy from 1937–1939. As well as these allusions to Witkacy's life, Treliński makes allusions to a range of cinematic genres, a strategy no doubt conditioned by the new popular tendencies in Polish cinema in which in contrast to the dominance of art cinema during communism, Polish versions of Hollywood genres had come to dominate local film production. We therefore see in Treliński's film elements of the gangster film, the thriller, the melodrama and popular comedy all of which Treliński is able to extract from the original novel; in other words Treliński's film attempts to cinematise Witkacy's novel through the use of popular genres, a process Witkacy would no doubt have been very wary of and yet which is a quite successful transposition of the novel into a cinematic mode of expression. A key feature of Witkacy's work, evident in Treliński's film is decadence, which is again expressed through cinematic allusions, this time to Visconti's The Damned and Bertolucci's The Conformist. For these reasons, Taras sees this film less as an adaptation than as a game with Witkacy, that is nevertheless the best cinematic realisation of his work, the one that 'gives the greatest voice to the catastrophism of the author of the theory of Pure Form.'

Insatiability and Impure Form: Grodecki's Insatiability

Witkacy's novel Insatiability, while not itself a work of Pure Form, nevertheless presents a political and historiographic vision of the desire for Pure Form, also evident in some of Witkacy's theoretical writings. However, even more than in Farewell to Autumn, Witkacy treated the form of the novel as a shapeless bag in which everything from the most erotic or banal experiences to abstract metaphysical observations could be thrown together with no attention given to the perfection of form; this led Witold Gombrowicz to consider the novel, despite flashes of brilliance an abject and even deliberate aesthetic failure, that is an act of self-destruction. Nevertheless the formlessness of the novel, epitomised by its information sections that give neutral reports on events that the novel does not narrate, is in many ways well suited to its subject matter of the insatiability of modernity and the destruction of European traditions and cultural decadence; it expresses fully both Witkacy's struggle against this decadence and modernity and at the same time his succumbing to it, while on the political plane it is extraordinarily prophetic.

While on the one hand the novel clearly belongs to the genre of the Bildungsroman and is filled with vivid and erotic descriptions of Genezip's progress to maturity, treated in a highly ironic or rather catastrophic way, its incessant philosophical and factual interruptions, and frequent digressions render it even less adaptable cinematically than most of Witkacy's other works. In Grodecki's 2003 adaptation, it is therefore no less a case of playing with rather than adapting Witkacy, although in this case it is less through cinematic allusions than through the filter of decadent eroticism. Despite, or perhaps because of this the film seems to lack both a real sense of eroticism and fails to capture Witkacy's social and intellectual world. One of the problems with the film is that it is dominated by its performers, especially Cezary Pazura who plays three roles in the film and was also an executive producer of the film. This means the film becomes more a case of playing Witkacy than playing with Witkacy, a series of performance pieces in which Pazura delights in playing the more grotesque characters of the novel like the paedophile composer Putrycydes Tengler. It does have the virtue of no longer focusing so much on the Witkacy legend scenes but rather on the work itself. If it does this for the most part by amputating the more philosophical aspects of the novel there are at least some scenes in which its decadent atmosphere is rendered cinematically of which the following from the chapter entitled in English either 'Deflowrfucked' of Sexphyxiation' is perhaps one of the best examples.

Abstract

In this essay the author discusses Cinema in the work of Witkacy, particularly its absence. He refers to many of Witkacy's Western contemporaries as being fascinated by this increasingly dominant 20th Century medium, which Witkacy seems to have ignored despite his interest and participation in a wide range of modern aesthetic practices including painting, photography, mass produced portraits, and theatre. Part of the explanation for this, it is suggested, may lay in the relative underdevelopment of cinema in Poland prior to World War II; most of the local cinema produced was in the form of highly conventional romances, with an avant-garde cinema only developing towards the end of Witkacy's life. The author continues to present a very succinct account of how Witkacy's work has been transmuted into the medium of Film and Television.

Dr. Michael Goddard
University of Salford

John D. Barlow

Witkiewicz's Theory of Pure Form and the Music of Morton Feldman[1]

1

Because Witkiewicz thought the notion of form was ambiguous, he coined the term "pure form" to describe his theory of form, form itself being simply "that which imparts a certain unity to complex objects and phenomena." When this "unifying of the many into the one comes about" and "directly affects us" and leads to "aesthetic satisfaction," it is pure form.[2] These observations are fairly consistent with ideas of formalism current in the arts in Europe in the first half of the twentieth century. However, Witkiewicz adds further conditions. He emphasizes the unity of the individual, both as artist in creating and as spectator in perceiving the pure form. This "unity in mul-

---

[1] This essay is based on my paper, Pure Form in Music, presented at the Witkacy 2009 conference in London on September 18, 2009 and part of my paper, Witkacy's Music, presented at the Witkacy 2010 conference in Washington on April 30, 2010.

[2] S. I. Witkiewicz: On Pure Form, trans. C. S. Leach, [in:] Aesthetics in Twentieth Century Poland, ed. J. G. Harrell and A. Wirzbiańska, Lewisburg 1973, p. 50–51.

tiplicity" is "the basic law of existence..., given to us directly in the form of the unity of our personality." All art, therefore, is "an expression of the unity of our personality," acting on us "in an immediate way by means of its very structuring."[3] Elsewhere he says, "Pure Form acts directly, calling forth in us... heightened 'metaphysical feeling.'"[4] This is different from most other modernist theories of form. Witkiewicz was introducing here personal and philosophical considerations about the making and reception of works of art, which other formalists, eager to discuss only the work itself, tended to avoid.

Witkiewicz was obsessed with the idea of unity in plurality and considered it the precondition for the "primal formal instinct of man"[5] and the attempt to deal with the questions, "Why am I precisely this being, and not some other? At this place in infinite space and at this moment in infinite time? In this group of beings, on precisely this planet? Why do I exist at all? I could not exist; in fact, why is there anything at all?"[6] Witkiewicz thought that the metaphysical disquietude that resulted from these kinds of questions was essential to enable the creative process to produce a unity of pure form, distinct from the unattainable unity in the multiplicity of the universe.[7] This artistic unity leads to the "heightened metaphysical feeling" mentioned above. According to Witkiewicz, art, which does not come into being in this manner, does not endure and tends to result in novelty and snobbery about the past.[8] In experiencing works of art in pure form, spectators theoretically perceive the artist's "heightened metaphysical feeling" in a sense related to their own individual condition. They participate in this unity and become part of it, identifying with the form. But if something that is not art is expressed or communicated, then the unity, as well as the thrill that comes from the sense of unity, will be compromised.

Witkiewicz defined music as "sounds set to rhythm,"[9] its essence, as with all art forms, not to be found in "emotional elements," but in a "formal construction that directly arouses metaphysical feeling."[10] Consequently, to talk

---

[3] Ibidem, p. 53–54.

[4] S. I. Witkiewicz: Second Response to the Reviewers of The Pragmatists, trans. D. Gerould, [in:] The Witkiewicz Reader, ed. D. Gerould, Evanston 1992, p. 154.

[5] Idem: Pure Form in the Theater, [in:] The Witkiewicz Reader, op. cit., p. 150.

[6] Quoted in D. Gerould: Witkacy: Stanisław Ignacy Witkiewicz as an Imaginative Writer, Seattle 1981, p. 146.

[7] See E. Makarczyk-Schuster: Raum und Raumzeichen in Stanisław Ignacy Witkiewiczs Bühnenschaffen der zwanziger Jahre, Frankfurt am Main 2004, p. 55–58.

[8] Ibidem.

[9] S. I. Witkiewicz: Einführung in die Theorie der reinen Form des Theaters, [in:] Verrückte Lokomotive. Ein Lesebuch, ed. A. Wirth, Frankfurt am Main 1985, p. 44.

[10] Idem: Pure Form in the Theater, [in:] The Witkiewicz Reader, op. cit., p. 148.

about pure form in music is to talk about both the structural shape of the music and its metaphysical implications. "For Witkacy," writes Daniel Gerould, "music is the purest form of artistic expression, since it is the art furthest removed from life and most capable of giving voice to metaphysical feelings that lie beyond language."[11] In music the pure form is captured in sound. All sound and noise act upon listeners physically, striking them with sound waves which, in themselves and unlike words, do not ordinarily carry content or outside information, so that the immediate reaction is a purely physical one, one that imprints the sounds on the physical being of the listeners. When the sounds are formally organized in relation to each other to become music, it reverberates physically through the bodies of listeners, getting literally inside them, so that they sense themselves almost channeled by the music, their sensibilities aligned to the music like iron filings aligned by a magnet. When this identification occurs between music and the listener, it is a particularly unique sense of form because it can occur without conceptualization and articulated meaning and can easily make listeners forget the everyday details and contingencies of their lives and give them a sense of intensity without actually drugging them, unlike the thrill of being carried away by sentimental and non-musical aspects of the performance. In perceiving the pure form of the music, listeners are physically participating in its unity. The pleasure comes from that experience of the formal oneness, a purely metaphysical identity because it is based entirely on artistic form. Witkiewicz thought, as did Schopenhauer and Nietzsche before him, as Artaud did at the same time, and as Beckett thought after him, that "all art is metaphysical."[12]

It is not clear what Witkiewicz meant by this heightened sense of "the unity of one's individuality,"[13] given his persistent public and social habit of taking on different personae, pretending to be different people, and his constant use of many different pseudonyms for himself. Commentators have noted Witkiewicz's sense of multiple personalities in himself and others, his view of the personality as a "battleground of two egos," and the many masks

---

[11] D. Gerould: Witkacy, op. cit., p. 257.

[12] Cf. J. Degler: Witkacy in the World, [in:] A. Micińska: Witkacy: Stanisław Ignacy Witkiewicz: Life and Work, trans. B. Piotrowska, Warsaw 1990, p. 297; A. Artaud: Seraphim's Theatre, [in:] Collected Works, trans. V. Corti, Vol. 4, London 1974, p. 166; U. Pothast: Die eigentlich metaphysische Tätigkeit. Über Schopenhauers Ästhetik und ihre Anwendung durch Samuel Beckett, Frankfurt am Main 1982, p. 11–12.

[13] S. I. Witkiewicz: Second Response to the Reviewers of The Pragmatists, [in:] The Witkiewicz Reader, op. cit., p. 154.

he lived behind.¹⁴ As Mark Rudnicki has observed, if one wanted a photograph to characterize the true Witkiewicz, which one would one choose? The "buffoon, drug addict, priest, doctor," or "madman?" Or maybe the one of him sitting in front of two mirrors, presenting four images of himself?¹⁵

The British philosopher Galen Strawson has argued in his book Selves that the use of the first-person pronoun "shifts between two different things" in one's thought and speech. "Sometimes 'I' is used with the intention to refer to a human being considered as a whole, sometimes it's used with the intention to refer to a self – two things that have quite different identity conditions,"¹⁶ the former referring to what Thomas Nagel calls a kind of "public human being, as when you say: 'I'll meet you in front of Carnegie Hall;'" the latter referring to the "subject of consciousness, as when you think, 'I hear an oboe.'"¹⁷ Witkiewicz's concern is for the second "I," the one referring to the subject of consciousness. This is the I he sees being drowned out by the public I in modern society. It is this subjective I which feels a sense of unity with the experience of pure form, both in the act of creation and in reception. As Witkiewicz's narrator in The Only Way Out says of the painter Marcell, "he expressed metaphysical convulsions and anguish in purely formal constructions, which likewise acted directly by means of their forms and called forth in the viewers the very same psychic state he had experienced at the time these forms came into being."¹⁸ The form's unity is experienced by both the creator and the perceiver as a personal unity, creating especially in music, a state of intensity at the moment of experience independent of the feelings and activities of everyday life. Whether Witkiewicz actually thought that there was a unified personality or not, his point of emphasis here is on the aesthetic experience of a sense of unity, a feeling of oneness, even though a continuity may not actually persist. The experience is a rush of energy unifying many impulses and inclinations that are often at odds with each other.

---

¹⁴ See T. O. Immisch, K. E. Göltz, U. Pohlmann: Witkacy – Metaphysische/Metaphysical Portraits, with essays by U. Czartoryska and S. Okołowicz, Leipzig 1997, p. 7, 19, 53.

¹⁵ M. Rudnicki: The Theater of Life or The Search for Self, http://info-poland.buffalo.edu/classroom/witkacy/mark.html, 1.

¹⁶ G. Strawson: Selves. An Essay in Revisionary Metaphysics, Oxford 2009, p. 6.

¹⁷ T. Nagel: The I in Me, "London Review of Books", 5 November 2009, p. 33.

¹⁸ S. I. Witkiewicz: The Only Way Out, [in:] The Witkiewicz Reader, op. cit., p. 299.

2

According to Witkiewicz the evolution of society was moving inevitably toward increased collectivity and diminished individual freedom. His fears were realized in the twentieth century most horribly with the fascist and communist tyrannies in Europe and Asia. It wasn't only the tyranny of these movements that Witkiewicz saw as a threat, but also their abilities to offer comfort and security as an alternative to the risks of personal freedom. Nowadays, some of these tyrannies still function and other kinds of mass movements have come into being, while new types of media technology and social manipulation further constrict individual development. Advertising and public relations steadily strive to manipulate and control individual decision-making. Material pleasure and success have become staples of personal development, both requiring, for the most part, accommodation and conformity to superficial social norms.

Witkiewicz also thought that the decline of the autonomy of the individual would carry with it a parallel decline of the significance of the arts, since pure form was so intimately connected with a sense of the unity of one's being. People would become more and more indifferent to art, treating it as a past-time or hobby, if not ignoring it altogether. Like most modernists, he advocated avant-garde forms of art to shock people out of their indifference to the arts, warning that "the feverish pace of life, social mechanization, the exhaustion of all means of action, and a blasé attitude toward art" would make it necessary for art to try to galvanize the public by being "complicated, or as the case may be, artificially simplified, artistically perverse, disturbing." Traditional styles and forms would only support and encourage superficial attitudes to art. Concern with what he called the "Secret of Existence" and attempts to understand it would become "inconvenient for a socially perfect, mechanized man."[19] Witkiewicz believed that art offered the only possibility of understanding what was happening in the evolution of society.[20]

In the public sphere, music is generally promoted as a kind of entertainment. Beyond entertainment, music is used both as a background and, in advertising, to get attention. It is used as accompaniment to just about everything we do: to stimulate us when we go shopping, to help relax us when we travel, to console us as we wait in the doctor's office, to keep us company on

---

[19] Idem: On Pure Form, [in:] Aesthetics in Twentieth..., op. cit., p. 55–56.
[20] Idem: New Forms of Painting and the Misunderstandings Arising Therefrom, [in:] The Witkiewicz Reader, op. cit., p. 107.

the telephone while we languish on hold, and even to make us feel at ease in someone else's house. Many of us work with music in the background. And that's not all: there is also the background music of TV shows and movies, not to mention those fanfare-like entities of sound used to support announcements and proclaim the commencement of various kinds of radio, television, and cinematic presentations, including even the news. All of this is music. The issue here is not about the kind of music, but about the fact that it is always there. Music of one sort or another is constantly surrounding us. So much so, in fact, that it becomes difficult to endure silence, and silence, as philosopher Vladimir Jankélévitch pointed out, is as necessary to music as non-being is to the sense of a meaningful life.[21]

If we are constantly surrounded by music as a background to most of what we do, the significance of music becomes diminished. Taken for granted, it relies on passive listeners who may never know the experience of listening to anything that might require concentration or extended attention. In addition, the use of music to manipulate the consumer reinforces the therapeutic view that music is either soothing to the troubled or stimulating to the bored. Music certainly can be stimulating and soothing, but constant over-exposure flattens out genuine stimulation and makes the music little more than some kind of wallpaper or half-conscious accompaniment to other public noises. Furthermore, most of the music used in public is by design familiar to a large majority of the public. Performing and playing familiar pieces over and over afflicts all kinds of music. A narcissistic population, seeking stimulation in the familiar and succor in things pertaining to its own perceived reality, makes music into a narcotic, which, like Witkiewicz's "Murti Bing pill," helps to influence the populace to abide in a state of contentment. Although Witkiewicz did not write much about music and left no specifications about the conditions of music in the future, this state of affairs, so much in line with other aspects of his predictions based on his theory of social evolution, provides a good testing ground for applying his theory of pure form to music. The application of his theory to forms of art upon which he had no historically direct influence demonstrates the vital relevance of Witkiewicz's theory of pure form, both in terms of the public use of music at the end of the twentieth and beginning of the twenty-first centuries and in the work of major twentieth-century composers.

---

[21] V. Jankélévitch: Music and the Ineffable, trans. C. Abbate, Princeton 2003, p. 132.

3

The music of Morton Feldman is an example of an extreme form of music that exhibits Witkiewicz's idea of pure form. Echoing the latter's demands for immediacy in art, Feldman explained in 1962 how the painting of the abstract expressionists made him "desirous of a sound world more direct, more immediate, more physical than anything that had existed heretofore." He acknowledged that the composers Edgard Varèse and Anton Webern had "elements" and "glimpses" of what he was after, but he said that he didn't find in them the level of "concentration" that he needed.[22] Feldman's main interest was sound, sound as it is in a pure and unadulterated state, as if being heard for the first time, without preconditioned notions or familiarity based on past musical practices and traditions. Like John Cage, he was interested "in liberating sounds from the formal concepts of European music,"[23] where, as he thought, a sound was only important as a part of a structure or development. Feldman was a large man, about six feet tall and weighing almost 300 pounds, loud and full of laughter. He had an enormous appetite for life and its pleasures. He was an endless talker.[24] This garrulous and noisy man paradoxically composed a music that is quiet, slow, and extremely delicate.

Eight years before he died in 1987, Feldman began creating pieces of great length, taking sometimes several hours to perform, written for solo performers or small chamber groups. There is nothing sonically grandiose in any of these pieces, nothing dramatic or bombastic and certainly nothing loud. Indeed, Feldman said in 1987, "There is no place for the drama of a gesture or an action in my music."[25] These long works developed partly from his impatience with the knee-jerk assumption that each composition be twenty-five to thirty minutes long, as well as Feldman's fascination with scale, influenced by Mark Rothko's huge panels and the large canvases of Jackson Pollack. He may also have wanted to allow "his quiet voice to be heard in the total isolation it required," as Alex Ross writes.[26] In a lecture in

---

[22] M. Feldman: Give My Regards to Eighth Street, ed. B. H. Friedman, Cambridge 2000, p. 5.

[23] E. Stiebler: Feldman's Time, trans. T. Jones, [in:] M. Feldman, Words on Music/ Worte über Musik. Lectures and Conversations/Vorträge und Gespräche, ed. R. Mörchen, Köln 2008, p. 18.

[24] See B. H. Friedman: Introduction to Feldman's Give My Regards to Eighth Street, p. XI.

[25] M. Feldman: Words on Music/Worte über Musik, op. cit., p. 710.

[26] A. Ross: American Sublime, "New Yorker", June 19, 2006, p. 87.

Toronto about the state of music in 1982, Feldman asked, "Do we have anything in music for example that really wipes everything out? That just cleans everything away, from some aspect of illusion and reality? Do we have anything like – Proust? Do we have anything comparable to Finnegans Wake?"[27] To be sure, he would repeat again and again his desire to strip away illusions, saying shortly before he died, in his typically bizarre syntax, "To me, the artist has only one duty, only one duty and no thing other than that one duty, is to strip away illusions about things... including myself. My whole life is that I'm trying to prove myself wrong, not right."[28] This remark is close to Samuel Beckett's statement, "To be an artist is to fail, as no other dare fail, that failure is his world and the shrink from it desertion, art and craft, good housekeeping, living."[29] In these two remarks, both Feldman and Beckett reject the notion of the artist as an all-knowing seer or the ultimate wise citizen, observing the world in serenity, and replace it with one of the artist as an experimenter, deliberately learning by error, never satisfied, and with little prospect of traditional success, a posture similar to Witkiewicz's repeated restless experimentation in different art forms. When asked about what sort of illusions Feldman wanted to strip away, he replied, "The illusion of progress, the illusion of an audience, the illusion of success, the illusion of what's exciting. Nowadays I would say the illusion of what is intellectual and what is not intellectual."[30] As was the case with Witkiewicz, Feldman was dismayed at the way all art was becoming devalued socially, complaining that art had become a "middle class toy for the educated."[31]

Feldman was also influenced in his later music by the Near Eastern rugs he collected, especially Turkish rugs where the patterns and colors are slightly irregular. He called it a "crippled symmetry."[32] He put this "crippled symmetry" into practice in his long pieces, where musical patterns are woven together over time with slight alterations. In listening to these pieces, one marvels, as the musicologist Catherine Hirata comments, at the way Feldman "could weave such a variety of different patterns," and follow them with the "various ways in which one pattern can be succeeded by another pattern." She notes that some listeners find Feldman very boring because

---

[27] Ch. Villars (ed.): Morton Feldman Says. Selected Interviews and Lectures, 1964–1987, London 2006, p. 136.

[28] M. Feldman: Words on Music/Worte über Musik, op. cit., p. 798.

[29] S. Beckett: Three Dialogues, [in:] Disjecta, ed. R. Cohn, New York 1984, p. 145.

[30] M. Feldman: Words on Music/Worte über Musik, op. cit., p. 800.

[31] Ibidem, p. 854.

[32] Cf. idem: Crippled Symmetry, [in:] idem, Give My Regards to Eighth Street, op. cit., p. 134–149.

nothing "happens" in his music. She suggests that those who are not bored may be practicing "a new way of listening: rather than waiting for something to happen, they are savoring what they are hearing now."[33] In the music's lack of forward thrust and in its emphasis on sound patterns assembled in the manner of Turkish rugs, the music eschews concepts of a defined beginning, middle, and end, as Feldman advocated,[34] and conveys a sense of an almost flat surface upon which the listener's attention roams. Feldman was sensitive to the fact that musical forms as forms of memory are a conventional basis for composition. The "crippled symmetry" of his music was a way to disorient the memory and permit the somewhat altered material to be taken on its own terms when it appears.[35] It is also a way of shutting off the voluntary memory to allow Proust's involuntary memory to be more active in listening.

The next to last piece Feldman wrote was called For Samuel Beckett. It is a tribute to another strong influence on his work and to a person with whom he identified. Though both did not like opera, they collaborated to produce an "opera" entitled Neither, which is actually a monologue for soprano and orchestra, one of three pieces of Beckett's set to music by Feldman. A good argument can be made for finding examples of pure form in Beckett's plays. Certainly the encapsulated space on stage, often indifferent to the realities of space and time, as well as the bewildered and bewildering interactions of the characters, are formal arrangements similar to those in Witkiewicz's theater of pure form. Neither could also be an example of pure form, oscillating as it does back and forth between "self and unself" and their incomprehensibility, but the music is dependent on its relationship to the text in a way that instrumental music is not. Only a small portion of Feldman's music was written for voice. He was not unlike Witkiewicz in this regard, who seems to have thought that the purest form of music was instrumental.[36]

There are no programmatic meanings or messages in Feldman's music. His music does not seek to express anything. In thinking about responses to his music, it helps to keep in mind Claude Lévy-Strauss's notion that the meaning of music, like myth, occurs in its reception and not in its transmission. "Music has its being in me, and I listen to myself through it,"[37] he wrote.

---

[33] C. Hirata: Morton Feldman, [in:] Music of the Twentieth-Century Avant-Garde, ed. L. Sisky, Greenwood Press, Westport 2002, 135.

[34] M. Feldman: Words on Music/Worte über Musik, op. cit., p. 706.

[35] See S. Claren: Neither. Die Musik Morton Feldmans, Hofheim 2000, p. 286.

[36] See D. Gerould: Witkacy, op. cit., p. 38, and S. I. Witkiewicz: The 622 Downfalls of Bungo, [in:] The Witkiewicz Reader, op. cit., p. 69.

[37] C. Lévy-Strauss: The Raw and the Cooked, trans. J. and D. Weightman, New York 1969, p. 17.

Consequently, a music that is going to make it possible for listeners to reflect on the "mystery of existence," as Witkiewicz expects, would need, in our time, where there is such an obsession with looking for meaning everywhere, to eschew any suggestion of message, lest it short-circuit listeners' responses by trying to program them as they listen. Program music and music with a message thrive on this short-circuiting, even frequently causing listeners to think that the music's programmed "meaning" is their own.

In his novel, Doktor Faustus, Thomas Mann has the fictitious composer, Adrian Leverkühn, define the essence of music as "an organization of time."[38] Lévi-Strauss considers music to be a machine "for the suppression of time."[39] But Feldman had a different sense of time in music. In 1969 he commented on a conversation he once had with the German composer, Karlheinz Stockhausen, who had admonished him for not having a rhythmic beat in his music. Feldman said, "I am not a clockmaker. I am interested in getting to Time in its unstructured existence. That is, I am interested in how this wild beast lives in the jungle -- not in the zoo. I am interested in how Time exists before we put our paws on it -- our minds, our imaginations, into it."[40] In Feldman's long pieces, the music embodies time. It is time itself that one perceives along with the music that one hears, time in the form of music. This might have something to do with the sense of loss or melancholy that some listeners perceive while listening to Feldman's music, because surely, any extended attention to time, to its nature, its constant passing and its moving closer to its ending, which is death, is bound to carry with it a feeling of loss. Time, as much as anything else, is at the basis of Witkiewicz's mystery of being, in one sense a matter of an individual life and its moments, in another the vast and almost incomprehensible multiplicitous life of the universe. The pianist Louis Goldstein has written of his experience playing Feldman's Triadic Memories, describing especially how the "sublimity of the ending, one hundred minutes into the piece," sometimes had the effect of "utter tragedy, when in spite of great effort, time finally does break down and an awareness of terrifying emptiness is discovered."[41]

The duration of these long pieces makes enormous demands on listeners and, especially, performers, both in the endurance required and in the diffi-

---

[38] T. Mann: Doktor Faustus. The Life of the German Composer Adrian Leverkühn as Told by a Friend, trans. J. E. Woods, New York 1997, p. 338.

[39] As quoted in E. Leach: Claude Lévy-Strauss, New York 1970, p. 125.

[40] M. Feldman: Give My Regards to Eighth Street, op. cit., p. 87.

[41] L. Goldstein: Morton Feldman and the Shape of Time, originally in: Perspectives on American Music since 1950, ed. J. R. Heintze, New York and London 1995, p. 67–80 and available on line at http://www.cnvill.net/mfgldstn.htm.

cult technique required to play it. This fits in with Witkiewicz's demand, mentioned earlier, for art that would be in some way challenging. An experience of listening to Feldman's String Quartet (II) without a break, in the six-hour and seven-minute recording of the Flux Quartet on an audio DVD, requires a commitment to time that is hard to achieve in a busy and noisy world; but once made, the figures and patterns heard become ends in themselves and one gets caught up in concentrating on how the "composition sounds, rather than how it is made."[42] The mind inevitably drifts, as well, both with the music and beyond it. The listener, solely in the presence of time and a sound undiluted by compositional rhetoric and virtuosity, finds himself in an unusual condition of heightened self-consciousness, oscillating between the music and what is going on in himself. The last dynamic indication of the entire piece, on page 76 of the 124-page score and two and one half hours before the end of this recording, is ppppp, a five-fold pianissimo. The affect of these two and a half hours of slow, barely audible and persistent music was intense and deep, but it depended on having listened to the previous three and a half hours, much as the impact of Time Regained depends on having read Proust's six novels that precede it. The feeling of a "vast stretch of time," to use Beckett's oft-repeated line from How It Is, combined with the moments of silence in the music, lead to a sense of huge pockets of empty space, perhaps the "emptiness" Louis Goldstein referred to above.

Many listeners have commented on their sense of solitude in listening to Feldman's music. Alex Ross has also noticed a "lonely, lamenting tone that runs through" the music, and how listening to this piece is to "enter into a new way of listening, even a new consciousness."[43] The composer Christian Wolf comments on a feeling of isolation in listening to the piece, even in public performances,[44] while the musician, Hans-Peter Jahn, writing on Feldman's music in general and also noting the sense of isolation, states, in a comment that would have been dear to Witkiewicz, "There is hardly any other type of music that lends itself so little to collective listening."[45] It would be crude to say that the listening described above resulted in a "heightened metaphysical feeling" plain and simple, but it was definitely a musical expe-

---

[42] Ibidem.

[43] A. Ross: American Sublime, "New Yorker", June 19, 2006, 88, 87; see also idem: The Rest is Noise: Listening to the Twentieth Century, New York 2007, p. 484–488.

[44] Ch. Wolf: Feldman's String Quartet No. 2, liner notes to the Mode CD and audio DVD of Feldman's String Quartet (II), mode 112.

[45] H.-P. Jahn: Isn't Morton Beckett... Samuel Feldman..., trans. R. Koch and Team, liner notes to the Kairos CD of Feldman's For Samuel Beckett, Kairos 0012012KAI.

rience far removed from both escapism and virtuosity and certainly metaphysical, affecting the listener directly at the core of individual being and giving some kind of a sense of unity in the midst of the confused multiplicity of everything else, as Witkiewicz advocated.

Abstract

In this paper I discuss how "pure form" applies to the music of composer Morton Feldman. Starting from Witkiewicz's idea that music is the purest form of art, I discuss his speculations on the "heightened metaphysical feeling" that results from aesthetic experience. I also look at Witkiewicz's rejection of sentimental music. I then take up the conditions of music in our time, where music is used as light entertainment. This exemplifies Witkiewicz's fears about the use of art as a distraction to keep people happy. I then examine the music of Feldman as an antidote to these trends. His music conveys a sense of a flat surface upon which the attention of listeners drifts contemplatively with the music, experiencing it as an end in itself. I try to show how his music affects listeners at the core of their being and gives them a sense of unity in the midst of the multiplicity of everyday life.

Prof. John D. Barlow
Indiana University (Indianapolis)

Gordon Ramsay

Futurism and Witkiewicz: Variety, Separation and Coherence in a Theatre of Pure Form

In this essay I want to explore the theoretical and dramaturgical relationship between Witkiewicz and the Italian Futurists, and in particular those elements that are predicated on binaries of separation and unity, singularity and plurality. In so doing I aim to identify Futurist precursors and influences and similarities and differences in Witkiewicz's development of models and practices.

Witkiewicz was well aware of the Futurists' work and declared that it conformed closely to his theory of Pure Form in the Theatre; however, he disliked their 'futurization of life'[1] and was hostile to what he perceived as the mechanisation of society and the threat to the individual. The Futurists of course looked forward to mechanisation and celebrated the human-machine interface, elevating it to an almost mythical status. Living in a time of accelerated invention and with huge developments in transport and communications, the Futurists extolled the force of the machine, its dyna-

---

[1] S. I. Witkiewicz: Pure Form in the Theater, [in:] The Witkiewicz Reader, ed. D. Gerould, London 1993, p. 152.

mism, power and speed, and in particular its ability to overcome the limitations of time and space.² This is made clear in their 1909 Founding and Manifesto of Futurism, with, as its centrepiece, a car race through the streets of Milan, passenger and vehicle transformed and mythologised, whose crisis point and anarcho-nirvana is the driver's near-collision with a bicycle.³ Witkiewicz on his part dislikes the confluence of human and machine, writing as he does of 'the gray soulless atmosphere of socially disciplined automatons.'⁴

In spite of these obvious philosophical differences, there are clear similarities between Witkiewicz's work and what the Futurists set out to achieve. This can be seen in the Futurists' Variety Theatre Manifesto (1913) and Synthetic Theatre Manifesto (1915); as well as in their very short plays or sintesi (sometimes only a minute or two long) that were written and performed from 1915 onwards. These similarities fall into three broad categories, though there is obviously overlap between them: the alteration of normal time and space; the disconnection of reality and identity; and the sense of the alogical.

The Alteration of Normal Time and Space

The Futurists' interest in the alteration of normal time and space is closely related to a desire for speed. With this speed, according to the Variety Theatre Manifesto, come new conceptions of time and space, as well as of perspective and proportion. The advent of the car (alongside the aeroplane and advancements in train travel) brings a shift of perspective: the landscape we travel through becomes 'a moving thing'. Danius points us to a precursor of the first manifesto, Proust's 1907 account of a car journey in Normandy, where the window becomes a framing device. Whilst it is the car that moves, the perspective of the passenger is such that it seems the surroundings themselves are coming to life and rushing towards the car.⁵

So speed and acceleration open up new perspectives and change our perception in an hallucinatory way. For Proust it is not the passenger but the church steeple that moves, as if animated. But these new perspectives are derived from other sources too, beyond travel and speed. From the world of

---

² See G. Berghaus: Italian Futurist Theatre, Oxford 1998, p. 3.

³ The driver was Marinetti himself. See F. T. Marinetti: Selected Writings, ed. R. W. Flint, London 1972, p. 39.

⁴ S. I. Witkiewicz: Pure Form in the Theater, op. cit., p. 151.

⁵ S. Danius: The Aesthetics of the Windshield: Proust and the Modernist Rhetoric of Speed, "Modernism/Modernity", 8.1 (2001), p. 113.

art, for example, there is the influence of cubism, and from the world of philosophy the influence of Bergson, who introduced the idea of a subjectivisation of time in his 1910 Time and Free Will: An Essay on the Immediate Data of Consciousness, predicated as it is on internal and external states of consciousness. His notion of the durée or duration allows for a simultaneity of past and present internal states. With this, notions of truth, consciousness and reality become negotiable.[6] This clearly subverts the idea of a single, immutable consciousness or truth and seems to be akin to Pandeus' view in Witkiewicz's Dainty Shapes and Hairy Apes, where he speaks of 'the dual comprehension of the uniqueness and identity of each moment'.[7]

Bergson's approach allows for a malleability, where one's sense of time can be altered by acceleration or slowing down.[8] In the Futurist Sempronio's Lunch, by Corra and Settimelli, a meal time is telescoped into five short scenes where a man ages rapidly from 5 to 90; in their Traditionalism a whole lifetime is compressed into two minutes. Likewise in Witkiewicz's The Water Hen, Elizabeth's arrival is introduced to Tadzio as though she had visited only five minutes earlier and he responds in a similar vein – in spite of the ten year gap between visits:

What? (Remembers) Oh! Show her in. Hurry up. I behaved so badly then.[9]

This subjective view of time also has an effect on the physical space that characters occupy. It leads not only to simultaneous action on stage, where two worlds sit next to each other, each unaware of the other's existence; but it also leads to moments of overlap, where these two worlds collide. In the Synthetic Theatre Manifesto The Futurists term this 'interpenetration'[10] or 'compenetration'[11] and it plainly echoes Bergson's own 'interpenetration of

---

[6] H. Bergson: Time and Free Will: An Essay on the Immediate Data of Consciousness, trans. F. L. Pogson, London 1910, p. 107.

[7] S. I. Witkiewicz: Dainty Shapes and Hairy Apes, [in:] idem: Seven Plays, ed. D. Gerould, New York 2004, p. 310.

[8] See M. A. Gillies: Henri Bergson and British Modernism, Montreal 1996), p. 12: "This explains that common experience of having time collapse or expand when an individual is under some stress; or of having time seem to fly when we want to prolong some particular experience, yet crawl when we would prefer to see the experience finished."

[9] S. I. Witkiewicz: The Water Hen, [in:] idem: The Madman and the Nun and The Crazy Locomotive. Three Plays (including The Water Hen), ed. D. Gerould, New York 1989, p. 70.

[10] F. T. Marinetti: The Futurist Synthetic Theater, [in:] idem: Selected Writings, ed. R. W. Flint, London 1972, p. 127.

[11] Ibidem, p. 128.

conscious states'.¹² This precedes Witkiewicz's idea of a plurality of realities. A Futurist example of interpenetration can be found in the sintesi Simultaneity by Marinetti where there seem to be two distinct worlds, one of a family in a sitting room and the other of a coquette at her dressing table, in a completely different world.¹³ When the family are asleep or otherwise occupied, the coquette without warning crosses into their space, goes to their table, hurls their homework and sewing to the floor and returns unnoticed to her own business at the dressing table in her own world.

This interpenetration, the displacement of one world – of one space, and all it connotes – by another, also occurs in The Water Hen, where the opening scene's pole, field and mound are replaced by a barracks. It is more than a simple set change, as the characters continue with the scene as before and are initially unaware of their new environment. It is only some time later that Edgar notices the change, having ironically just remarked that 'nothing happens' and 'there's no change.'¹⁴ The opening setting is returned to later, bringing with it a reprise of the original context – Edgar shooting the Water Hen. This is clearly a form of simultaneity. However, it does differ from the Futurist example in that in Simultaneity the worlds of coquette and family are initially separate and here, the two worlds of mound and barracks collide and coalesce; and there is also a period where Edgar and Tadzio might be in both spaces at once or in no space at all. The scenographies do not co-exist at the same time.

The scenography in Act Three of The Beelzebub Sonata is entirely simultaneous and meets the Futurist notions of such. The division is of two apparently separate worlds: Baroness Jackals' salon in her castle on the outskirts of Mordovar, presented on stage on a narrow strip running alongside the footlights; and Baleastadar's Hell which will later be revealed behind the upstage curtain. We first sense that something is amiss when Hilda enters the salon through this curtain – it is not a normal entrance point as the stage directions indicate that the doors are on the left and the right. When the curtain opens moments later, hell is revealed, with the characters of Bealeastadar and Istvan present. The stage directions indicate that the salon on the forestage remains as it is, instead of being subsumed within the deep red hell. Yet both sets of characters co-exist: and while De Estrada from the salon is nervous, he does not query the sudden intrusion of this other world, any

---

¹² H. Bergson: Time and Free Will..., op. cit., p. 107

¹³ T. F. Marinetti, E. Settimelli and B. Corra: Il Teatro Futurista Sintetico, Milan 1915, p. 21.

¹⁴ S. I. Witkiewicz: The Water Hen..., op. cit., p. 49.

more than the other characters do. The two worlds are at once unified and distinct.

There are nonetheless boundaries between these places and as Witkiewicz writes in the stage directions, there is a 'threshold of hell.'[15] At first sight the scene seems like a medieval morality play, as characters consciously choose to enter the space and become Baleastadar's subjects or choose to remain outside, and thus escape his control. But when Jackals and Hilda enter hell, and Jackals shoots Hilda before turning the gun on himself, his death brings about the immediate suicide of his mother in the salon, as if one causes the other. The two spaces, salon and hell, are joined not only by virtue of the spatial interpenetration, but also by what might be called a psychic interpenetration. The coquette's intrusion into the living room in Marinetti's Simultaneity (impossible in terms of the normal laws of space and time) is also symbolic of a metaphysical perforation, in Marinetti's own words 'a synthesis of sensations'.[16] In both cases the intrusion results in disorder, whilst uniting the dramatic space.

This simultaneity, of spatial and psychic overlap, may be said to be an example of dramatic brisure, a term that springs from the work of the artist Delaunay and indicates a disruption of time, space and causality.[17]

Just as in Simultaneity there are two separate worlds that bleed into one, but with neither fully yielding to the other, so too are there two worlds in The Beelzebub Sonata, a bleeding together of salon and hell, each retaining their separateness. They are at once unified and distinct. We see one through the other, as with the point of brisure on Delaunay's canvas.[18]

The Disconnection of Reality and Identity

Allied to the alteration of time and space is of course the reappraisal of reality as well as identity. When these norms are altered, the stability of character, relationship and self becomes vulnerable and open to question. The contexts that one has taken for granted become unreliable. New facets of identity are revealed and this can cause disturbance and surprise: sometimes this is shown by surprise or confusion in the characters but sometimes the surprise is ours, as audience. We may even be surprised that the charac-

---

[15] Idem: The Beelzebub Sonata, [in:] idem: Seven Plays, op. cit., 2004, p. 377.

[16] F. T. Marinetti, E. Settimelli and B. Corra, op. cit., p. 21.

[17] See S. A. Buckberrough: Robert Delaunay: the Discovery of Simultaneity, Ann Arbor, Michigan 1982, p. 25.

[18] Delaunay's 1909 Self Portrait.

ters are not surprised – and that may be surprising in itself. A character and a situation become disconnected from that which has gone before. Reality and identity seem to be no sooner established in a particular form than they are revised or entirely changed (indeed, the one reliable element in a character's life is transformation). Sudden transformations called for in the Variety Theatre Manifesto, influenced in part by the skill of the Italian quick-change artist and the architecture of the variety format, are key to narrative and character. This can also be said to be a characteristic of Witkiewicz's plays, albeit in a very different context. The Futurist play Alternation of Character by Ginna and Corra highlights this sense of transformation, of disconnection of identity and relationships: a husband and wife switch, line-by-line, from declarations of love to declarations of hatred in rapid succession. Their emotional states are keenly felt but are in a state of turmoil and it is impossible for audience and character to discover or establish reliable connections between statement and response. Identity begins to founder. And it is not just emotional cogency that is hard to divine: the characters too become uncertain about their consciousness and the reliability of their personal narratives. So in Cangiullo's First Class Fantasy a traveller in a railway waiting room is confronted by the sudden apparition of a quick change artist, Fregoli, performing his act.[19] When the traveller wakes from sleep we are uncertain as to whether he is waking f r o m a dream or waking i n t o a dream, and whether the companion he was speaking to was imaginary or real.

This sense of disconnectedness, with past events, with the present, with friends, relatives, spouses and lovers, this sense of the tenuous, pervades the work of Witkiewicz too. The feeling and tone of living in a dream, sometimes with moments of torpor, is never far way. In The Water Hen Tadzio sees his existence as a series of dreams from which he fears to be awoken. In The Beelzebub Sonata, De Estrada gives the clear impression of being very much a stranger in his own narrative:

De Estrada: Now I see that none of this makes any sense. Once in Mordovar, as soon as I left the station, I went straight to a house totally unknown to me, and then with this young lady here, whom I saw for the first time in my life, I came here to this cabaret in an abandoned mine.[20]

---

[19] See Vela Latina, Anno 111, No. 51, 23/31, Dicembre 1915, Napoli, [in:] Vela Latina: Pagine Futuriste 1915–1916 (Firenze: S.P.E.S. – Salimbeni, 1979), p. 22.

[20] S. I. Witkiewicz: The Beelzebub Sonata, op. cit., 2004, p. 359.

The clear sense that he has no control over his life (and little understanding of it) mirrors that of the situation in Folgore's play, Shadows + Puppets + Men, where three characters who claim to have never met before appear together at a country house:

Blue: Gentlemen I don't know how I find myself in your company!...

Maxim: It's a ridiculous situation. I can't understand. I got off the transatlantic liner this morning after three years of travel.

Blue: Me too. But I don't know you.

Job: Curious. The three of us to have travelled aboard a liner and never met.[21]

However, we have already seen that they have met each other earlier: it is just that they seem to have no recollection of this. They have been disconnected from the reality already established and are now uncertain as to their relationship. This flavour of fatalism, of the human as an instrument of forces beyond their control, contradicts Futurist notions of will and control and foreshadows Witkiewicz and the theatre of the Absurd.

However, it is not the case that reality is purely determined by the subjectivity of the characters. The disconnection between different states of reality (and the commensurate uncertainty of identity that this engenders) is clearly demonstrated to the audience. In Chiti's Constructions we see a man being knifed to death only to return to life and fall into good-humoured badinage with his murderer, as the directions note, 'one of those usual discussions where a real dead person talks to a real murderer. One of those incoherent discussions where, without knowing, life experiments with its own surprising geniality.'[22] Their conversation is polite, rational, and even logical given that the situation confounds our understanding. Audience perceptions of life and death are similarly under scrutiny in Tumor Brainiowicz when the audience sees Gamboline throw the baby Isidore out of the window. A few moments later Balantine tells the distressed Gamboline that the baby is not dead at all, and Iza reassures her uncomprehending mother that it was only a dream. The audience are as uncertain as the characters and cannot tell where (if anywhere) reality lies. Similarly, in Metaphysics of a Two Headed Calf, we see Patricianello's mother and Mikulini die in Act Two only to be told by Parvis in Act Three that he has seen them driving around town.

---

[21] F. T. Marinetti et al., op. cit., p. 29.
[22] Ibidem, p. 25.

Patricianello's response to this may be surprisingly cool ('Ten mothers, a hundred Mikulinis can come here') but it is matched by his mother's own indifferent response at seeing him when she does indeed reappear:

Patricianello: Mother, Mother! It's me!

Mother: Well, what of it? Stay there on the ground with your Mirabella. Don't let me bother you.[23]

As far as she's concerned, he barely exists for her. To all intents and purposes they are dead to each other. Their current identities have little bearing on what has gone before-though one cannot ignore Patricianello's sense of excitement and how this is at variance with his earlier indifference. These disconnections in relationships, often surprisingly sudden, may not be as absurdly depicted as they are in Alternation of Character (the grotesqueness of which is aided and abetted by the play's brevity), but are nonetheless a notable part of the warp and weft of Witkiewicz's drama.

Shifts of familial identity may seem to be casual and capricious and at times accepted with indifference by those involved. These can be seen through the prism of the Bergsonian view of time in which case all realities are true (in Chwistek's terms, a plurality of realities). In Witkiewicz's drama, relationships often exist on different footings in different contexts and a sense of linear continuity is therefore absent. In The Water Hen Edgar may be the Water Hen's lover but to her he also seemed to be like her child and her father.[24] Sudden revelation of a character's relationship to another may be surprising to the audience but as with the apparent mortality (or not) of the baby Isidore or Patricianello's mother, the other characters' response to the revelation, loss or gain of a family relationship may also be surprising. This is demonstrated when the young Tadzio appears (from virtually nowhere), and the Water Hen introduces him as Edgar's son.[25] Edgar's reaction is more one of frustration as yet another layer of reality is revealed: 'For all I know I might even be your father.' He adds, with brutal indifference, 'although I can't stand children' which savagely undercuts the child's sense of identity and (emotional) reality.[26] But even this is provisional, with transformation an ever present condition: thus when Edgar later discovers

---

[23] S. I. Witkiewicz: Metaphysics of a Two-Headed Calf, [in:] The Winter Repertory 7: Tropical Madness, Four Plays, ed. D. Gerould, New York 1972, p. 226.

[24] S. I. Witkiewicz: The Water Hen, op. cit., p. 46.

[25] Ibidem, p. 48.

[26] Ibidem, p. 62.

Tadzio is also the Water Hen's son, he experiences a feeling of shock and surprise. Edgar is at once disgusted by and 'insanely attached' to the boy.[27] He inhabits a contradiction of states, an 'alternation' of character and identity, which he has the awareness to recognise, yet is powerless to alter.

While indifference in relationships plays a part in the Futurist sintesi (and this disconnection is heightened and schematised as much by the brevity of the form as by the creators' political outlook), it is a given, and does not impinge on our initial understanding of the character's identity: we generally know where we are from the outset, whether this is an ageing couple in Traditonalism, a young couple in Pratella's Night, or the mechanistic paternalism of Cangiullo's Of all the Colours. In Witkiewicz's plays, such indifference has an altogether different impact, in that it is invariably introduced in such a manner as to challenge and subvert our existing understanding of the characters' identity. In Along the Cliffs of the Absurd, Piggykins' reaction to being told that Wahazar is her father is that she thought it was 'pure chance' that she 'loved him so much.'[28] Her rationalisation, as well as her indifference to his being taken to the lab for the necessary transplants to take place, nonetheless amaze her mother, whose surprise is akin to our own surprise at the emotional disconnection between daughter and new-found father. Other examples abound, underscoring the fragility of what and who characters believe themselves to be, in relationship to what we as audience have taken to be their significant others. The Gravedigger in The Anonymous Work, disinterested in the fact that he may be the father of Prince Padoval (and anyway unsure which children he does have); Claudina offering herself as a daughter to the Professor as a sort of surrogate (while his son Plasmonick is in prison for fifteen years); or the same character offering to look after Rosa's little girl, Sophie (who Rosa has just realised she herself had forgotten all about): each demonstrates relationships to be quixotic, casually abandoned, casually adopted. In The Cuttlefish, Rockoffer has no memory of his mother, in The Beelzebub Sonata Istvan is informed by Rio Bamba that he is in fact his uncle, while in Metaphysics of a Two Headed Calf Patricianello believes it is possible to have two mothers, one dead and one from his dream.[29] Even little Tadzio in The Water Hen has to check with Lady Nevermore why Edgar is his father: 'Mama, I forgot why He's my papa.' The response is disarmingly offhand: 'It doesn't make any difference if you have.'[30]

---

[27] Ibidem, p. 65.
[28] Idem: Along the Cliffs of the Absurd, [in:] The Winter Repertory 7: Tropical Madness, Four Plays, ed. D. Gerould, New York 1972, p. 168.
[29] Idem: Metaphysics of a Two-Headed Calf, op. cit., p. 207.
[30] Idem: The Water Hen, op. cit., p. 58.

In Witkiewicz's work, relationships seem to be tenuous and arrived at by chance; embarked on, surrendered and rebuffed at times with a staggering ease at once perplexing and funny. In pyrotechnical terms, Futurist surprise in the short-burn sintesi is generally a one-off event, a reversal usually occurring at the finale like the punchline of a joke.[31] With Witkiewicz, the firework is of a very different order, its form and duration permitting a series of surprises, whereby we are constantly reminded of the existence of more than one plane of reality and simultaneous worlds.

The Futurists' distrust of conventional representations of reality and identity stems from their hostility to passéist theatre, and this includes a deep antipathy to that which is comprehensible and predictable, to the play where 'the audience understands in the finest detail the how and why of everything that takes place on the stage, above all that it knows by the last act how the protagonists will end up.'[32] This approach is mirrored by Witkiewicz in Pure Form in the Theatre where he views realistic expression as synonymous with a rationalistic utilitarianism in which art should have purpose, meaning and solution:

> We turn away in disgust from the work under discussion, swearing more or less politely and repeating triumphantly, "I don't understand". We do not want to grasp the simple truth that a work of Art does not express anything in the sense in which we have grown accustomed to use the word in real life.[33]

Yet however similar to the Futurists' instinct to confound an audience's expectations of form, Witkiewicz's treatment of relationship is very different. The format of the sintesi, which have brevity at their heart, mitigates for the most part against the establishment of emotional scenarios and therefore against any significant subsequent subversion of same. Relationships between lovers or husbands and wives are largely givens and frequently (though not always) shaped by chauvinistic conceptions of women as femmes fatales or stultifiers (Parallelipiped, The Big Problem, The Bachelor Pad, Towards the Conquest, The Green Plums) or alternatively as objects to be used or humiliated (Devourer of Women, Of All the Colours, The

---

[31] Such as the 'properly' behaved lady visitor turned seductress in Boccioni's The Bachelor Pad, the lover in Boccioni's The Body That Rises being sucked up the outside of the building by his girlfriend so the landlady does not see him using the lift and the soldiers in Marinetti's The Communicating Vases obstructed by the wings of the theatre and falling back in surprise.

[32] F. T. Marinetti: The Futurist Synthetic Theater, op. cit., p. 125. See G. Berghaus, op. cit., p. 19 for the theatrical conventions against which Futurists were writing.

[33] S. I. Witkiewicz: Pure Form in the Theater, op. cit., p. 149.

Womaniser and the Four Seasons, Call-Up Council, Parallels, The Contract, Woman + Friends = Front, The Invulnerable). Romantic love sans emasculation and objectification is generally ignored or disavowed (though there are exceptions in such pieces as The Displeasure of the Apron, The Little Theatre of Love and Moonlight).

These concerns may be present in Witkiewicz, but given his larger canvas there is opportunity for more complex developments. Here the relationships of partners and lovers are subject to surprising moments of disconnection, where past events and feelings that audience and/or character have relied upon are swept aside. This can leave characters out of kilter with each other, with one feeling the same as they had before, and the other occupying an entirely different emotional space. This is more than the travails of unrequited love, as the connections and disconnections are frequently allied to characters who are at times fully aware of their impotence and vulnerability. As Rockoffer says in The Cuttlefish, after suddenly deciding to break off his engagement with Ella, 'You'll have to pardon me, but unknown perspectives are opening up before me.'[34] This may indeed be the case, but only a dozen lines before he declared to Ella, 'now I really love you for the first time.' The speed of the formation of these relationships as well as their fracture is remarkable; and although like the Futurists in their reversals, they are unlike them in that relationships are contingent on a presentation of love that might be said to be 'character-led' – even if that character is driven by forces and perspectives apparently outside of their control. In The Water Hen, Lady Nevermore's sudden announcement that she is to be Edgar's wife causes Edgar a mild hesitation but he falls in with his new life more or less immediately.

Similar emotional transformation is seen in The Anonymous Work. No sooner has Rosa's Tzingar been strung up by the crowd than she awakes from what she calls 'a horrible nightmare,' says she does not love him any more, and declares her love for Plasmonick instead.[35] He, however, wakes from a nightmare of his own and declares that he no longer loves her. He takes a razor to Rosa's throat and kills the person he professed to love on the spot. Mirabella's connection with Patricianello is ruptured with similar speed in Metaphysics of a Two Headed Calf. As he is gagged and bundled into the car, she is clearly distraught at being left without him but within a moment of the shadowy figure nearby revealing himself, she is immediately captivated by this apparent replacement:

---

[34] Idem: The Cuttlefish, [in:] idem: Seven Plays ed. D. Gerould, New York 2004, p. 267.
[35] Idem: The Anonymous Work, [in:] idem: Seven Plays, op. cit., p. 232.

Mirabella: Will you love me?

Figure: Naturally I will.[36]

In Tumor Brainiowicz, Brainiowicz's decision to divorce Gamboline is also extremely sudden, at odds with the subject and tone of their preceding dialogue, and Gamboline meets it with similar indifference. These sudden moments of emotional disconnection confound the audience's expectation.

Context is everything and characters are not always simply disconnected from reality. They can also be aware of the existence of multiple realities. For every character emotionally disconnected there is another that is bewildered by change. The multiple realities can add to the confusion, compounded by the fact that disconnections are not necessarily absolute, in love as much as in anything else: as Brainiowicz says to Iza, 'If it weren't for this insane heat and my new thought about an nth-class of tumors, I don't know if I wouldn't fall in love with you all over again.'[37]

While characters may accept the general philosophical idea that there is an uncertainty of self, they are at other times far less sanguine about the impact it has on their own particular lives and their feelings fluctuate accordingly. In The Water Hen Edgar is at times quite relaxed about this state of affairs – 'I should have been somebody, but I never knew what, or rather who. I don't even know whether I actually exist [...]'[38] However, in The Cuttlefish Rockoffer is terrified by a similar uncertainty. Tumor Brainiowicz, who wonders if he exists at all, suffers from despair and anguish. Yet for all the giddying sense of paralysis, Edgar himself and Price in Tropical Madness are both enervated by the possibilities that uncertainty offers: the opportunity for a fresh start and new adventures.

The Sense of the Alogical

The alogical is a further characteristic which the Futurists and Witkiewicz share. In the Synthetic Theatre Manifesto the Futurists suggest that the autonomous and the unreal are part of the alogical, indicating a theatrical form that makes sense entirely within its own terms. As Kirby writes:

---

[36] Idem: Metaphysics of a Two-Headed Calf, op. cit., p. 234.
[37] Idem: Tumor Brainiowicz, [in:] idem: Seven Plays, op. cit., p. 74.
[38] Idem: The Water Hen, op. cit., p. 49.

> The acrobat and juggler do not aid in the development of a narrative or pretend to be anywhere other than where they really are. Nor do they generally embody abstract ideas and concepts: the trapeze artiste flies without representing flight.[39]

The alogical evidently stems from variety entertainment, a populist form offering short, fast, discrete scenarios where psychological analyses on the part of the audience is unnecessary. In this context, there are no anxieties about a lack of narrative progression and continuity. We do not ask what a sword-swallower or a contortionist 'means' – they just 'are' and we appreciate them (or not) on their own terms. If there is coherence it is not contingent on what precedes or follows but on the here-and-now territory of the act itself. Whereas conventional theatrical semiotics normally depends on connotations and meanings, the Futurists' alogical performance, like the variety show, depends on attention being paid to denotation rather than representation. The act of the trapeze artiste, whose body is the site of performance, each flex and release of muscle and limb an immediate and unmediated display of physical virtuosity, needs no explanation or narrative development in order to engage the audience.[40]

Alogicality is put into practice in the sintesi themselves, most obviously in pieces where language is abstract (Chiti and Settimelli's Wandering Madmen, Depero's Colours), non-existent (Cangiullo's Detonation and Not a Soul, Marinetti's Public Gardens and The Officer's Room, Marinetti and Corra's Hands) or, at the very least, secondary to physical performance (Marinetti's Bottom Halves). Between them these sintesi show a range of alogical elements, whether absurd, autonomous or unreal. Futurism, however, is a broad church, one where theory is not always followed-up in practice and where there is a tension between the alogical, with its subversion of aesthetic expectation, and the political and cultural concerns of the movement itself. And, as many of the sintesi are in fact aiming for clear political and social meaning, the signs pointing indexically to such issues as war, gender, pacifism and bourgeois and academic inertia, alogicality is regularly and necessarily ignored.

Witkiewicz, whose political and cultural outlook is obviously different, achieves a more consistent sense of Futurist alogicality ('A theatrical work in Pure Form is self-contained, autonomous, and in this sense absolute'), and does so in a more sustained fashion.[41] Instead of the variety format of the

---

[39] M. Kirby: Futurist Performance, New York 1971, p. 22.

[40] A fine example of this could be seen in the Rebecca Leonard's aerialist/trapeze artiste's act in the Futurist show ScrABrrRrraaNNG, Glen Morris Studio, Toronto, November 6th to November 8th, 2008.

[41] S. I. Witkiewicz: Pure Form in the Theater, op. cit., p. 151.

sintesi, with its overt disconnections and blanks (and with its equally overt recognition of audience and frequent willingness to involve and implicate them in the theatrical moment), Witkiewicz presents an audience with alogicality within a more conventional theatrical form.[42] It is a form that offers a sense of narrative continuity and development, but, as we have seen in discussion of time, space, reality and identity, it is also a form that questions its own reliability, logic and coherence. Compared to the discrete alogicality of the trapeze artiste, Witkiewicz's scenes point us to meanings and understandings, only for these to vanish as the narrative road continues. This is less a sleight of hand, a Futurist trick, a plan of deception where the writer 'outwits' the audience (and tells them so), than it is an expression of a plurality of separate alogical realities that coexist. This provisionality clearly affects the characters themselves:

> Their past experiences can in no way concern us, unless they are formally linked with the present, and the same is even more true for their future.[43]

Like the trapeze artiste, the Witkiewicz scenes 'just 'are' and we appreciate them on their own terms. If there is coherence it is not entirely contingent on what precedes or follows but on the 'here-and-now territory of the act itself.' It is this sense of the alogical that Witkiewicz has in mind when he writes that 'we should find ourselves in the world of Formal Beauty, which has its own sense, its own logic and its own TRUTH.' Witkiewicz has removed the alogical from the variety format, and re-presented it within a sustained form, where contiguity is present but often ephemeral.[44] In so doing, he asks very different questions about the human condition and also paradoxically provides a sense of coherence to the disparate, the surprising and the unreliable. The variety or plurality of meanings and perspectives that he expresses is unified not only by a pervasive atmosphere of dream, hallucination, unreality or displacement but also by the constant if ultimately fruitless attempt to make sense of things. In this Witkiewicz might be said to achieve what he deems to be 'the most profound principle of existence: unity in plurality.' It is an achievement that follows on in no small measure from the work of the Italian Futurists.

---

[42] Bennett refers to the productive nature of breaks and Iser's blanks in performance. See S. Bennett: Theatre Audiences, London 1997, p. 44.

[43] S. I. Witkiewicz: Pure Form in the Theater, op. cit., p. 152.

[44] Ibidem.

Abstract

This article will consider Witkacy's theatre plays alongside his contribution to dramatic theory with the Theory of Pure Form. In particular, it will examine the interplay between a sense of unity and a sense of the alogical, a term first used by the Italian Futurists. Focusing on The Water Hen but with reference to other plays as well as Futurist theoretical and dramatic counterparts, the article investigates on the one hand the interruption of narrative and linear progression, and uncertainty as to existence, identity and relationship; and on the other hand the persistent continuous underlying anxiety within the characters themselves and their sense of journey and destination. I suggest that his use of a series of arresting visual images and theatrical transformations unifies the scenes within a single dream-like world, bringing an order, however opaque, to the chaos.

Dr. Gordon Ramsay
University of Nottingham

Agnieszka Marczyk

The Witkacy – Cornelius Correspondence, or how to Cure Gout with Transcendental Philosophy

> That we can so easily consider our own body as one of the objects of the external world depends on the quality of the sense of sight. When we close our eyes and only [apprehend] ourselves and objects through the sense of touch, we immediately feel an immense bodily difference between ourselves and the outside world... I am my body and not a unity of personality which is accidentally connected with this "complex of qualities."[1]

Witkacy addressed these words to the German philosopher Hans Cornelius in the context of their epistolary debate which lasted from 1935 to 1939. For

---

[1] S. I. Witkiewicz: letter to Hans Cornelius, June 25, 1936. Reprinted as item no. 100 [in:] H. Kunstmann: Stanisław Ignacy Witkiewicz (Witkacy) im Briefwechsel mit dem deutschen Philosophen Hans Cornelius (The Correspondence Between S. I. Witkiewicz and the German Philosopher Hans Cornelius), Teil I, Part I, "Zeitschrift für Slavische Philologie" 1977, No. 39, p. 60–156. Teil II, Part II: ibidem, No. 40, 1978, p. 150–213; citation from Part I, p. 105.

Witkacy, as for Schopenhauer, reflection about the human body was a necessary element of ontological inquiry. No philosophy could correctly characterize reality, Witkacy believed, if its descriptions of the body were inadequate. And he was convinced that Cornelius drastically underestimated the body's special importance for philosophy. This would not have mattered if Cornelius were a logical positivist, a pragmatist, or any other stripe of philosopher whose work Witkacy could dismiss as immature reductionism. In Witkacy's estimation, however, Cornelius' philosophical system was among the best in Europe, and it deserved careful scrutiny and criticism. This conviction inspired him to write to Cornelius and his letter started a friendship which soon became deeply empathetic and affectionate, a friendship which contrasted strongly with the political crisis that was quickly enveloping Europe. As Witkacy and Cornelius wrote about philosophy, art, and their personal lives, Europe was collapsing under the expansionist politics of Nazi Germany.

Their quixotic friendship first received scholarly attention in the 1970's when Heinrich Kunstmann discovered more than one hundred letters from Witkacy in the Cornelius archive in Munich.[2] Kunstmann edited and published the letters in 1977, and within a year a number of them were translated into Polish.[3] Since most of Witkacy's personal papers were destroyed during World War II, Kunstmann's discovery was greeted with great enthusiasm and the letters became an important biographical source.[4] The scholarly analyses of the correspondence itself, however, remained relatively cursory. Without access to Cornelius' replies to Witkacy, scholars could only give general descriptions of what seemed to have mattered to the two thinkers, but they could not reconstruct the dialogue between them. Above all, the letters came to symbolize the purity of intellectual kinship, extended like a

---

[2] H. Kunstmann: introduction, Briefwechsel, Part I, p. 60–68.

[3] Idem: Nieznane Listy Witkacego (Witkacy's Unknown Letters), "Przegląd Humanistyczny" 1979, nr 6, p. 133–136; S. I. Witkiewicz: Listy do Hansa Corneliusa (Letters to Hans Cornelius), "Przegląd Humanistyczny" 1979, nr 6, p. 137–157. Continued in "Przegląd Humanistyczny" 1980, nr 2, p. 87–112, all three translated by J. Dalecki and W. Kleman: Listy St. I. Witkiewicza do Hansa Corneliusa (S. I. Witkiewicz's Letters to Hans Cornelius), "Twórczość" 1979, nr 35 (4), p. 113–123, translated by H. Opoczyńska; S. I. Witkiewicz, Listy do Hansa Corneliusa (Letters to Hans Cornelius), "Dialog" 1978, nr 5, p. 90–100, translated by S. Morawski.

[4] See for example J. Degler: Witkacego portret wielokrotny: szkice i materiały do biografii (1918–1939) (Witkacy, a Multifaceted Portrait: Sketches and Materials for a Biography (1918–1939)), Warszawa 2009; A. Micińska: Istnienie poszczególne, S. I. Witkiewicz (A Particular Existence – S. I. Witkiewicz), ed. J. Degler, Wrocław 2003; and D. Gerould: The Witkiewicz Reader, Evanston 1992.

fragile bridge over the abyss of the increasingly menacing German-Polish politics of the late 1930s.[5]

In what follows I seek to provide a new perspective on the Witkacy–Cornelius correspondence by drawing on archival materials which were not considered in previous studies.[6] On the one hand, Cornelius' papers and copies of some of his letters and postcards to Witkacy allow for a much fuller reconstruction of their philosophical arguments than has been possible so far. On the other, they reveal that while Witkacy and Cornelius hardly ever explicitly mentioned politics, a political dimension was by no means absent from their friendship. In the present context I will limit myself to two themes which are particularly interesting and significant. I will first explore how Witkacy and Cornelius treated the body in their philosophical and personal discussions, and I will then briefly analyze the political elements in the correspondence and in Cornelius' memory of the friendship during World War II.

When Witkacy first wrote to Cornelius, it was after more than thirty years of studying his works.[7] Although this first letter is missing, from Cornelius' reply from April 19th 1935, we know that Witkacy expressed great

---

[5] For the most recent analysis which idealizes the friendship as a symbolic triumph of rationality over divisive political forces see A. Jonas: Mit Dir nur in der Ferne... Der Briefwechsel zwischen Stanisław Igancy Witkiewicz und Hans Cornelius (1935–1939) (With Nothing but you in the Distance [...] the Correspondence between S. I. Witkiewicz and H. Cornelius, 1935–1939), "Zbliżenia, Polska–Niemcy" 1994, nr 3, p. 33–43.

[6] The documents which are included in this analysis but which were not published by Kunstmann seem to have been added to the Cornelius archive after Kunstmann had consulted it. Kunstmann found and published a carbon copy of one of Cornelius' letters to Witkacy and his letter to Czesława Oknińska; he was aware that Jan Leszczyński might have preserved some letters from Cornelius to Witkacy but did not have access to these (see his introduction to the correspondence, as cited above). The materials I consulted are photocopies of postcards and letters from Cornelius to Witkacy, which seem to have been sent from the library of the Polish Academy of Science in Kraków. There are 7 letters and 17 postcards written between April 19, 1935 and September 15, 1938. The envelope in which they were placed includes an order slip (No. 42, dated April 10, 1976), which indicates that Mrs. Zofia Leszczyńska requested that a microfilm of the letters be made at the PAN library in Kraków. No information is provided about how or when the envelope with photocopies was sent to Munich. I also use a carbon copy of Cornelius' letter to Witkacy (Box 19), which is undated and which was not published by Kunstmann. Its content and Witkacy's responses suggest that it most likely comes from October 1936. Finally, I use Cornelius' correspondence with the General Command of the German Army in Berlin (March 1943), Boxes 13 and 21.

[7] Based on Witkacy's correspondence with his father, Kunstmann suggests that Witkacy started reading Cornelius with the Einleintung in die Philosophie (Introduction to Philosophy, 1901), see Kunstmann, "Przegląd Humanistyczny" 1979, nr 6, p. 134.

respect and admiration for Cornelius and introduced himself as his student. He also immediately announced, however, that he was "15%" his opponent.[8] Cornelius did not succeed in attracting many students or followers in Germany, and he was thrilled to hear from a Polish admirer. His enthusiastic reply invited further discussion and in the weeks and months that followed their letters became friendly and direct. Enjoying both the intimacy and the distance of written correspondence, they wrote frankly about their personal lives, discussed their artistic interests (both shared a passion for painting), and gave each other books and photographs. When Witkacy sent Cornelius one of his novels, he added that he was quite pleased that Cornelius was unable to read this "terrible" book.[9] Cornelius, for his part, was already studying Polish, and in the next letter he warned Witkacy: "but only wait, sir, I will procure a Polish dictionary, and then woe to you! Then I will read it!!!"[10] It was not until May 1936, however, that Witkacy finally wrote the all-important "philosophical letter" which he had been promising Cornelius from the very start.[11] In this outpouring of passionate arguments, Witkacy attempted to explain to his "master" (as he often called Cornelius) how his philosophy was flawed.

Between 1901 and 1934 Cornelius published several treatises in which he put forward the principles of a system which he called 'transcendental idealism.'[12] His goal was to overcome the limitations of both idealist and materialist philosophies and propose a new epistemological framework. His primary focus was on the mind's representations of the world, but he did not believe that reality was reducible to mental images. Critical of Bishop Berkeley and inspired by Kant, Cornelius defined objects as "ever-present laws," which the mind deduces from the stream of constantly changing perceptions. Like Kant, he believed that objects have mind-independent existence.

---

[8] Postcard from Cornelius to Witkacy, April 19, 1935, Ana 352, Box 19.

[9] Witkacy to Cornelius, November 1935, Briefwechsel, item, No. 10, p. 80. Kunstmann suggests that the "terrible" book in question was Insatiability.

[10] Cornelius to Witkacy, November 4, 1935, Ana 352, Box 19, emphasis in the original. For Cornelius' remarks that he has started studying Polish with the book Witkacy sent him see his letter from August 5, 1935, Ana 352, Box 19.

[11] Witkacy to Cornelius, two-part letter, part I sent on May 21, 1936, part II sent on June 25, 1936. Both appear as a single item in Briefwechsel, item, No. 25, p. 99–108.

[12] The most important of these were Psychologie als Erfahrungswissenschaft (Psychology as an Empirical Science) Leipzig 1897, Einleitung in die Philosophie (Introduction to Philosophy), Leipzig and Berlin 1901, and Grundlagen der Erkenntnistheorie, Transcendentale Systematik (Foundations of Epistemology, Transcendental Systematics], Munich 1916. Later publications were shorter versions of earlier works, see for example Das philosophische System von Hans Cornelius. Eigene Gesammtdarstellung (The Philosophical System of Hans Cornelius in his own Overview), Berlin 1934.

Unlike Kant, however, he did not think that the mind's intrinsic structure is what governs the processes of perception. Cornelius claimed instead that the mind apprehends objects by extracting regularities which belong intrinsically to the objects themselves. He attempted to explain this in a variety of ways, one of which was an example of an observer walking around a book. At first the book appears as a "complex of qualities" – it has a specific shape, colour, texture, and so on. Some of these qualities change, however, as the observer looks at the book from different vantage points. From one angle the book might appear as a large flat rectangle, from another as a long and narrow one, from yet another as a parallelogram. Such images have no mind-independent existence, Cornelius argued, but this makes them neither illusory nor infinitely variable. They change predictably and the observer quickly learns what to expect with each step. Cornelius therefore claimed that the real book, the "book in itself" is the invisible source of this predictable variability – it is the objective law according to which the book's qualities must change in an observer's mind.[13] To the mind the book thus appears as a lawfully organized "complex of qualities," in itself the book is an ever-present law which cannot be directly perceived by the human senses.

Witkacy found this unsatisfying – he agreed neither with Cornelius' definition of objects, nor with the consequences this definition had for theories of the self. In his two-part letter from May and June 1936, Witkacy told Cornelius that philosophy should strive, above all, to describe the world as it is, without any preliminary attempts to eliminate complexity. He argued that one must both respect the irreducible dualism of existence, and differentiate the body from all other types of objects. The notion that objects are "complexes of qualities" or "laws of regular correlation" (depending on how one thinks of them) was unacceptable to Witkacy because it could not describe the human body. Because one always experiences the body both from within and from without, he argued, one can never describe it exhaustively in either materialist or idealist terms. One cannot think of the body as nothing but a "complex of qualities," and the idea of an "ever-present law" is much too ambiguous. Purely materialist descriptions, Witkacy pointed out, necessarily neglect the body's inner life, they cannot account for the sense of 'inner touch' which informs the mind about pain, hunger, pleasure, or exhaustion.[14] Conversely, idealist philosophies, even those as sophisticated as Cornelius', ignore the body's self-subsistent existence in the world. Mental representations of the body, Witkacy claimed, are not images of an ephemeral "complex

---

[13] H. Cornelius: Eigene Gesamtdarstellung, op. cit., p. 26–27.

[14] For an excellent analysis of the history of the concept of "inner touch" see D. Heller-Roazen: The inner touch: archaeology of a sensation, New York 2007.

of qualities" but arrows which point to something real, something immediately and undeniably present, something which is exists independently of the mind. To call that something an abstract law is to betray the commitment to remain true to the richness of reality.[15]

By the mid-1930s Witkacy was working on his 'biological monadology,' an original and imaginative, if not a particularly verifiable, system of ontological claims.[16] In his letter to Cornelius, he interspersed critique with his own findings and expected Cornelius to grasp the truth of his statements. Reality, he wrote, consists of an irreducible multiplicity of "Particular Existences," or living monads, each of which has independent existence, it subsists "in itself." Each person is a Particular Existence, but monadology does not end there. All that appears to be inanimate matter is actually a composite of vast numbers of infinitesimal monads. Unity of consciousness, just like sounds and colors, has a scale of intensity, and the tiny monads have self-awareness and self-unity appropriate to their simple structures. Each is thus endowed not only with a body but also with a primitive personality.[17] One can only imagine Cornelius's surprise when Witkacy told him that biological monadology was a direct outgrowth of his transcendental idealism.[18] Witkacy's letter was effectively a plea for Cornelius to further articulate the truths already inherent in his philosophy.

What he received instead of the expected offer to join forces was a very disappointing outline of all the ways in which he had misunderstood Cornelius's thought. Cornelius' reply was a letter of a self-assured teacher di-

---

[15] Witkacy to Cornelius, letter from May 21, 1936 (Part I) and June 15, 1936 (Part II), reprinted in Briefwechsel, item, No. 25, p. 99–108. Whereas in the early 1920s Witkacy privileged the body and consciousness equally, between 1934 and 1936 he began to give ontological primacy to the body, for further discussion of this shift see M. Soin: Filozofia Stanisława Ignacego Witkiewicza (The Philosophy of S. I. Witkiewicz), Wrocław 2002.

[16] His most extensive articulation of this system was Pojęcia i twierdzenia implikowane przez pojęcie istnienia: 1917–1932 (Concepts and Propositions Implied by the Concept of Existence: 1917–1932), Warszawa 1935.

[17] Witkacy discussed these concepts in his May–June 1936 letter to Cornelius, explaining some aspects in detail and only mentioning others, he returned to the themes in later letters, see especially the Briefwechsel, item, No. 100 (November 1938), p. 192–194.

[18] Witkacy often emphasized Cornelius' role in the development of his thought but other influences, which Witkacy did not discuss, might have been very important as well. See, for example Janusz Degler's discussion of the importance of Witkacy's stay in Russia during World War I and the popularity of Leibniz's monadology among Russian intellectuals during that time - editorial note in the most recent critical edition of Witkacy's Pojęcia i twierdzenia (Concepts and Propositions), Warszawa 2002, p. 458–465.

rected at an uncomprehending student. He carefully and patiently restated his own understanding of reality, and emphasized that in his system the body has no special epistemological significance. It is an object given to the mind no differently than any object in space – as a complex of qualities which change in lawful, predictable ways. Touch, Cornelius reminded Witkacy, whether internal or external, gives the mind as much or as little information as all the other senses. It provides nothing but fleeting perceptions which, by themselves, are incapable of pointing to anything that exists beyond the mind. He suggested that Witkacy's remarks about statistics revealed his limited training in the natural sciences, but did not remark about Witkacy's monadology. Nor did he ask about the evolution of Witkacy's thought.[19]

Witkacy was immensely disappointed by the accusation of misunderstanding Cornelius' philosophy and with his typical verve proceeded to convince Cornelius that he understood his system quite well because he had "lived through it" for years.[20] In the exchange of letters that followed in the fall of 1936 Witkacy's tone ranged from respectful gratitude to emotional outbursts of frustration and subsequent apologies.[21] The letters did not bring any more mutual understanding or conceptual clarification. In October 1937, Witkacy invited Cornelius to come to Poland and they enjoyed long walks in the foothills of the Tatra Mountains. Even their conversations and the fluidity of the spoken word, however, seem not to have helped them to come any closer to comprehending each other's most fundamental premises. Their letters from 1938 and 1939 still resounded with frustration and accusations of misinterpretation. Cornelius maintained that his system effectively overcame the traps of idealism and believed that Witkacy never truly understood his theory of objects. Witkacy remained convinced that Cornelius made the cardinal mistake of neglecting the unique epistemological priority of the body.[22]

---

[19] Cornelius to Witkacy, undated carbon copy of a letter, most likely written in October 1936. Bavarian State Library in Munich, Ana 352, Box 19.

[20] Witkacy to Cornelius, letter from November 5, 1936, item, No. 41 in the Briefwechsel, p. 127.

[21] See Witkacy to Cornelius, Briefwechsel: item, No. 28 p. 109, item, No. 32, p. 112, and items, No. 36–46, p. 117–134. See also Cornelius to Witkacy, postcard July 16, 1936, Ana 352, Box 19.

[22] Cornelius' report about his lectures and meetings in Poland appears in the Briefwechsel as item, No. 68, and in Polish in "Twórczość", nr 30, 1974, p. 72–79. For further philosophical exchanges between Witkacy and Cornelius Briefwechsel, items, No. 51, 70, 73, 76, 80, 83, 100, and 102 (the last item is Cornelius' letter to Witkacy, the others are Witkacy's letters to Cornelius).

If we focus only on the philosophical elements of this correspondence we have before us a story of misunderstandings. Witkacy and Cornelius could not find a common language precise enough to transform their exchange of philosophical views into dialogue. They were locked into their own technical terms and their own linguistic spaces. Cornelius never learned Polish well enough to read Witkacy's philosophical texts, and Witkacy's German was anything but precise. He wrote passionately and without much regard for order, he often left his clauses and his sentences incomplete, and more than once made German words out of Polish ones. Sometimes he wrote in sinister depression, sometimes in excited fury, and sometimes he confessed to being half-drunk but pressed on with philosophical arguments nonetheless. As his Polish friends often attested, Witkacy felt the intensity of philosophical questioning to the very core of his being, and this did not always support his efforts to make his claims clear. Cornelius' philosophy, on the other hand, even if expressed in perfect and perfectly detached academic German, was full of conceptual gaps and vague claims which were open to misreading.

It is therefore remarkable that the misapprehensions and frustration did not upset the genuinely warm and caring friendship that developed between the two men. It appears that the very act of conducting an honest and engaged philosophical discussion created a sense of solidarity which was far more important than all the conceptual gaps. A fascinating contrast, moreover, emerges from the letters: whereas Witkacy and Cornelius could not see eye to eye when it came to philosophical treatment of the body, they fully understood each other's struggles with bodily ailments and shared both advice and empathy. Some of the linguistic obstacles which plagued their philosophical discussions were also prominent when they wrote about personal issues but the obstacles did not matter nearly as much. Experiences of the aging and vulnerable body gave Witkacy and Cornelius a shared reference point which brought them as close, if not closer, than their passion for philosophy.

Gout was the worst culprit. At times it made it impossible for Cornelius to type, and it pushed Witkacy to experiment with all kinds of dietary remedies. The two were tireless in exchanging ideas about cures and medicines which might bring relief. Witkacy advised Cornelius to drink salt water, eat pickled vegetables, and abstain from meat. He also described his own attempts to control attacks by abstaining from beer. Cornelius, in turn, provided long lists of mixtures and tinctures and sent Witkacy his short, light-hearted booklet about gout. There were other ailments and other attempts to help. The most humorous perhaps was Cornelius' initiation into the world of Polish folk medicine. When he suffered from bronchitis Witkacy sent him a package of thick glass cups (bańki) along with detailed instructions for applying this rather unusual instrument of healing. Cornelius was baffled, and when he asked Witkacy for a better explanation he remarked: "it seems that you did not understand my concept of the object quite right, just as I did not correctly understand your instructions concerning the glass cups."[23]

The body also appeared in the correspondence as a visual object of great emotional importance and as the unwieldy cause of erotic troubles. As a painter of psychological portraits, Witkacy used painting as a mode of understanding people's personalities. He requested a picture of Cornelius so that he could make his portrait, and when he received the photograph he kept it by his bed. Cornelius likewise expressed joy when he saw a picture of Witkacy on the cover of one of the books Witkacy sent him. He later commented on Witkacy's handsome and expressive features which, he felt, suggested a particularly nice personality.[24] Cornelius was Witkacy's senior by twenty two years, and Witkacy treated him not only as a mentor, but also as a father-figure and a most trustworthy friend. He confided in him when his problems with women became overwhelmingly complicated, and shared his fears about the isolation and bitterness that would come with aging. When Witkacy and Czesława Oknińska-Korzeniowska experienced their worst crisis, he asked Cornelius to plead on his behalf and Cornelius obliged.[25]

Given the context of late 1930s, it is surprising that there seem to have been no exchanges of political views between Witkacy and Cornelius. Aside from Witkacy's occasional statements about his premonition that a global catastrophe was near, there is only one explicit reference to contemporary politics in the preserved correspondence. In a letter from October 9th, 1938, written ten days after the Munich Conference and German annexation of the Sudetenland, Witkacy joked that both his ability to finally turn to the critique of the Vienna Circle and the Munich Agreement succeeded in averting a world catastrophe. He told Cornelius, however, that Hitler "is still the greatest man of our times."[26] We do not have Cornelius' response to this remark. We do know that two years earlier, in Niemyte Dusze (Unwashed Souls), Witkacy put forward a rather different assessment of Hitler. Niemyte Dusze

---

[23] See, for example, Briefwechsel, items, No. 4, 7, 8, 11, 12, 13, 19, 23, 31, and 32; Cornelius to Witkacy, letters from September 20 and November 4, 1935, letter from January 29, 1936, postcard from July 16, 1936 (includes the cited quote), postcard from February 22, 1937, and postcard from September 15, 1938, Ana 352, Box 19.

[24] See Briefwechsel, item, No. 21, and Cornelius to Witkacy letters from August 5, and September 20, 1935.

[25] See, for example, Briefwechsel, items, No. 49, 50, 54, 67, 86–92, see also Cornelius to Witkacy, letter from November 24, 1937, Ana 352, Box 19.

[26] Briefwechsel, item, No. 96, p. 189.

was Witkacy's analysis of Polish society, its position in Europe, and its structural problems. It was an attempt to raise individual and collective sense of responsibility among his fellow Poles, and a decisive departure from his earlier credo of abstaining from socio-political engagements. Witkacy devoted much attention to what he saw as a particularly Polish "inferiority complex," and bemoaned the fact that, with all his shortcomings, Piłsudski was the only great man in Poland since the sixteenth century. Regarding the future of Europe, Witkacy confessed that he had once placed high hopes in Hitler's assertive leadership but these hopes were sorely disappointed. Hitler, he argued, failed to carry out a revolution from above and create a just and a radically socialist order, free from both militarism and utopian excesses. Instead of being Europe's benefactor, Witkacy predicted, Hitler would one day find himself running for his life.[27]

Political views thus seem to have been either bracketed or edited in the Witkacy–Cornelius correspondence but political realities intervened powerfully with the outbreak of World War II. At that point the personal and the political could not longer exist in separate spheres. The fusion of personal and political tragedy in Witkacy's death is well known. In September 1939 German troops invaded Poland, and Witkacy, who was 54, attempted to enlist in the Polish army. He was turned down on account of his age and his failing health, and together with Czesława he joined the refugees who were traveling east. On September 18th, a day after the Soviet invasion, he committed suicide.

The intimately personal and the political came together for Cornelius in a very different way. He learned about Witkacy's death from Jan Leszczyński in January 1940.[28] Later that year he wrote to German authorities on behalf of Tadeusz Kotarbiński's son who was interned at a prisoner of war camp close to Cornelius' home town.[29] In June 1942, the White Rose student dissidents began their pamphlet campaign at the university in Munich where Cornelius was still a part-time professor. In February 1943, Christoph Probst and Hans and Sophie Scholl were sentenced to death and executed for their activism. Cornelius' two sons were in the German army at the time. A month later, seemingly unprompted, Cornelius wrote to the army command in Berlin with a surprising offer. He reported that during his trip to Poland in 1937 he was told about rich oil deposits near Zakopane, and he wanted to share

---

[27] S. I. Witkiewicz: Narkotyki. Niemyte Dusze (Narcotics. Unwashed Souls), Warszawa 2004, footnote on p. 241. Comment about Piłsudski, p. 233.

[28] Briefwechsel, item, No. 119.

[29] Cornelius met Tadeusz Kotarbiński through Witkacy during his trip to Poland. For the Cornelius–Kotarbiński correspondence (1940–1942), see Ana 352, box 20.

this information to support the war effort. When prompted for more details, he wrote that the oil deposit was near the home of his friend who was now deceased, and he provided Witkacy's address and directions to his home. The letter ended with an empathetic "Heil Hitler!"[30] Cornelius survived the war, he died in Gräfelfing in 1947.[31]

Abstract

By drawing on archival materials that were previously considered missing, the author examines Witkacy's epistolary friendship with the German philosopher Hans Cornelius, a friendship which lasted from 1935 to 1939. She explores how Witkacy and Cornelius discussed the body as an object of philosophical speculation and personal experience, and then briefly turns to the political elements in the correspondence, and in Cornelius' recollection of the friendship during later years. Witkacy and Cornelius did not find a common language precise enough to transform their exchange of philosophical views into genuine dialogue, but their friendship became more intimate with time. It seems that the process of engaging in honest and passionate philosophical dialogue helped them develop a personal friendship which was more important than their conceptual misunderstandings.

Dr. Agnieszka Marczyk
University of Pennsylvania

---

[30] See Ana 352, Box 21 for carbon copies of Cornelius' letters to the army command unit in Berlin, and Box 13 for replies Cornelius received from a Dr. Bentz.

[31] Some aspects of Cornelius' personal reckoning with how he and other Germans dealt with Nazism and the war can be glimpsed from his personal papers and his open letter to the Americans, Ana 352, Box 28. For an analysis of the Nazification of the German university see H. Sluga: Heidegger's Crisis: Philosophy and Politics in Nazi Germany, Cambridge 1993.

Paweł Polit

Philosophical Marginalia by Stanisław Ignacy Witkiewicz[1]

Philosophical marginalia are the lesser known form of Stanisław Ignacy Witkiewicz's creative activities. They embrace the notes and drawings that the artist and writer made in the 1930s in the margins of the philosophical books he read. Witkacy's marginal notes constitute often humorous comments on the texts he studied and are intertwined with notes of a personal nature; the drawings he added on the edges of pages, frequently acting as illustrations, suggest motifs known widely from his paintings.

Witkacy's philosophical annotations have been preserved on the pages of over thirty books that are currently in the collection of the Library of the Institute of Philosophy of Warsaw University. They constitute unusually valuable documentation of Witkacy's intellectual explorations and passions just before World War II, in the period when he no longer focused upon the painterly practice congruent with the principles of the theory of Pure Form, but concentrated upon developing the principles of his philosophical system.

---

[1] This text is a fragment of an essay: Pawel Polit: Fragment, rama, seria. O wizualnych aspektach marginaliów filozoficznych Witkacego, [in:] Stanisław Ignacy Witkiewicz. marginalia filozoficzne, exhibition catalogue, ed. P. Polit, Centre for Contemporary Art Ujazdowski Castle, Warszawa 2004.

It is not possible to treat Witkacy's marginalia merely as a side effect of his encounters with the text he read; quite on the contrary, they seem to express in an intriguing way the sense of his creative attitude. As Jadwiga Witkiewiczowa, the artist's wife, commented upon the experience of reading in Witkacy's intellectual biography:

> He devoted himself to reading with passion. I could not figure out how he did manage to read that much while being engaged in that many activities, such as writing, making portraits, while living that intensely as he did. He employed a certain system which seemingly stood in opposition to any system one could employ in daily life. He strove not to waste any moment in his life; in the pockets of his coat he used to have some book of an appropriate format – at the final stage this was the volume of writings by Leibniz – which he read when riding by tram or by bus. He even visited the toilet with some book – this was called the "toilet reading" in his vocabulary – and that book remained there in the pocket of his pyjamas or dressing gown until he finished reading it.
>
> Most of the reading he did was philosophy. He knew languages: English, French, German and Russian. His library – not especially numerous – embraced primarily philosophical books. Most of them were lost in Warsaw in 1939, with the exception of a number of books which survived in Zakopane. I sold these books to the Philosophical Seminary of the University of Warsaw; they contain a large number of annotations, even short humorous verses, which could be of great value for the explorer's of my husband's output. Stasio's way of reading was not a common reading – this was already the critique of a given work itself.[2]

The adversaries of Witkacy's polemical remarks inscribed in the books' margins were the leading figures of Polish philosophy of the interwar period: Roman Ingarden, Maria Kokoszyńska, Tadeusz Kotarbiński, Joachim Metallmann, Alfred Tarski. The list also includes foreign philosophers, such as Emil Boirac, Ludwig Busse, Arthur Stanley Eddington, Bertrand Russell or Alfred North Whitehead (the latter's ideas were commented upon by Witkiewicz on the margins of Joachim Metallmann's dissertation). The list of Witkacy's readings in philosophy, however, are not limited to these names only. There are records of his exploration of writings of Edmund Husserl, the initiator of phenomenological movement; he also devoted extensive texts to theories of the philosophers of language – Ludwig Wittgenstein, Rudolf Carnap and other logical positivists of the Vienna Circle – the texts which later became incorporated in one of Witkacy's major philosophical works – The Psycho-Physical Problem (Zagadnienie psychofizyczne).

---

[2] J. Witkiewiczowa: Wspomnienia o Stanisławie Ignacym Witkiewiczu, [in:] Spotkanie z Witkacym. Materiały z sesji poświęconej twórczości Stanisława Ignacego Witkiewicza, Jelenia Góra 1979, p. 100.

In his polemical statements – marginal annotations and, subsequently, expanded critical texts – Witkiewicz accuses most of the authors of introducing serious distortions into philosophical subject matter: of suppressing or serious misconstruing ontological questions. The theories they proposed disguise, according to him, in this way or the other, the fundamental problem of psycho-physical dualism: the functioning of a living entity – the Particular Existence – on the crossing of two orders: the temporal one and the spatial one. These authors also conceal the related type of dualism, the one which manifests itself on the existential plane: the gap between the Particular Existence and the rest of the world – and neutralize the resulting experience of one's own exceptionality and solitude: the "metaphysical feeling" of astonishment with the inexplicable fact of one's own existence and the strangeness of the surrounding world.

Coping with the problem of psycho-physical dualism, Witkiewicz opposes any kind of minimizing of the essential, in his opinion, philosophical subject matter. His polemical discussions could be qualified as a kind of psychoanalysis of the philosophical language; in his marginalia and the related critical texts, Witkiewicz enters into a "conversation" with the authors he read with an aim to reveal the artificial character and the falsehood of their concepts and to reach the level of repressed concepts and statements which are grounded – as it is suggested by the title of his most important philosophical work – in the very notion of Existence.[3]

The method of "unmasking" the philosophical concepts employed by Witkiewicz has been described by Bohdan Michalski in his book Polemiki filozoficzne Stanisława Ignacego Witkiewicza. In Michalski's view, Witkiewicz used to prove that each theory which makes attempts at eliminating the psycho-physical dualism and rejecting the notion of the self is constrained, "in the last instance, to admit, in a disguised manner [...] the substitutes of all fundamental concepts which it aimed to erase from our view of the world."[4] These concepts return, according to Witkiewicz, in the guise of "masked concepts" which are competitive to "true, i.e. necessary, concepts, which necessarily refer to each existence – concepts which would grasp the psycho-physical duality of Existence."[5]

---

[3] S. I. Witkiewicz: Pojęcia i twierdzenia implikowane przez pojęcie Istnienia, Warszawa 1935.

[4] B. Michalski: Polemiki filozoficzne Stanisława Ignacego Witkiewicza, Warszawa 1979, p. 120.

[5] S. I. Witkiewicz, Stosunek wzajemny nauki i filozofii, [in:] idem: Pisma filozoficzne i estetyczne, Vol. III, Warszawa 1977, p. 87; quoted after B. Michalski, op. cit., p. 119.

Witkiewicz reproaches the representatives of philosophy of language (such as Carnap, Kotarbiński, Tarski, Wittgenstein) for improperly reducing the problematics of ontology in their research concerning the foundations of logic and the principles of construction of linguistic expressions. He ascribes the philosophers, who take as their point of departure the results of particular sciences, the tendency to cultivate what he called 'pseudophilosophical monism' by means of introducing notions which obliterate the fundamental, in his opinion, difference between the objective and subjective spheres. He also suspects the thinkers of the phenomenological circle (Edmund Husserl, Roman Ingarden, Jan Leszczyński) of hypostasizing certain abstract notions and abandoning the realistic attitude by admitting the concept of pure consciousness as the founding centre for the contents of an experiencing subject.

Philosophical annotations inscribed by Witkiewicz on the texts' margins frequently served as the point of departure for his criticism of a given author's ideas in an extended polemical text. During the process of reading, he usually creates a preliminary scheme of argumentation, which he would eventually develop and complete in the full length polemical text; he sketches out his own ideas, drafts the arrangement of questions to be addressed. The activity of annotating provides him also with an occasion to make an inventory of philosophical notions and problems, carefully inscribed in some books, together with the index of relevant pages, on the empty pages neighbouring the title page, or on the inside back of the book's cover. It seems, though, that Witkacy's philosophical marginalia, in addition to performance of their role as an auxiliary function, before they serve as a preliminary plan for philosophical argumentation, constitute a sphere of a purely disinterested game, related to the domain of an aesthetic experience. Within this border-line zone, situated somewhere between the activity of reading and an attempt to construct a complex structure of concepts in the form of an extended philosophical text, the schemes of polemical discussions, drawn on an enormous number of pages, degenerate into form, to become grotesque or fantastical creatures then visible to comment upon philosophical problems, or indeed remain indifferent to them.

What seems to be of significance in this 'conversation' with adversaries, is the theatrical metaphorics of 'masking' and 'unmasking' the concepts they propose – with the metaphorics recurring in Witkacy's polemical statements. When reading his philosophical marginalia, it is frequently difficult to resist the impression of witnessing the course of a philosophical discussion animated by the protagonists of one of his dramas or novels. In these 'essential conversations,' performed on the pages of books studied by Witkiewicz, the flow of philosophical argument is interrupted time after time with the cut of Witkacy's reply; numerous invocations to the authors and remarks formulated in ad personam mode which emphasize the dialogical character of the text. Lines of reference, reaching far into the paragraph of the printed text, sometimes creating a dense network, bring to the mind the notion of theatrical score. Tiny drawings, interspersed with lines and verbal inscriptions, in addition to oval, wavy or angular forms enclosing concise statements, seem to endow Witkacy's marginalia with the character of stage directions, in which it would be difficult not to specify the names of the drama's protagonists; on the cover of one of the brochures – the one containing the text by Alfred Tarski – we find a whole list of fictitious characters: Oneric Picton, Belferic Montero, Kiernozjan Trichinienko, Tryndaljon Oniniwalenko, Miendorlan Purdyfietko... On the cover of the brochure containing a text by Jan Wortman we find the sketchy description of some complex narrative depicting 'common sense philosopher reaching the stage of monadism via animism' – the short annotation being, perhaps, the record of a dream, or inscribed under the influence of drugs.

All of this provokes the suspicion that the operation of 'unmasking' the concepts in his marginalia provide Witkiewicz with an opportunity to 'mask' the characters. He not only introduces real philosophers and fictitious protagonists on the stage, but also introduces his own character – not unlike the procedure he employed for the scenes he enacted for various photographic shots – engaging in the intricate disputes and inscribing his own inimitable text on the fabric of a pre-existing one. Utilizing the very method he employed in his dramas – the method consisting of super-imposing the narrative transparencies one upon the other – he endows any such text with the character of palimpsest; in his hands, the 'found' text becomes the material for creating the new one, reinterpreting the content of the former and transferring it into an altogether different, extra-philosophical dimension. Accordingly, during the course of his reading of the major work by Alfred Tarski, Pojęcie prawdy w językach nauk dedukcyjnych (The Concept of Truth in Formalized Languages), the cover carries the new alternative title – Unitas multiplex – expressing the notion of unity in multiplicity, so fundamental to Witkacy's thinking. In another instance, the invocation placed on the title page of the same book, but later erased, evokes the mysterious figure of "God of tiny quantifiers."[6] The dramatic aspect of Witkacy's philosophical marginalia is emphasized by the inscription 'Spłyciarze i pogłębnicy' – 'the shal-

---

[6] This transcript has been preserved in the form of typescript made by Jadwiga Witkiewiczowa, now in the collection of Książnica Pomorska in Szczecin.

lowers and the deepeners' which written on the inside cover of a history of philosophy book by Friedrich Schwegler; this inscription tells us of the radical polarisation of attitudes commented upon by Witkiewicz – and not only the philosophical ones, it seems. So for Witkiewicz, in this way the experience of reading a philosophical text becomes the equivalent for Witkiewicz to an endeavour to reinscribe it, and the polemical discussion with a particular author is transformed by him into a dramatised, 'conversation of essence.'

Abstract

This article develops the idea which stood behind the exhibition entitled Stanisław Ignacy Witkiewicz – Philosophical Margins held at the Centre for Contemporary Art Ujazdowski Castle, Warsaw, in 2004. This exhibition focused upon the hitherto unknown forms of Witkiewicz's creative activities: it presented the notes and drawings that the artist and writer made in the 1930s in the margins of the philosophical books he read. Witkacy's marginal notes constitute often humorous comments to the texts he studied and are intertwined with notes of a personal nature; the drawings he added at page edges suggest motifs known widely from his paintings. The purpose of the exhibition was to draw an analogy between Witkacy's artistic concepts and his philosophical thinking. The article is meant as a reflection upon the question of place and role of philosophy in his output as a whole.

Paweł Polit
Centre for Contemporary Art Ujazdowski Castle, Warsaw

Bryce Lease

Cutting the Romantic's Throat: Witkacy's Nasty Nightmare

This crucial turn in the twentieth century is not only reflected in the techniques of Modernism (e.g. a focus on the Self qua interiority, the mythic apparent in the everyday), but in a pervasive – and, therefore, less isolationist – world outlook. As many scholars have noted, Witkiewicz's plays in the 1920s reflect a world in which modern totalitarian regimes will reign supreme. This is not restricted to Witkiewicz's belief that the upper classes, of which he was a member, were crumbling – indeed, he believed this was a 'well-deserved catastrophe'.[1] He was interested in portraying the 'boredom and despair of modern civilization"[2] on an international level. It is precisely in Witkiewicz's shift in focus away from Romantic values that we discover his ability to traverse the Polish nationalist fantasy.[3]

Bezimienne dzieło (1921) (translated as The Anonymous Work: Four Acts of a Rather Nasty Nightmare) deals with the devastating effects of revolution,

---

[1] D. Gerould: Twentieth-Century Polish Avant-garde Drama: Plays, Scenarios, Critical Documents, Cornell NY 1977, p. 35.

[2] Ibidem, p. 35.

[3] This shift from Romantic values is no doubt one of the major contributors to why Witkiewicz's work was so unpopular in his own lifetime. Most critics, however, focus on the anti-realistic nature of his writing in relation to his unpopularity.

and the mode in which even the greatest causes can be mere pretenses for the power-hungry. In this play, Witkiewicz is interested in exposing the mechanisms of ideology, the hopelessness of any large-scale utopian revolution, and the inevitable loss of the individual that such social shifts ensure.

The plot focuses on Rosa van der Blaast, a famous composer who is in love with the leader of a social revolution, and Plasmonick Blodestaug, a consumptive painter who is desperately in love with Rosa. As opposed to the Woman in the final scene of Mickiewicz's Dziady, who is interpellated by her love for Konrad into the nationalist cause, Witkiewicz gives us a cold and calculating female character who is able to manipulate men for her own pleasure. In short, Witkiewicz creates one of the original femmes fatale. Most significantly, in the relationship between Rosa and Plasmonick, Witkiewicz exposes both the lure and the apparatus of fantasy.

At the beginning of The Anonymous Work, Plasmonick, the protagonist, is about to be tried for espionage. He has recently received a large sum of money from Rosa van der Blaast, who is also to be tried as an espionagette, under mysterious terms. It is clear by the second act that Rosa is having an affair with Józef Tzingar, a social activist and leader of the faction who wishes to bring down the current monarchy. When Plasmonick discovers that Rosa will be sent to prison he also claims to be guilty of espionage, though we know he is innocent and merely wishes to share a cell with her in prison. Rosa does not contest Plasmonick's (false) admission of guilt, nor does she then try to prove her own innocence, as this allows Tzingar to freely pursue his revolutionary work.

In Act III, we are confronted with Rosa and Plasmonick sharing a prison cell, fighting about the nature of art: whether form or content is more important, painting or music, etc. We are led to believe, however, that such quarreling merely conceals a much deeper rupture in their relationship. Plasmonick does not understand why Rosa allowed him to falsely admit his guilt, and believes, rightfully, that she is protecting a lover. What repulses Rosa in this scene is not Plasmonick's outright musings on the true identity of her lover – thus exposing her desire – but rather the revelation that Plasmonick conceives of her as an esponiagette. What Plasmonick fails to realize here is precisely the mode in which he has fashioned Rosa into an object of his fantasy, an object devoid of any material content; in other words, we see the exact mode in which desire is metonymic. Desire tolerates shifts from one set of contents to another (Rosa as composer, as upper-class citizen, as lover, as espionagette), as long as it remains within the boundaries of the fantasy wherein Rosa returns Plasmonick's desire. In this example we see clearly Lacan's point that desire is the desire of the other. That is to say, desire is never direct, but caught in a self-reflective trap that is inherent to the (barred-by-language) subject's relationship to the symbolic network. To put it simply, Plasmonick's desire for Rosa is not straight but curved – it does not directly seek its target but requires a curvature of space; in short, his desire requires Rosa as a fantasy object rather than as a subject – it does not indicate a desire to simply be near her in the prison cell. If this were the case then Plasmonick would be troubled by Rosa's espionage. The fact that this revelation has no effect on his desire whatsoever does not indicate flexibility and compassion in Plasmonick's love for Rosa, quite the contrary. Once Rosa divulges her secret – the reason why she did not defend herself after Plasmonick's confession was because she actually loves Tzingar – she renders Plasmonick's desire for her impossible:

Plasmonick: (Inwardly shaken) Don't talk that way… I'm not reproaching you because you took spy money for your music, only because you could love him so much that to save him you'd go to prison and deceive me for such a long time. When I loved you so…

Rosa: That wasn't love; that was just weakness. [...]

Plasmonick: But how are we going to go on living? Fourteen years! No – I've got to get out of here. I simply can't – I can't love you anymore [...] It's all a stupid hideous dream. It's got to come to an end.[4]

Rosa functions as a femme fatale[5] not because she is aware that Plasmonick's fantasy will lose its consistency and dissipate with the divulgence of her secret, but rather because she is the means by which Plasmonick experiences 'subjective destitution.'[6] Plasmonick alludes to his state of subjective destitution as a result of Rosa's revelation when he says to his father, 'I'm in

---

[4] S. I. Witkiewicz: The Anonymous Work: Four Acts of a Rather Nasty Nightmare, trans. D. Gerould, [in:] Twentieth-Century Polish Avant-Garde Drama, London 1977, p. 134–135.

[5] Rosa's status as a femme fatale is solidified at the conclusion of the scene when in response to Plasmonick's plea, 'You don't know how monstrously you're torturing me,' Rosa declares, 'I do know – I know perfectly well [...] Torture is the absolute essence of love' (142). Is this declaration not stricto sensu one of the key features of film noir's femme fatale?

[6] Plasmonick, however, puts Rosa into an impossible position, and this is why we see her eruptive response. What Rosa acknowledges is that as an object of Plasmonick's fantasy, she is loved for everything except the one substance that gives her subjectivity its consistency, that is her love for Jozef Tzingar – the man for whom she was willing to sacrifice her life and go to prison.

a state of great inner transformation, Father. For me the world has turned round a hundred and eighty degrees at least.'[7] It is at this point in the play that we should recall Lacan's formula 'woman is a symptom of man.' This is not a misogynist notion that implies a woman has no ontological consistency unto herself; instead, Rosa functions as a symptom for Plasmonick without whom 'reality' as such would have no positive uniformity. Rosa subtracting herself from Plasmonick's fantasy is the equivalent to Plasmonick losing his symptom. And if we take into account Lacan's later writing on symptom, no longer as an attribute that will simply dissolve when it is appropriately symbolized, but as the feature which endows the subject with their very ontological consistency, then we can make sense of Plasmonick's outburst, 'I'm destroyed;' an outburst which should be taken literally:

> If [...] we conceive of the symptom as [...] a particular signifying formation which confers on the subject its very ontological consistency, enabling it to structure its basic, constitutive relationship to enjoyment (jouissance), then the entire relationship is reversed: if the symptom is dissolved, the subject itself loses the ground under its feet, disintegrates.[8]

Here we should detect the seeds of the conclusion, the point at which Plasmonick overcomes his love for Rosa, and feels as if he has 'woken from a dreadful nightmare.'[9] It is precisely in Plasmonick's ability to traverse his fantasy, that is to overcome Rosa – quite literally, in fact, for he cuts her throat with a razorblade – that we see Witkiewicz has really left behind the Romantic universe, that is, the symbolic network that refused to renounce the desire for desire – the very form of drive – that could not surpass the fantasy for its own aim (that is, autonomous 'nation') without renouncing the desire for this desire. In doing so, does Witkiewicz not expose the paradox of Polish Romanticism? In other words, freedom and desire are indeed exclusive; the metonymic nature of desire (versus the repeated staging of loss we encounter in drive) is always-already related directly to the subject's fundamental fantasy, that inaccessible fantasy which anchors the subject to his social field. Which Romantic character is able to attain freedom from their symbolic networks to such a radical degree as Plasmonick accomplishes? When Plasmonick cuts Rosa's throat he accomplishes an act in the strict Lacanian sense. The act is that which resounds outside of the Symbolic, which cannot be incorporated or sutured into it. Just before committing

---

[7] S. I. Witkiewicz, op. cit., p. 137.
[8] S. Žižek: Enjoy Your Symptom!, New York, London 2001, p. 155.
[9] S. I. Witkiewicz, op. cit., p. 150.

the act, Plasmonick says, 'I'm going back to prison. And in order not to be tempted out again' – in other words, in order to renounce the 'new world' that will come about as a result of Tzingar's coup d'état, in order to renounce the symbolic field that constitutes his identity – 'I've got to do something appropriately monstrous.'[10] The act is always monstrous insofar as it disturbs the laws of the symbolic network – it literally has to break the law in order to undermine the law from within. For a moment, the onlookers believe Plasmonick will kill himself; instead he kills the object of his fantasy – Rosa – the symptom which endowed his notion of 'reality' with some consistency. From this point on, Plasmonick has confirmed his life-long prison system, cut off from the 'terror' of Tzingar and Lopek's revolutions that preclude all (metaphysical) individuality, a revolution that will see the individual reduced to the grey mass of unidentifiable workers.

Should this act not be directly contrasted with Konrad's (false) act at the conclusion of Mickiewicz's Dziady, the point at which Konrad transcends the earth on a golden chariot – an act that not only fails to renounce the symbolic field but, in a process of sublimation, confers consistency on Polish nationalist identity? What's more, do we not encounter an important cut here between Mickiewicz and Witkiewicz, surrounding not just the object of desire, but the 'object of negative magnitude,' the object which gives consistency to our reality? At the end of Dziady, the Woman misrecognises Konrad's glance, and believes that it is intended solely for her. Of course Mickiewicz's real intention is for the entire audience to perceive this glance as intended solely for them. It is here we see the paradox of interpellation, when one moment of radical contingency changes the entire field of subjectivity. Konrad's glance is both intended for everyone and for each individual in particular. How is this possible? The only satisfying answer concerns the nature of objet petit a. As Žižek explains in The Plague of Fantasies, 'the object which functions as the "cause of desire" must be in itself a metonymy of lack – that is to say, an object which is not simply lacking but, in its very positivity, gives body to lack.'[11] In other words, the lack itself, the gap which constitutes subjectivity, is unbearable because it provides no consistent model of selfhood. This is why we have Konrad, the Romantic hero, as the Thing (das Ding), the 'negative magnitude:' 'if our experience of reality is to maintain its consistency, the positive field of reality has to be 'sutured' with a supplement which the subject (mis)perceives as a positive entity, but is effectively a negative magnitude.'[12]

---

[10] Ibidem, p. 151.
[11] S. Žižek: Plague of Fantasies, London 2009, p. 81.
[12] Ibidem.

Rather than carrying on this process of nationalist interpellation, attempting to supply the supplement that secures meaning for a nation that is 'nationless,' as in the Mickiewicz example, Witkiewicz is here revealing the very nature of this relationship to desire, subjectivity and the role of the Thing. It does not matter to Plasmonick that Rosa might be an espionagette, beause the nation-as-cause is not the supplement that secures Plasmonick's life with meaning and consistency as it does for the Romantic subject. Rather than favoring love as a cause worthy for this position, the position of the Thing, Witkiewicz exposes the very negative dimension of any object which functions in this role; in short, he shows that this object (Konrad, Poland, Rosa) is simply the embodiment of a lack. It is for this reason that Plasmonick is so devastated when Rosa reveals that she is not only Tzingar's mistress, but that she never loved Plasmonick in the first place. Despite Plasmonick's earlier protestations that nothing could stop him from loving Rosa – this is the primary reason he gives to coerce Rosa into confessing her secret – his whole subjective field is thrown into turmoil: 'Plasmonick: Aaaah! What monstrous swinishness! I've plunged down from the loftiest heights to the very bottom. I'm completely destroyed.'[13] The 'I' Plasmonick uses here is the subject of the enunciated, the subject around which 'being desired by Rosa' ensured consistency. This self-reflecting mechanism of desire that compounds subjectivity – and forms the fundamental fantasy – is the same mode that categorizes the abstract relationship between Mickiewicz's Konrad (and Wyspiański in his assimilation of the character in The Deliverance) and the spectator. Mickiewicz's project is only successful insofar as the audience believes Poland desires them (a desire which is summed up in the nationalist slogan 'Poland Needs You!'), desires that they join the nationalist cause on its behalf. This is an example par excellence of a belief in the big Other founding symbolic identity, wherein Poland is conceived of as a material value, as an object capable of desiring its citizens.

It is also here that we must problematize Konrad as a Christian 'call to action' for the Polish to take up arms against their oppressors. The moment that Konrad is put onto the stage is there not an injunction to sit back and enjoy Romanticism nostalgically? In other words, in understanding the difference between Wyspiański, who 'realized' Konrad, and Witkiewicz, who parodies him, do we not have to take into account the role of 'primordial substitution'? Žižek often speaks of the role of canned laughter in television sitcoms as the subject who laughs for you, and points out that the very virtual nature of this laughter – although you as the viewer may never directly

---

[13] S. I. Witkiewicz, op. cit., p. 133.

laugh out loud – in no way hinders its efficacy. In other words, when after a long day at the office you sit down to watch television, the canned laughter actually relaxes you, as if you yourself have been laughing. The crucial point Žižek makes in relation to this process is the more primordial substitution that takes place with the signifying structure – that a signifier acts on behalf of the signified: 'a signifier is precisely an object-thing which substitutes for me, acts in my place.'[14] In the same mode that canned laughter laughs on your behalf – you can literally laugh through another – the signifier acts on your behalf. This is the status of Konrad for Wyspiański, who successfully conjoined modernist trends with Romantic themes, in his legendary 1901 production of Dziady at the Teatr Miejski in Krakow. By surrendering one's innermost content, fears and anxieties to Konrad, by applauding his speeches from the audience, one is relieved of one's duty to directly participate in revolutionary activity: 'when the Other is sacrificed instead of me, I am free to go on living with the awareness that I did atone for my guilt.'[15] The pacifying element in seeing one's nationalist fantasy staged – wherein the practice of emancipation happens on one's behalf; 'spectating' is sufficient action, it 'atones for our guilt' – is the very distinguishing characteristic of 'primordial substitution.'[16]

If one was still stuck in the Romantic universe, the play would conclude with Plasmonick's endless longing, similar to Gustaw who has lost his love in Part II of Dziady and wanders the earth in utter despair. But Witkiewicz is able to break the Romantic deadlock. Plasmonick will indeed be sent to prison, but this should be understood as an act of liberation rather than confinement qua desire. My point is that Plasmonick's prison sentence is the counterpoint to Konrad's ascension (sublimation) to heaven. And this moment of liberation is characterized by Plasmonick's refusal to accept a 'forced choice' as such, but rather to experience the forced social choice as a real choice, thus opening up the possibility of free will.

Plasmonick's father suggests that his son come home and enjoy some 'coffee and nice fresh rolls.'[17] Instead of taking this option, a forced choice – an option that appears to be a choice, but whose acceptance is the mandate of any social bond – Plasmonick commits the 'monstrous' act and murders Rosa. This is the moment he awakes from the nightmare, when he successfully traverses his fantasy. He actually treats his father's invitation as some-

---

[14] S. Žižek: Plague of Fantasies, op. cit., p. 109.
[15] Ibidem.
[16] Is not the fear of just such a 'primordial substitution' lodged directly in the rejection of Romanticism that drives Słowacki's Fantazy?
[17] S. I. Witkiewicz, op. cit., p. 151.

thing to be accepted or declined – when, in reality, rejection was always prohibited. Plasmonick's act is subversive because he treats his father's choice (to go home with his father and take up his position as the Head of the National Gallery under the new totalitarian regime) as a real choice, and 'in accomplishing this act, the subject suspends the phantasmatic frame of unwritten rules which tell him how to choose freely.'[18] As Žižek points out, it is no wonder that such an act has catastrophic consequences; it breaks down the social contract that sustains our symbolic field. In The Anonymous Work, one can say that the social rules are literally 'unwritten', which is why Plasmonick remarks, 'I assume that even in a new state [...] such crimes will have to be punished.'[19] Although a new 'constitution' has not been written, our behavior must already presuppose its existence and we must act accordingly...

Witkiewicz's genius stroke is that the characters do not react to Plasmonick's act. In order for the symbolic field to remain intact his act must be completely ignored. The last lines of the play have Plasmonick's father repeating the 'forced choice' of restored order in which everyone will carry on as if nothing has changed. 'That Plazy really is a madman,' the father says, and then repeats his invitation to all those left onstage, 'I'm inviting all of you for coffee and nice fresh rolls.'[20] It is this repetition of – and the characters' implicit agreement to conceal – the 'forced choice' that recreates their social solidarity, which marks the counterpoint to Plasmonick's choice of freedom; freedom rendered here, with irony, as a prison.

Witkiewicz's fundamental achievement in this text rests with his acknowledgement that fantasy not only sustains desire and social roles, but that the very mechanism of authority is a semblance. The crucial warning of The Anonymous Work resides in the perverse nature of confusing the leader with the locus of power, precisely the confusion that leads to totalitarianism. As Claude Lefort (1988) points out, democracy reminds one the place of power is an opening that can never fully be assumed. This is why, in a democracy, every leader remains a usurper, in direct opposition to the figure of the monarch who appears to fit the role 'naturally.' This is the danger for such totalitarian leaders as Stalin, who believe in the direct equivalence between their person and their position. This is also the role of the pervert for Lacan, the one who directly acts as an instrument for the big Other. 'A madman is not only a beggar who thinks he is a king, but also a king who thinks he is a king – that is, who directly grounds his mandate in his immediate

---

[18] S. Žižek: Plague of Fantasies, op. cit., p. 29.
[19] S. I. Witkiewicz, op. cit., p. 151.
[20] Ibidem, p. 152.

natural properties.'²¹ This is the mistake Tzingar makes as he edges towards power; the day before his revolution, he confuses the 'greatness' of his position directly with his own physical 'greatness.' Tzingar becomes a 'pervert' in that he 'wishes to work for the Other's enjoyment, to become an object-instrument of it',²² which embeds him in the totalitarian universe. While in prison, Tzingar and Plasmonick argue about Tzingar's position:

Plasmonick: [...] I've got to admit you're a monstrous scoundrel, Mr. Tzingar.

Tzingar: You're wrong. The position I now occupy has ennobled me. Napoleon was an ordinary crook at the start of his career. But leading France to glory made him truly great – the way he was at Waterloo. Now I would be utterly incapable of being a spy.

Plasmonick: What megalomania! Rosa, can't you see he's a disgusting clown, that darling Tzingar of yours?

Rosa: Can't you see what a clown you are? No, Plazy, he has true greatness in him. We can't begin to evaluate him properly; we're seeing him too close up. Only history can judge him.²³

It is no coincidence that Tzingar calls on Napoleon as an example here, the textbook example of one who believes himself to fully personify the place of power as the embodiment of the Will of History, the one who crowns himself emperor. It is testimony to Tzingar's own ignorance that he should evoke Waterloo, the precise moment of Napoleon's defeat – Witkiewicz incorporates some Romantic irony, for the very evening in question will prove to be Tzingar's Waterloo, when Lopak overtakes his theocratic revolution with a 'communist' one.

Rosa's reaction is equally insightful, as she explains to Plasmonick, 'we're seeing him [Tzingar] too close up' to judge. This position – which is fully founded on a belief in the mystique of power, that power should not be seen too close up or it will disintegrate; a position which clearly disavows the fact that power is merely a semblance, whose efficacy can be destroyed by viewing it 'too close' – is the opposite of Giers, president of the military tribunal that is investigating Rosa's espionage. In Act I, Lopak tries to convince Giers to join the revolutionary faction. Giers resists at first, saying that he might

---

²¹ S. Žižek: Plague of Fantasies, op. cit., p. 142.
²² Idem: For They Know Not What They Do: Enjoyment As A Political Factor, London 2002, p. 271.
²³ S. I. Witkiewicz, op. cit., p. 141.

'become [Lopak's] worst enemy.'[24] However, Tzingar convinces Giers that there the revolution will be successful, and Giers changes sides, admitting that 'power is power'. This last acknowledgment is not a mere tautology, but should be read as 'power is (the semblance of) power.'

Tzingar, in Act I, is able to convince Giers of his plans because he has not yet assumed the perverted position in which he confuses himself with his position of power. In the beginning, Tzingar is fully prepared to manipulate 'power as a semblance', as a means whose efficacy is dependent on faith.

> Tzingar: [...] the only thing that's needed is to create a new type of state ruled by priests. What other churches weren't successful in doing because of their real faith and the concessions they had to make for the sake of that faith, we'll be able to do quite consciously as a pragmatic, systematic swindle [...] Believe me, people today are far more inclined to adopt any old belief than the totem worshippers in New Guinea. There must be belief – even if we have to make use of spiritualism and table-tipping.[25]

Tzingar's defeat coincides with his perception that power is no longer an element to be manipulated by means of faith – in other words, the point at which Tzingar treats power as a semblance – and begins to treat himself as the direct embodiment of authority. In this way he can be related to the capitalist in commodity fetishism: although Tzingar knows there is a gap between the locus of power, its universal position, and the particular content that seeks to fill this space, the Leader, he acts as if there is a magical element that renders the particular immediately universal. And it is precisely this confusion that leads to totalitarianism. Witkiewicz's work not only breaks the deadlock of desire qua symbolic identification in Romanticism, insofar as it presents us with the true choice of freedom by treating the 'empty gesture' as a genuine choice, he also warns us, in an Orwellian move, against the lure of totalitarian power.

Abstract

This text, based on Witkacy's The Anonymous Work, explores the devastating effects of revolution and the mode in which altruistic causes function as pretenses for power mongering. Witkacy exposes the mechanisms of ideology, the hopelessness of a large-scale utopian revolution. It is in Plasmonick's ability to traverse his fantasy to overcome his love for Rosa, whose ideological interpellation is strictly contained within the coordinates

---

[24] Ibidem, p. 114.
[25] Ibidem, p. 115.

of Romantic ideals, that Witkacy leaves behind the Romantic universe, the symbolic network that refuses to renounce the desire for desire. In so doing, Witkacy exposes the paradox of Romanticism: freedom and desire are exclusive; the metonymic nature of desire is always-already related directly to the subject's fundamental fantasy, that inaccessible kernel which anchors the subject to his social field.

Prof. Bryce Lease
University of Exeter

Witkacy: 21st Century Perspectives

Mark Rudnicki

The Profane and the Sacred in Insatiability

In his lifetime Witkacy was strongly aware of his philosophic and artistic isolation among his Polish contemporaries; however, once placed on the world stage, his work seems to have found more than a few kindred spirits. Artaud, Strindberg, Shaw, Nietzsche, Heidegger have all been the subject of comparative analyses with the Polish avant-garde writer, but points of intersection between Georges Bataille and Witkacy have yet to be investigated. From a brief biographical comparison, one can see striking similarities: Both wrote in the first half of the 20th Century and were not well respected during their lifetimes, both underwent psychoanalysis, and both wrote philosophical as well as literary works. More important than common biographical details, their works have many recurrent themes, most notably, the theme of transgression. Bataille placed a great deal of importance on the topic of transgression; in fact, he devoted entire works to the subject, such as Eroticism and Tears of Eros. Witkacy, on the other hand, did not explicate the theme in his theoretical works, but he does ascribe a great deal of significance to it in his literary work, Insatiability. In this essay, I would like to investigate Witkacy's novel, Insatiability, with the aid of Bataille's socio--philosophical explorations of transgression and the limits of reason.

Insatiability and the "Mystery of Everything"

"Awakening," the opening chapter of Witkacy's novel Insatiability, sets the tone for Genezip Kapen's (a.k.a. Zip) erotico-philosophical adventure. Based on a dream, in which he asphyxiates a stranger, and his first intimate encounters, the hero experiences both a sexual and existential epiphany: "All at once the mystery of his dream and his erotic future became the mystery of Everything: it encompassed himself and the whole world. It embraced not just the inscrutability of life's each and every moment but the stunning mystery of the entire universe." And so begins Zip's adventure to solve this mystery of everything without fear or "else perish," yet he still wonders "why this drive for the all?"[1]

Embedded in Zip's quest, we find Witkacy's theory of unity in multiplicity. In his most developed philosophical work, Concepts and Principles Implied by the Concept of Existence, Witkacy explicates this theme by an examination of the structures of being, i.e. what makes an individual existence unique in a world composed of multiple existences. Ultimately, he was unable to reconcile the duality of an Individual Being viewed externally, its corporeity, i.e. its multiplicity "for others," which determines its membership in the species, with an Individual Being viewed internally, its consciousness, its unity "for itself," which makes it unique.[2] For Witkacy, an individual's awareness of this fracture between "Self" ("I") and "Other" ("Not-I") evokes a metaphysical unrest or a feeling of strangeness because the recognition causes both an awareness of the uniqueness of personality – an occasion to rapture or wonder – and an awareness of the horror of being differentiated.

As noted above, Zip relates this existential mystery of everything to the erotic. Bataille's work on the erotic proves useful in exploring this connection. For Bataille, the erotic and our relationship to sexuality always involve anguish: "In essence the domain of eroticism is the domain of violence, of violation."[3] This violation in eroticism, related to reproduction, involves shifts between discontinuous states, i.e. separate beings, and continuous states, i.e. connected beings. Each individual being is distinct from all other beings. Beings that reproduce are distinct from each other, and the offspring is distinct from the parents. While the events of the life of the offspring may be of interest to the parents, the individual experiences his birth, life, and death alone, separate, discontinuous from others. "Between one being and another there is a gulf, a discontinuity." This gulf cannot be eliminated, but "we can experience its dizziness together."[4]

---

[1] S. I. Witkiewicz: Insatiability, trans. L. Iribane, Northwestern University Press, Chicago 1996, p. 15.

[2] See B. K. Michalski: A System of General Ontology, or Stanisław Ignacy Witkiewicz's Universal Science of Being, "Dialectic and Humanism" 1985, No. 2, p. 169–190.

[3] G. Bataille: Eroticism: Death and Sensuality, City Lights Books, San Francisco 1986, p. 16.

[4] Ibidem, p. 12–13.

Bataille begins the explication of eroticism by focusing first on asexual reproduction in simple organisms and then on sexual reproduction in complex organisms, including human beings. In human reproduction, in most cases, a process of transition from two individual beings in states of discontinuity in the act of sexual reproduction achieve "one moment of continuity" in which there is dissolution of the boundaries of bodies.[5] After this moment of continuity, the individual beings return to a state of discontinuity as separate beings. The play of this shifting, Bataille claims, is the feeling of eroticism. Ultimately, Bataille argues that as discontinuous beings, we strive for continuity. Our "ephemeral individuality" is difficult to accept, so "there stands our obsession with a primal continuity linking us with everything that is."[6] Bataille emphasizes that the continuity of existence is not knowable, but "it can be experienced" at certain moments. "The whole business of eroticism is to destroy the self contained character of the participants as they are in their normal lives;"[7] the result of this dissolution is contact with an experience of the sacred.

It is this fracture, this metaphysical "mystery of Everything" that Zip sets out to explore through his erotico-philosophical adventures, for while this mystery cannot be explicated fully through philosophical discourse, for Witkacy and Bataille, it could be experienced beyond the limits of reason during intense physical and emotional moments that occur in sacred time.

The Sacred and the Profane

To understand how eroticism connects to the sacred and inner experience, Bataille employs the Roger Callois theory that human time is divided into profane and sacred time. Profane time is considered "normal" time, the time of work, during which taboos are respected; sacred time, on the other hand, is considered the time of celebrations, during which taboos are transgressed. In other words, sexual life, murder, war, and death in general "are grave if not overwhelming disturbances where work is concerned."[8] For Bataille, work has been of central importance in human development; however, the world of profane time in a mechanical observance of the dictums of project and work has denatured our existence by removing it from the sacred, inner

---

[5] Ibidem, p. 14.
[6] Ibidem, p. 15.
[7] Ibidem.
[8] Ibidem, p. 257–258.

experience. Only through the intense emotions of sacrifice and the erotic can the sacred be reintroduced thereby ending the abuse of our existence in profane time and restoring the inner experience.

Bataille's insight is applicable to *Insatiability*, in which Zip recognizes a clear contrast between the world of work and eroticism:

> Zip could not stand the sight of his father's workmen without shuddering and getting queasy in his lower gut. [And yet wasn't there something erotic about it too? Erotomania? No – but a person shouldn't stick his head in the sand while thugs are carving up his next door neighbor.] An immense sadness brought on by two irreconcilable contradictions – the life of the species versus the life of the individual – took possession of him now as he sat there contemplating this picture.[9]

Zip intuits the two "worlds:" the life of the species, associated with the world of work and automatization, and the life of the individual associated with the sacred and metaphysical intrigue. However, the world of work is not only relegated to the obvious factory setting. Zip prided himself on his intellect at an early age as he excelled in the natural sciences, but elementary school tasks dulled his "metaphysical wonder" of his place in the universe, and instead became, what the narrator calls, "forced labour." Furthermore, as he matures into a young man, his quest leads him through many philosophical conversations on ontology, existentialism, fine arts, and socio-political issues. Ultimately, he concludes that philosophy has reached a "dead end" and contains nothing more than "dead concepts", unable to gain access to life's inherent mysteries. In fact, philosophy as a "system of concepts" becomes a project associated with labour in the world of work because it attempts to justify rationally the horror of existence and not affirm/experience it.[10] Bataille would agree with this assessment. Philosophy, for Bataille, as an "undertaking is work" and is only the sum of certain well defined experiences aimed at knowledge." It "excludes without even deigning to notice" the outer most reaches of human life and "moments of intense emotion."[11] The world of work, therefore, sets a rational limit that for Zip must be transgressed, so he must continue his existential quest in the realm of the sacred.

Zip's prioritization of the sacred over the profane is evident early in his life. In fact, in contrast to the laborious elementary school lessons, his cousin

---

[9] S. I. Witkiewicz: Insatiability, op. cit., p. 30-31.
[10] See: idem: New Forms in Painting.
[11] Idem: Insatiability, op. cit., p. 258–259.

Toldzio "introduced him to a new world of autoerotic perversions" from which they attained a "diabolical thrill of some ineffable, eternally mysterious, unachievable lust".[12] In addition to this initiation, Zip recalled finding "indecent prints" in an "insecurely shut drawer" in a family friend's library, and "[h]e gazed like a spectator to some lewd effigy, upon her naked figure..."[13] Interestingly, in a library filled with philosophical and literary texts, Zip seeks the taboo; he opts for the erotic images which are located not on the shelves with the great works, but on the margins in a locked desk drawer.

Embedded in this prioritization of the sacred is the question of utility and uselessness. For Bataille, there is a clear distinction made between eroticism and animal sexuality. The latter was primarily for the purpose of biological reproduction, while the former was human non-reproductive useless pleasure. Abandoning the utility of procreation, eroticism revels in its uselessness and thus serves as a transgressive act of expenditure opposed to the profane working world, which always seeks to save or accumulate. This antisocial wastefulness is the sociological importance of eroticism:

> Erotic conduct is the opposite of normal conduct as spending is the opposite of getting. If we follow the dictates of reason we try to acquire all kinds of goods, we work in order to increase the sum of our possessions or of our knowledge, we use all means to get richer and to possess more. Our status in the social order is based on this sort of behavior. But when the fever of sex seizes us we behave in the opposite way. We recklessly draw on our strength and sometimes in the violence of passion we squander considerable resources to no real purpose. Pleasure is so close to ruinous waste that we refer to the moment of climax as a 'little death.' Consequently anything that suggests erotic excess always implies disorder.[14]

Bataille explored eroticism as one of the few recourses left with which to combat society's obsession with production and accumulation. The erotic experience is seen as being one of the few activities that involved useless expenditure; hence, it served as a release of energy for an individual in a society that no longer understands the value or need for such a release. For this reason Zip cannot stand to look at his father's factory workers and their obsession with utility and production, opting instead to follow the path of the useless activity of the erotic/sacred. Moreover, Insatiability contains no

---

[12] Ibidem, p. 5.
[13] Ibidem, p. 10.
[14] G. Bataille: Eroticism: Death and Sensuality, op. cit., p. 170.

discussion of procreation as a possible outcome of sexual intercourse, except for a brief statement that Zip's wife Eliza was barren.[15]

The concept of uselessness is carried to an even greater extreme in the novel. Insatiability contains numerous references to, what Bataille calls, ruinous waste, and they are evident in almost all of Zip's significant transformations. For example, in the chapter entitled Demonism, while witnessing the Princess and Toldzio's sexual encounter, Zip engages in autoerotism; the result of which is uselessly dispersed on the bathroom floor. In another reference to waste, he compares the Princess's first name Irina to urine. Lastly, he explicitly and frequently uses the term excremental to describe various things, including an idea, a city, and even a friend.

Sacrifice and the Summit

Zip's transgressions intensify in his three mature relationships: the Princess, who initiates Zip; Persy, who tortures him; and Eliza, who acts as a maternal figure. Led by insatiable desires in these relationships, he violates the most basic taboos including sexual "deviant" acts and murder. In each of these encounters, he attempts to solve the "Mystery of Everything" by reconciling, albeit temporarily, the fissure between Self and Other. These transgressive, self-destructive acts reveal, what Witkacy called, a primordial contradiction: Zip gains a heightened awareness of self, but at the same time his very identity is nearly annihiliated.

Zip's "drive for the all" through a reconciliation of self and other draws a striking similarity to certain aspects of Bataille's philosophy:

> To ask oneself before another: by what means does he calm within himself the desire to be everything? Sacrifice, conformity, trickery, poetry, morality, snobbery, heroism, religion, revolt, vanity, money? Or by several means together? Or all together? A wink of an eye in which glimmers a deceitfulness, a melancholy smile, a grimace of fatigue together betray the disguised suffering which the astonishment at not being everything, at even having concise limits, gives us.[16]

---

[15] Significantly, erotic activity parallels Witkacy's theory of the creation of Pure Form in the work of art: just as erotic activity lacks any utility, one of the essential criteria for the creation of art is that it in no way have any utility, which would make assessment of its "value" based only on how well or badly it fulfills its use.

[16] G. Bataille: Inner Experience, translated by A. Boldte, State University of New York Press, Albany 1988), p. XXXII.

Bataille further claimed that we cannot escape our desire to be everything, to become one with the whole of being. In other words, there is the attempt to surpass our limited existence; however, an individual simultaneously desires autonomy, individuation. Bataille argued that there is an "uncertain opposition of autonomy to transcendence," and the individual's will for autonomy struggles with and occasionally succumbs to the temptations to unite with the "whole."[17]

The contradictory tendencies to be at one with everything yet autonomous are evident in Zip's first erotic encounter with the Princess. During this interaction, his fragile personal identity is in danger of disintegration, as he "fought back with the sheer instinct of personality against the herd and against the multiplicity of existence that personality engenders out of metaphysical necessity."[18] His resistance, however, proves futile, as he and the Princess experience the loss of self in this interaction:

> Their bodies meshed, interlocked, and Zip perceived that life was really something. She had the same sensation, only on the brink of death. And that young stud truly went berserk, gorging himself on the fatal passions, both his and hers [...], now melted into one floorless ocean of insanity. She became for him the embodiment of life's essence: insolent, naked to the point of excoriated... He had been annihilated, so to speak.[19]

Clearly, for Zip, erotic conduct reconciles momentarily self and other "into one floorless ocean of insanity." He experiences "life's essence" to the point of the "little death," i.e. the loss of individuation. This is the beginning of his addiction to the erotic and the sacred as an approach to life's existential mysteries, and similar to a drug, it requires increased doses to attain the same heightened effect.[20] Subsequent, perpetrated acts must therefore, go to greater lengths to test the limits of societal taboos in the profane world of work.

Zip's next transgression occurs during his courtship of the actress, Persy. Persy plays a metaphysical "game" of insatiability, i.e. she prefers the sexual expectation without consummating or satiating the desire. The culmination of the game comes about when Zip, unable to quench his passion, finds

---

[17] Ibidem, p. 85.
[18] S. I. Witkiewicz: Insatiability, op. cit., p. 134.
[19] Ibidem, p. 142.
[20] Similarly, Witkacy claimed that artists must attempt more elaborate experimentation to access the world of Pure Form and the metaphysical strangeness of existence.

release not in the sexual act, but in murder. Colonel Sump fails in his attempt to use rational discourse to calm Zip, who, in a state of temporary insanity or insatiability, "gripped the hammer... and with all his might struck the bearded, bushy-blonde, brute skull..." In Freudian terms, the pleasure principal was not sublimated to the reality principal, the world of a functional society concerned with production. Immediately after the murder a sense of freedom sets in, but Zip once again doesn't recognize himself: "He was tasting true freedom now, an unprecedented levity. 'Gawd! Who am I?' he thought, going down the stairs." Despite this exhilarating feeling of freedom in the loss of identity, in the very next paragraph he expresses the beauty of necessity and uniqueness, how things could not be otherwise, once social laws are seen as nothing more than fictitious human constructs:

> [...] the sense of 'thisness' as opposed to 'otherness' – how wonderful to apprehend the quality of absolute necessity in this outrageous kingdom of chance and nonsense such as is raw existence when it is stripped of fictitious social laws concealing the most abominable contingencies.[21]

Fictitious social constructs which allow for society to exist become exposed and the trangressive act is the only manner to achieve some form of heightened self.

Zip's transgressions escalate from childhood experimentation to sexual intimacy with the Princess to the murder/sacrifice of Colonel Sump. The final transformation takes place on his wedding night. After a period of abstinence, due to the Devamesque B pills, Zip and his wife Eliza consummate their wedding vows. Zip realizes that his efforts to reconcile the contradictions of self and other for any extended duration were futile: "He stopped loving her at that very moment. And why? For his having been liquidated alive: because he could never be himself and her at the same time..." The climactic conclusion of his quest occurs on his wedding night, when he commits the ultimate transgression. Zip, in a manner which bears a striking similarity to the dream that began his quest, asphyxiates his bride. Only through erotic/sacrifice can he simultaneously destroy and become united with the Other:

> He [...] dug his hands into that detestable neck. Eliza's eyes bulged from their sockets and became even more beautiful than before. She offered no resistance, evidently preferring to drown in ecstasy. Pain became fused with pleasure, death with eternal life in

---

[21] S. I. Witkiewicz: Insatiability, op. cit., p. 401.

praise of the unfolding mystery of Panexistence, which was on the verge of being illuminated. She took a deep breath, but it was no longer a living breath that came out of her body. Her body shook in the final convulsions of death. [...] At last he could love Eliza in his own way; at last they were one.[22]

Through reaching such heights, Zip completely loses the ability to experience metaphysically. Zip had already recognized that after attaining such summits of becoming one with the other, existence becomes utterly banal and a horrific boredom sets in:

> Oh to wed life's contradictions for a hundredth of a second and then hold out a split second longer! But, alas, all the joy lies in the overextension; don't count on any orgasm there; climax is nothingness incarnate. Woe to one who holds out for too long; he or she will return to a boredom the likes of which the planet has not seen yet. And only by boredom shall he or she know what death is actually like...[23]

Here we witness Zip experiencing, what Bataille refers to as, the summit and the decline. As mentioned earlier, all erotic acts entail violence, which shatter social boundaries. Transgressions of eroticism and death, performed without an appeal to reason, can leave us with a sense of a summit. The summit takes tragic intensity to its limit: "Essentially, the summit is where life is pushed to an impossible limit. I reach it, in the faint way that I do, only by recklessly expending my strength..."[24] Once the summit is reached or, more precisely, approached, since it can never be truly reached, decline sets in. Decline results from exhaustion, from fatigue. In decline the being is restored to preserving rules of morality, and ultimately boredom sets in.

For Bataille, Zip's final sacrifice approaches a sense of the 'summit because this crime is a clear expression of violent passions and is devoid of reason. It is not carried out with a specific goal, such as monetary gain or political ambition, but his actions are rather an end in themselves. In this moment of extreme passion achieves for a moment his desire for the all, i.e. union of self and other. However, due to such intense experience of the erotic and death, the decline or "the little death" is just as extreme. As a result, Zip experiences the horrific boredom of life. Zip's quest ends and he loses the sense of metaphysical wonder, which coincides with the new society where the world of work, i.e. the world of utility and morality, is prioritized, providing no time for intense emotions and metaphysical experiences.

---

[22] Ibidem, p. 566–567.
[23] Ibidem, p. 309.
[24] G. Bataille: On Nietzsche, trans. B. Boone, Continuum Press, London 2004, p. 39.

Abstract

In this essay I examine Genezip's effort to solve the mystery of existence by employing the theoretical and social insights of Georges Bataille. I argue that Bataille's division of human time into profane and sacred time is applicable to Zip's adventures as he follows sacred/erotic passions as opposed to the world of the profane/work to encounter the mystery. I examine this dichotomy as it is prevalent throughout the novel from Zip's earliest encounters with sexuality and observations of his father's factory workers. He abandons the world of profane not only in the forms of manual labor, but also in the forms of philosophy and literature. Instead, Zip opts for the sacred/erotic as he is initiated into the world of bohemia and experiences self individuation ironically at moments of transgression.

Dr. Mark Rudnicki
George Mason University

Ewa Wąchocka

Identity Traps in Witkacy's Dramas

> I am not a minister, factory director, social agitator, nor a general. I am a man with no profession and with no future. I am not even an artist.
>
> Edgar Wałpor in The Water Hen

> I'll teach you the genuine technique of imaginary life - penetrate your nothingness to the very bottom, be convinced that you are a born fool, an idiot, and a duffer [...] and then create, in the ideal vacuum that nucleus of gravitational field which, expanding, will sustain, without support, the enormous edifice of your new 'self'.
>
> Master in Janulka, Daughter of Fizdejko

It would not be difficult to demonstrate that at the cross-roads of the above two statements is the problem of identity. This is typical for so many characters from Witkacy's plays. That is: the need or compulsion to self-create together with the awareness of the inevitability of defeat. The consistent consideration of the issue of mutability of the subject is generally recognised to be a legacy not only of Polish Modernism, but Modernism in general. This style of thought was characterized by the ardent defence of the individual paralleled with a fear that the individual would dissolve in the nameless mass. This style in literature brought new artistic and deeper psychological descriptions of the processes of "self" disintegration. Meanwhile, it seems that what is so characteristic of the modernist experience of identity crisis has perhaps an equally valid connection with the situation of the subject and its depiction in contemporary life.

The difficulties and problems which Witkacy's characters encounter with the issue of their own existence seem to chime in, not only with the fairly common conviction of our time that the individual is relatively free to experiment not only with his or her own sense of identity but also with the concept of individual self. This is very much akin to the approach which functions within the Social Sciences. It, therefore, seems evident that it is possible to see a definite commonality between Witkacy and contemporary discourse on the question of identity.

On the one hand, Witkacy approaches the characters in his plays with active, creative formation of themselves; some of these get entangled in it, others enjoy a delusive sense of freedom. Alternatively, he outlines the dramatic conflict between their individualistic aspirations and the extant pressure of the society and culture in which they exist. Techniques, which have their origins in the Social Sciences, permit us to take a different perspective on the relationship between the process-driven nature of identity, i.e. self-creation of the "I" through game and mystification and the conviction that borders are delineated by cultural pressure and social discipline. The drama of in-authenticity of Witkacy's characters locates them in the sphere of such contemporary constructs of conceptualizing the "I." It is argued that this indeed is the case with both Lacan's psychoanalysis as well as Foucault's thought, while negating the strength of subjective causative influence; they do not restrict themselves to revealing the pressure of institutionalized forms of life, and show such influence already at the micro level.

Contemporary approaches to the notion of the subject have been significantly influenced by the ideas of Jacques Lacan. This applies in particular to those which derive from his discovery of the fundamental role played by the mirror in developing the identity of the child. That is, according to him, the subject obtains a feeling of distinct character by means of visual identification with its own reflection in the mirror. This is at complete variance to the approach propounded by both Descartes and Husserl whereby the subject obtains a sense of distinct character from within.[1] Thus, according to this thesis, the image reflected in the mirror is something external in relation to the subject, something alien in relation to it; this leads to an erroneous

---

[1] J. Lacan: Phase of the Mirror, [in:] idem: Ecrits. The first complete edition in English, trans. by B. Fink, H. Fink, R. Grigg, W.W. Norton & Co, New York 2006.

recognition and consciousness of oneself. Thereby, identity as such is believed to be derived from a fallacious inspection, a false suggestion concerning the "I," which remains with us till the end of our life, as an ideal ego. Lacan's concept of the mirror phase provides a paradigm of the way, in which something that remains outside, something else – in this case a mirror – attaches an imaginative shape to the self. A double, as a reflection may also be such a projection, the impersonation of the hidden part of personality. Therefore, the primary experience of erroneous recognition, which occurs as a result of reflection, constitutes the basis of all further experiences on the plane of relationships with other people, including those within the immediate family and above all those relationships which are intimate. The individual becomes locked into the world of appearances.

In Witkacy's dramas, games with identity or indeed for identity are often connected with the structure of the doppelganger. In this scenario, family relations play a fundamental role. The double, along with the shadow or reflection in the mirror has for centuries enabled the objectivization of the multidimensional internal space. This has permitted the possibility of what is split and not in harmony in the individual to establish separate personae. Parents and the family, for Witkacy, appear to be the centre of relations of a social character, which to an immense degree determine the identity of an individual. It is the authority of this kind that the individual is usually not able to set him or herself free. As Erich Fromm recollects, "Family is a psychological agency of society;"[2] it is a medium through the intervention of which society imposes the mark of its structure upon a child, thus also upon a grown-up. In both instances the presence of the other turns out to be of essential significance: "an other through the relation with whom an update of the identity of the 'I' takes place."[3] Michel Foucault suggests in his study, Words and Things, that the contemporary subject, which appeared in the 19th century and distinct from the classical subject of the philosophy of Descartes and Kant, searched for its truth not in the thought, but in the subconscious and in the other. Indeed, the reference made to the surrounding persons, whom are in turn, as pointed out by Charles Taylor and Anthony Elliott, of crucial importance for the process of self-identification. That is how the subject perceives itself and therefore it is apparent for individual self-

---

[2] E. Fromm: Kryzys psychoanalizy. Szkice o Freudzie, Marksie i psychologii społecznej (The Crisis of Psychoanalysis), Polish translation by W. Brydak, Rebis, Poznań 2000, p. 159.

[3] R. D. Laing: "Ja" i inni (The Self and Others), Polish translation by B. Mizia, Rebis, Poznań 1997, p. 92–93.

-narrative.⁴ Although Witkacy's characters are not capable of establishing genuine relationships, it is doubtless, that only in contact with the other, with some micro-community, can they make their desires come true, the desires to reach some ultimate, "metaphysical" limits of being. This metaphysical dimension of identity attains much more significance in Witkacy's world than in the concepts of authors quoted above, perhaps with the exception of Taylor. Thus, the sense of man's unity with himself, in moments of deepest feelings or sensations, is manifested at the same time as a feeling of being at one with the totality of being.

The threat to a given individual is, however, not just about the necessity of yielding to the pressures of the external world, but also about those pressures being internalized. The perception of self, according to Lacan, attains its structure by means of projecting the external images. This may undermine the possibility of the subject controlling it and obtaining full autonomy, whereas the emphasis is on the opposite trend of segmentation, cracking, and cleaving, which Lacan refers to by the collective notion of fragmentation. Therefore, the family as understood by Witkacy – apart from the closed groups of sects, which appear in some of his plays – is a model space, where the complementary nature of human relationships manifests itself, so according to this thesis, the "I" is filled or supplemented by others. At the same time, however, nowhere more than in the disciplining world of family does the half-conscious internalization of more than individual norms and rules, principles of collective life occur. A similar mechanism of internalization may also be manifested by means of the double figure. The double, as Otto Rank was to observe at the beginning of the 20th century, reveals the complex relations between the individual and its "I."⁵

The aim of Witkacy, the devotee of the idea of Pure Form in art, is thus to demonstrate the process of leveling the Particular Entity, the process undermining culture at its very foundations in such a way as to separate the family drama from naturalist ideology and aesthetics. In The Water Hen, the personality of Edgar is both co-originated and at the same time differentiated by the configurations of the remaining male characters. Here the old Wałpor represents the social order and the power of the oppressive cultural

---

⁴ C. Taylor: Źródła podmiotowości: narodziny tożsamości nowoczesnej (Sources of the Self: the Making of the Modern Identity), Polish translation by M. Gruszczyński et al., ed. by T. Gadacz, introduction A. Bielik-Robson, Wydawnictwo Naukowe PWN, Warszawa 2001; A. Elliott: Koncepcje „ja" (Concepts of the Self), Polish translation by S. Królak, Sic!, Warszawa 2007.

⁵ O. Rank: Don Juan et le Double. Études psychoanalytique, translated [from German] by S. Lautman, Payot, Paris 1973. The first version of Otton Rank's book about the double came into being in 1914.

mechanisms. This is in the name of whose rules he wants to make Edgar an artist. He is the 'other,' the one who attempts to impose upon the "I" the unwanted identity, albeit that not only because of him Edgar remains under the rule of the system of the false "I," which makes him feel like "a dummy, a puppet." Tadzio and Ryszard de Korbowa-Korbowski, already performing definite doppelganger roles, personify the contradictory sides of the hero's personality and consciousness. In Korbowski, everything that is alien, rejected, abominable, and at the same time contaminated with the stigma of unwanted kinship is focused. Edgar, as Alicja's husband, with matchmaking enforced by the father to strengthen trade interests, does not differ much from his rival, who is Alicja's kept man. In a deeper sense, the hated intruder continuously demonstrates the not-too-distant, yet really probable and gloomy perspective: who Edgar could have become or would have to become in the future. On the contrary, the adoptive son Tadzio, who initially seems to be a kind of superconsciousness of the main character, as he so openly expresses the metaphysical issues, which the latter superseded. Applying the psychoanalytic encoding, one could perhaps assert that Tadzio represents the – dwarfish or perhaps latent, superseded – inner self; manifesting itself at a higher level than the protagonist himself could manifest, the self-observing self, the transcendental self. The "I," which strives to maintain its identity and freedom by not being incarnated, thereby avoids capture, thus escapes the trap of being seized. Such an "I," which in principle desires to be a pure subject, deprived of objective existence, thus also of all, and therefore able to avoid the commitments and obligations enforced by other people or indeed any community.

This readable system of doppelganger structures, the 'unity in multiplicity' captured in theatrical form, breaks down, however, in act III of the drama. The mature Tadeusz rivals his 'father' for the favour of Water Hen; he tries to walk in the footsteps of Korbowski, while in the end, as the former, joins the rebellious crowds in the streets. Here then, the 'extraordinary child' and, typical for Witkacy, the 'common new man' who were initially the incarnations of contradictory elements of the protagonist's personality, in the finale of the play become alike. They do this, following Edgar's suicide, such that they manifest in an emblematic way that we are led to see the inevitable absorption of an individual by the future mechanized society.

In another domestic drama, The Metaphysics of a Two-headed Calf, Witkacy takes the same approach, but this is more literal than the mainly symbolic perspective taken in The Water Hen. He methodically reveals the process of the modeling of the identity of an individual, which concludes with the individual 'fitting into' the social framework. The criticism of competing, seemingly different systems of upbringing and therefore the criticism of society and culture, takes place here by means of a parody of domestic drama. Here we see the perfect knitting together of the question of ambiguous paternity, confused family connections and indeed erotic complications. The issue of unresolved biological paternity is an even more marked demonstration of the disappearance of paternity than the pedagogic activities of Wałpor. That is: the disappearance of the figure of 'patriarchal' father, or to use the terminology of Lacan: the symbolic father. For Witkacy, one of the most significant symptoms of the fall of the old social order is, undoubtedly, the collapse of the father's authority, as well as that of various institutions which support such authority; in short, the collapse of the social "super--ego."[6] Despite the shaking of both prestige of parents and the institution of the family, Karmazyniello, a protagonist in Metaphysics..., is ruthlessly entangled in the family-society, and utterly subordinated to it. As noted by Hermann Lang when commenting upon Lacan's thought: "parents do not constitute the ultimate instances determining the life of a subject, but are mediated and mediating elements of a certain order, which determines their entire existence."[7] The network of complicated connections between characters, as well as the grotesquely accumulated complications of the plot, even more emphatically draws out this particular determinism. Children are compelled to repeat the fate of their parents as well as their faults and indeed their crimes too. Family relations, as well as erotic ones, the basis of social organization appear in consequence the irreducible factor which makes it more difficult or even renders impossible the process of self--identification of an individual, and that process – in the light of incidents of this play – will be neither guaranteed nor simplified by any system of upbringing.

Confirmation of this may be seen in the attempt, made by Karmazyniello, to rear children in his own chosen way. This ended in a defeat and paradoxically, underlined the impossibility of disentangling from family and social dependencies. What should self-socialization be like? Should this be an apparent source of grandeur? Witkacy does not even try to show such utopian notions beforehand. In his anthropology, man is not capable of creating himself in absolute isolation from others; an individual cannot become separat-

---

[6] Cf. P. Dybel: Anty-Edyp po polsku. Transformacje Freudowskiej hipotezy kompleksu Edypa w pisarstwie Witkacego, [in:] Wokół Freuda i Lacana. Interpretacje psychoanalityczne, ed. by L. Magnone, A. Mach, Difin, Warszawa 2009.

[7] H. Lang: Język i nieświadomość. Podstawy teorii psychoanalitycznej Jacques'a Lacana (Sprache und das Unbewußte), Polish translation P. Piszczatowski, słowo/obraz terytoria, Gdańsk 2005, p. 257.

ed from the community or group, with which she or he is linked by birth or in other ways and cannot function with complete independence. Instead of the possibilities of self-dependent development of identity narrative, what is left is some kind of speeded up education – the awareness of utter submission to social rules, the desire to kill the father, then finally and most importantly, the experience of existential ennui. Such experiences, in particular the latter seem to be obstacles, difficult to overcome, for the formulation of – as counter-proposal against somebody else's – one's own projection of the self. It therefore follows that the identity of an individual seems to be something internally torn apart, ontologically unsure, due to constraints and lack of possibilities of individual, free development, both within and outside the system.

In Act III the resurrection of the parents killed earlier has a particularly cruel meaning. A situation such as this brings the illusion of self-development to a definite end and at the same time we see the motif of family and social pedagogy somehow summarized. These parents not only do not consider renouncing their rights, guaranteed authoritatively by the organization of society, but with a redoubled strength take up the task of socializing, which will be even more efficient, as the Mother (Matka) rules out any bonds of feeling, any subject bonds, to replace them with a relation that is purely functional, that is the privilege of wielding power. The victory of the upbringing programme of the Mother (Matka) and Mikulini leads to the restoration of the shaken order, while it, in fact, leads to a catastrophe. "You evil phantoms of abominable people. [...] You are not here at all," repeats Karmazyniello, oblivious of the fact that the rules of existence of humankind cannot be impaired. Parents, as envoys of the community, are the guardians of the order compulsory in the Western world; parent-ghosts are a representation of such a type of dependency, which cannot be removed from the consciousness by any power, whatsoever. The reflection of social and parental pressure is internalized by the individual. This is a strong indication of the effect of the power of such systems, as argued by Michel Foucault, which causes man to imprison himself at the level of the self and subjectivity. This threat is brought about by regularly enforced or mechanical, pretended internalization of values, principles, social attitudes, against which an individual cannot defend her or himself, as is the case of The Water Hen or in The Mother. In Metaphysics..., the threat, personified in the ghosts of parents, stands for the past, which turns into inevitable future.

In his work, Foucault demonstrates the complex interdependencies, such as the issue of finding, shaping, and transforming one's person is always considered in the context of social ruling and reigning. The concept of self, which emerges from Foucault's thought, is linked directly with the process of subjugation – by various ways – in which identity is constructed by social forces and subdued by them. Whereas in his later work, in which he set out to develop such a theory of identity, which would transgress normalizing activities, he developed the idea of 'self techniques,' that however did not imply the invalidation of control mechanisms, but rather the interest in their functioning 'in hiding.' Such an approach on the one hand enabled him to provide characteristics of various ways of creative constitution of identity by individuals. Conversly this enabled him to recognize manifestations of power, such as those which limit or attenuate the various forms of self--expression.

Internalized authority, such as that which is not connected with overt compulsion, yet with apparent space for choice and freedom, makes itself known in Witkacy's experiments of the subject with her or his own identity. It is the more dangerous than those experiments which are about 'metaphysical' goals, which as we know is the one thing of the highest order in Witkacy's writing. Furthermore, of particular significance here is the experience of oneself as the other, which is manifested in a doppelganger relation. In The Water Hen, besides the antithetic pair Tadzio – Korbowski, the split personality of Edgar is co-developed by yet another relationship – that with his late friend. Young Wałpor has learnt about the death of Edgar Nevermore soon after the symbolic introduction – the shooting of Water Hen and the "birth" of Tadzio, after which he pronounced the following: "something strange happened. I am on the verge of another life. As if beyond the grave..."[8] Still, Nevermore "lives" on – he lives in the consciousness of Edgar. The futile struggle against the influence of the Prince and his aspiration to live the life of the artist consumed ten years. The 'Other,' as the second "self" becomes autonomous and thus evokes the feeling that his situation has lost balance. As in the classical literary formulations of Poe, Stevenson, or Dostoevsky, the doppelganger gains control of the self and subordinates it, while every contact with 'him' (the double) entails falling into constraint. Despite his declared disinclination for 'creation in life,' Wałpor failed to overcome the past enough to take up work towards building an independent identity, in the same way as he was unable to free himself from the dictate of his father's social directives. It is Nevermore, or in fact his un-obliterated image, that seems to write an inner scenario, with which Edgar does not identify fully; however, neither is he able to cope with it. The friend from old days

---

[8] S. I. Witkiewicz: Kurka Wodna, [in:] idem, Dramaty II, ed. by J. Degler, PIW, Warszawa 1998, p. 289–290.

becomes his rival, the one who had the freedom of self-determination – thus being an antithesis of Edgar's own nothingness – that is why he is recognized as internal enemy, admired and despised at the same time.

The staging of the voluntary tortures is clearly an attempt of imitative repetition of the circumstances of Nevermore's death, as the latter – bitten by a tiger – 'suffered terribly,' yet 'died beautifully.' This is an act of in-personalization, which consists of receiving a part of the personality of the other, by imitating his behaviours, or – as Lacan would formulate it – by narcissistic identification, meant to drown the feeling of emptiness. This act turns out to be only its own parody – the awareness of being locked in the vicious circle of imitation fails to enforce change; the doppelganger makes one realize the impossibility of absorbing the subjectivity of the other. The true awakening of Edgar, which ultimately allows him to understand both imitation and self-isolation in the social game, derives from the Act III repetition of the situation from Act I. This seems to equate with arrival at the end of existence. It may no longer lead to breaking with the imitation of the imposed identity, but to breaking with life itself.

A different variant of the impact of hidden authority, of authority deeply mediated, upon a subject is presented in the doppelganger relationship of Karmazyniello and Parvis in Metaphysics of a Two-headed Calf. Their relationship, sealed by the bonds of blood, reminds one of a relationship of teacher and disciple, originally devoid of the stamp of oppression. Karmazyniello willingly gives up the authority over himself to Parvis, recognizing in him his spiritual father. The Prince, unlike the parents, tempts with the alluring prospect of developing 'wild power', intended to be a guarantee of the unlimited possibility of development. In a fashion which seems to echo Nietzsche's 'will to power,' he tempts with the vision of an individual man, not dependent on anybody or anything. In fact, the only thing he really has to offer is erotic initiation.[9] The 'powerful' personality project says almost nothing about the conditions of truly individual existence, such as separateness, or the will to establish one's own place in the world. The influence of Parvis is based on the illusion of extending the 'inner space' of the disciple, as he represents what is in prospect, what has not been yet perceived, although it soon turns out he is also the one, who unveils the fearful sides of affinity. Likewise, in the Wałpor – Nevermore relationship, the doppelganger is the figure, which reveals the primary tension within the subject, i.e. the tension between the imaginary identification with the subjective self ("I") and the

---

[9] Cf. L. Sokół: Witkacy i Strindberg: dalecy i bliscy, Wiedza o Kulturze, Wrocław 1995, p. 371–374.

inability of reaching the level of that imagination in external reality, i.e. the dissonance between what a given person is in her or his own eyes (being-for-oneself) and what she or he is in the eyes of others (being-for-others).[10] At the same time, in both of these cases the doppelganger structures, by showing the subject as the 'Other,' deprive it in a sense of its "uniqueness," impairing its individual (subjective) status.

Witkacy's characters are unable to evolve a fortunate narrative of identity, as for them latter represents an area of enslavement, or mystifications and experiments, as a result they lose in the fight for themselves. The problem of identity is, at the same time, founded on a profound paradox. An authentic and autonomous existence is something extremely desirable, yet at the same time the characters, those characters which undertake such a search, are perhaps aware of nothing else more than of knowing that the state of unity with oneself may never be attainable for them. The writer's diagnosis remains very close to contemporary ways of recognizing the subject's situation, which question the subject's autonomy, while formulating the subject's vicissitudes as a much more complex phenomenon than just the determination of an individual by social structures. We are of course aware that in contemporary discussions about identity, the issue is not only how to analyse the impact of institutionalized systems, and the influence of processes at the macro level, but rather how to reveal ways in which the power of community and cultural compulsion work at the micro-level. So, we are more concerned with not so much a collection of rules, imposed by specific groups, but a force that functions with the mediation of language, behaviour patterns, and the order of interpersonal interactions. Witkacy consistently described the fall of the individual in consequence of mass phenomena behind which there are anonymous social forces. Yet, he also presented the equally distressing threat at the level of individual consciousness – play, illusions of self-creation, strategies of subordination, and private zones of coercion.

Abstract

That 'crisis of identity' is one of the central problems addressed by the dramas of Witkacy is primarily linked in the mind of critics to the tradition of modernism. In this contribution I would like to suggest a change of viewpoint, and to present this problem rather from the

---

[10] R. D. Laing: Podzielone „ja". Egzystencjalistyczne studium zdrowia i choroby psychicznej (The Divided Self: an Existential Study in Sanity and Madness), Polish translation by M. Karpiński, Rebis, Poznań 1995, p. 44–45.

point of view of contemporary discourse concerning identity. The problems that Witkacy's characters have with their own existence are in accord, not only with today's quite common conviction that individuals can experiment with their own sense of identity with relative freedom but also with the concepts of the individual ego, derived from the realms of the Social Sciences.

Prof. Ewa Wąchocka
University of Silesia

Dorota Niedziałkowska

Witkacy's Self-Portraits as Manifestations of the Dandy Figure[1]

It would seem that the history of art demonstrates that one of the most notable strategies of auto creation is dandyism. To illustrate this, it is enough to recollect the images of the young Albrecht Dürer Self-Portrait at 22 (1493) or Self-Portrait at 26 (1498). Here the painter appears in outstandingly sophisticated clothes, both with headgear and indeed a thistle. Similarly, young Gustave Courbet presents himself (1842) set against the background of a landscape, dressed as a Parisian Dandy, with long hair, pipe in hand, a walking stick, a book and a black dog. Clearly these are only two examples from the historically long tradition of the self-portrait,[2] which was to serve

---

[1] This paper is a modified version of the article Autoportrety Stanisława Ignacego Witkiewicza – twarze dandysa. Strategia autokompromitacji, [in:] Przyszłość Witkacego, ed. T. Pękala, Kraków 2010, p. 227–241. I presented different aspects of this subject (as Autoportrety Stanisława Ignacego Witkiewicza – twarze dandysa. "Wyszlachetnienje podozritielnoj licznosti" kontra "Le vrai visage du maître") at the session Witkacy: bliski czy daleki, organized in September 17th to 19th, 2009 by the Museum of the Middle Pomerania, which is to be published separately.

[2] F. Ried: Das Selbstporträt, Berlin 1931; L. Goldscheider: Fünfhundert Selbstporträts von der Antike bis zur Gegenwart. Plastik-Malerei-Graphik, Wien 1936; E. Götz: Selbstbildnisse niederländischer Maler des 17. Jahrhunderts, Berlin 1971; E. L. Smith, S. Kelly: The Self Portrait: A Modern View, London 1987; J. L. Koerner: The Moment of

as a source of inspiration for Stanisław Ignacy Witkiewicz (1985–1939),[3] a brilliant artist, draftsman, painter, photographer, writer and philosopher. Some other models of auto creation, which may frequently be encountered, I should like to nominate as 'provocation' and 'auto disgrace.' In some senses within the range of self-discrediting strategies there are many variations of artistic provocation. We are thinking here of those emerging from nakedness (Albrecht Dürer, 1507 or Egon Schiele, 1911), the macabre (Caravaggio, David with the Head of Goliath, 1605–1606; Ludwig Kirchner with his cut off hand, 1915) or death (Arnold Böcklin Portrait of Myself, with Death Playing a Violin, 1908, James Ensor, My Portrait 1888).

For the purposes of this essay I have undertaken a study of Witkacy's self-portraits to discuss the significance of dandyism for his artistic stance. Whilst remaining within the domain of dandyism, the artist chose a specific variation, namely that of a self-discrediting strategy, which to a certain extent renders Witkacy exceptional in this respect.

A list of the most celebrated dandies would surely include the following: George B. Brummel, George G. Byron, Alfred de Musset, Charles Baudelaire, Aubrey Beardsley and Oscar Wilde.[4] Marcel Duchamp, Salvador Dali and Andy Warhol were, in turn, described as the dandies of 20th century art. It must, however, be remembered that dandyism is viewed as being not only excessive care for refined elegance and a product of a particular social code of behaviour, it is also an attitude towards life, a "para artistic expression of personality that is conveyed through refined elegance, the cult of fashion and evanescence, indifference, nonchalance, eccentricity and scepticism."[5] As an ideology, dandyism, on the one hand, seems to be connected with decadence and aestheticism. On the other hand, it is not limited to these concepts. As a form of struggle for a sense of individuality in life, preservation of

---

Self-Portraiture in German Renaissance Art, Chicago–London 1993; J. Woods-Marsden: Renaissance Self-portraiture. The visual construction of Identity and the Social Status of the Artist, New Haven and London 1998; Five Hundred Self-Portraits, ed. J. Belle, London–New York, 2000. In polish for example: M. Wallis: Autoportret, Warszawa 1964; idem: Autoportrety artystów polskich, Warszawa 1966; A. Kowalczykowa: Świadectwo autoportretu, Warszawa 2008.

[3] B. Zgodzińska: Recepcja schematów formalnych i tradycyjnych tematów sztuk plastycznych w obrazach i rysunkach Witkacego, [in:] Powroty do Witkacego. Materiały sesji naukowej poświęconej Stanisławowi Ignacemu Witkiewiczowi, Słupsk, May 7–8, 2004, ed. J. Tarnowski, Słupsk 2006, p. 103–134.

[4] R. Okulicz-Kozaryn: Mała historia dandyzmu, Poznań 1995.

[5] G. Grochowski: Dziwactwa i dzieła. Inspiracje dandysowskie w twórczości Stanisława Ignacego Witkiewicza, [in:] Osoba w literaturze i komunikacji literackiej, eds. E. Balcerzan, W. Bolecki, Warszawa 2000, p. 133.

one's own world and one's authenticity, dandyism originates in the problem of existence. A dandy appreciates art and culture only in opposition to nature. The only dictate in this case is seen to be the shaping of life as a work of art and the only absolute value is beauty. What results from this belief is the cult of youth and narcissism. The dandy is also possessed of an inclination for satire and self-irony. For the dandy life is built on legend by the use of anecdote and the bewitchment of the audience through intellectual play. The need for auto creation becomes a force organizing his whole life – a dandy is an actor and a director at the same time.[6]

The topic of dandyism in Witkacy's oeuvre has also been discussed by Bożena Danek-Wojnowska, Wojciech Sztaba, Stefan Okołowicz, Anna Żakiewicz, Radosław Okulicz-Kozaryn, Jan Błoński and Jan Gondowicz.[7] In addition, Lech Sokół noted the special significance of dandyism in Witkacy's life and work: "Dandyism is one of the most important issues in both the biography of Stanisław Ignacy Witkiewicz and his artistic creations such as; the visual arts, literary and dramatic work."[8] Grzegorz Grochowski has shown us that Witkacy's Narcotics is not only useful journalistic writing, but also steeped in the spirit of jocular provocation, constantly breaking the rule of decorum, inviting the readers to join a perverse game, auto ironic dandy text.[9] Grochowski also studied the influence of the dandy attitude on different aspects of this artist's activity.[10] The author characterizes some basic elements of Witkacy's dandyism: the self-discrediting strategy, intertextuality, the autobiographical theme, dilettantism, the domination of dis-

---

[6] B. Sadkowska: Homo dandys, „Miesięcznik Literacki" 1972, nr 8, p. 86.

[7] S. Witkiewicz: Listy do syna, eds. B. Danek-Wojnowska, A. Micińska, Warszawa 1969; W. Sztaba: Gra ze sztuką. O twórczości Stanisława Ignacego Witkiewicza, Kraków 1982; S. Okołowicz: Przeciw Nicości, [in:] E. Franczak, S. Okołowicz: Przeciw Nicości. Fotografie Stanisława Ignacego Witkiewicza, Kraków 1986, p. 11–46; A. Żakiewicz: 'Cierpienia ich muszą być brzydkie i dziwaczne'. O związkach młodzieńczej twórczości Stanisława Ignacego Witkiewicza z prozą Romana Jaworskiego, [in:] Przed wielkim jutrem. Sztuka 1905–1918, ed. T. Hrankowska, Warszawa 1994, p. 285–300; R. Okulicz-Kozaryn: Dziwna przyjaźń. O Romanie Jaworskim, Stanisławie Ignacym Witkiewiczu i dandysowskim ich pokrewieństwie, [in:] Fakty i interpretacja. Szkice z historii literatury i kultury polskiej, ed. T. Lewandowski, Warszawa 1991, p. 326–345; J. Błoński: Nerwowcy, dandysi, nadludzie, [in:] idem: Witkacy na zawsze, Kraków 2003, p. 55–67; J. Gondowicz: Upadek rozpatrywany jako jedna ze sztuk pięknych, „Twórczość" 2006, nr 8, p. 88–104.

[8] L. Sokół: Dandyzm u Witkacego: gra i metafizyka, [in:] Witkacy w Polsce i na świecie, ed. M. Skwara, Szczecin 2001, p. 197.

[9] G. Grochowski: Trudna sztuka mówienia głupstw. O 'Narkotykach' Stanisława Ignacego Witkiewicza, „Pamiętnik Literacki" 1998, nr 3, p. 115–141.

[10] Idem: Dziwactwa i dzieła..., op. cit.

course over the world presented, the graphic importance of gesture and the collecting of odd things. Witkacy did not want to feel subordinate to any of his arts: in his novels, one can find philosophical debates, he insults his readers and his philosophical discourse consists of a number of frivolous pokes. The novel is denied the rank of art and the Portrait Company is limited to the role of a manufactory of portraits. Grochowski argues that dandyism is a consistent component of many works of the author of The Only Way Out[11] and that its impact on his artistic creation is far greater than previously thought.

Grochowski was primarily concerned rather with Witkacy's literary work and journalistic output. Whereas here it is intended to pursue this undertaking from the point of view of the History of Art and consider what we have already referred to as Witkacy's self discrediting strategy in the realm of dandyism. It would appear that this self-discrediting strategy is based on the voluntary assumption of roles which normally have negative cultural connotations. In reference to this strategy, we can point to effeminate self-stylization and the acting out of roles such as those of a megalomaniac, a snob and a dilettante. Subsequently, I will endeavour to discuss the implementation of this 'strategy', and I will try to discuss this on the basis of a dozen or so examples which I find the most suitable for purpose of illustrating my argument.

Whereas, on the one hand, the specificity of the self-portrait relies on conventionalization, on the other hand, the challenging of this conventionalization enables the author to introduce certain visual games to the audience. Witkacy's collection of painted and sketched self-portraits consists of eighty two images,[12] within which one can find well-rounded representational portraits, psychological studies, hasty sketches drawn under the influence of drugs, as well as self-caricatures with humorous commentaries. This collection is rendered an even more interesting subject of investigation because of various transgressions of the conventions of the self-portrait. Nonchalant

---

[11] All titles (works of art, books, articles) translated by the author.

[12] The authors of the catalogue of paintings (Stanisław Ignacy Witkiewicz (1885–1939). Katalog dzieł malarskich, ed. I. Jakimowicz in cooperation with A. Żakiewicz, Warszawa 1990) have defined the collection of self-portraits as consisting of 74 works. There is also An officer's portrait from the year 1917 that is considered to be a self--portrait and Self-Portrait with a Samovar from February 17th, 1917 discovered in 1998. I also include in this set the collective self-portraits: With her attendants, Battlepiece, caricatures: An astral tea, "Let me tickle your chin..." and three self-portraying drawings from letters: a profile sent to Helena Czerwijowska on March 30th, 1913, My portrait by my secretary for his wife from July 25th, 1925 and Stanisław's likeness offered to Helena Maciakowa on May 6th, 1935.

disregarding of obligatory conventions seems to be clearly linking Witkacy with the stance of the dandy. An endeavour to undertake a fresh and more profound reading of self-representational art by Witkiewicz which includes auto-photographs and a series of faces is rendered realizable courtesy of the phenomenon of dandyism.

Among Witkacy's works, one can find numerous examples challenging the conventions of the self-portrait. This is particularly so with respect to the portrayal of male subjects with traditionally feminine characteristics. The feminine mask is easy to portray by means of a painting. In the pastels dated 1922 (Witkacy en beau for his Mother and The Last Cigarette) an oval mirror on legs placed in the atelier reflects Stanisław Ignacy's face. Feminisation is also evident in the depiction of the hands and facial features, most notably in the exaggerated form of lips. Further, in the representational self-portrait dated 1913, the effeminacy is evident in the form of a shiny thumb nail. In the decorative drawing from the years 1922–1924, depicting the model in an elegant, colourful, pinkish and green garment, a big vase with flowers serves to emphasize the hands, slender fingers and filed, shiny, pointy nails. In addition, one's attention is drawn also to a watch with a traditionally feminine thin strap. Further evidence is found in the self-portraits dated 1913, 1930, 1931 and 1938 where Witkacy enlarges his eyes and mouth and highlights the colour of his lips.

Another of Witkacy's challenges to the self-portrait convention is the use of long hair. The self-portrait from October 21st 1930 (pencil and crayon) shows a head slightly tilted forwards, captured en trois quarts in a very tight display frame with long, straight hair depicted through the use of parallel, gentle, wavy lines. Irena Jakimowicz describes the face as elderly, with flabby, unhinged features.[13] The eyes focused on a point somewhere ahead and the leaning of the head give the impression of melancholy, sadness and helplessness.

In a work bearing the date October 11th, 1927 Witkiewicz portrayed himself unequivocally as a woman in the work: Self-portrait as a Woman. Irena Jakimowicz claims that this representation is an extreme manifestation of searching for an opposite to one's personality.[14] The painting depicts a torso captured en trois quarts turned to the left on an abstract background. In constructing his feminine version, the painter makes himself much younger, his face slimmer and chin more prominent. His high forehead is

---

[13] I. Jakimowicz: O rozmaitym użytkowaniu lustra, czyli autoportrety Witkacego, „Rocznik Muzeum Narodowego w Warszawie" 1987, nr XXXI, p. 499–531.

[14] Ibidem, p. 519.

covered with smoothly combed hair and his ears with locks. Instead of the usual neatly shaped mouth, he draws himself with wide, full, dark lips, the artificiality of which would be noticeable even today in terms of a portrait of a woman. The huge, asymmetric, dark blue eyes look straight ahead giving little impression as to the thoughts of the subject. The orange and blue garment with a 'v'-neck décolletage reveals a long and slender neck. We know well that Witkiewicz was certainly capable of adding gentleness and charm to the face of a woman; however, this representation reveals no such qualities.

Effeminate self-stylizations were universal attributes of dandies. Baudelaire glorified lipstick before Witkacy's Postscriptum to Unwashed Souls praised rice flour as face powder. Jarry was famous for women's footware, Duchamp created self-portraits dressed in feminine garments entitled Rose Sélavy. Characteristic features of the dandy's relation towards femininity were captured by Sartre: "a dandy – like a woman – does not work and does not occupy himself with useful actions, but is to be «looked at and fancied like a woman»."[15] In the article O dandyzmie zakopiańskim from 1921 Witkiewicz claimed that the woman endowed with instinct and the characteristic of acting before thinking is a role model for the Zakopane dandy – a "psychologically bisexual monster" that lives to bewilder himself. Therefore, "Zakopane dandyism is by principle assumed to be masculine."[16]

Witkiewicz, for example, described himself as a dilettante by placing a negative opinion of himself on his painting. The painter "when dissatisfied with the artistic level of his portrait [...] would add T.U. (failure or death of the artist's talent)."[17] The abbreviation appears to be constructed in a fashion analogical to the typology of the products of the Portrait Company (types A to D.) He believed that the self-portraits dated 1922 and 1929 should be self-criticized.

The role of a dilettante – especially a graphic artist or a painter who is amateurish in his work – is best to be portrayed by means of caricature. Witkiewicz uses this technique willingly – for example in his charcoal drawings Remorse (in the self-portrait with Irena Solska and Stanisław Witkiewicz, Witkacy stylizes himself as a pierrot), as well as in the drawings entitled Les ésprits de Messaline (1928) and Stanislaw's likeness (1935). The exposure of an elongated nose, jutting chin, protruding ears or disheveled

---

[15] G. Grochowski: Dziwactwa i dzieła..., op. cit., p. 137.

[16] S. I. Witkiewicz: O dandyzmie zakopiańskim, [in:] idem: Bez kompromisu. Pisma krytyczne i publicystyczne, ed. J. Degler, Warszawa 1976, p. 506.

[17] B. Zgodzińska: Witkacy in Słupsk: "The S. I. Witkiewicz Portrait Painting Firm", Słupsk 2010, p. 17.

hair appears also in official self-portraits, for instance in Choromański puking at me (1928). In this work, Chromański was depicted as a huge leech in the center of the composition and Witkacy himself below, as a humanoid figure raising its head. Additionally, in the drawing An astral tea (1928) Witkiewicz presents his friends as fantasy characters and himself as a worm with bearded face. In the portrait dated as January 13th/14th 1930 Witkacy presents himself with dragon's spikes on his neck.

Another example of Witkacy's use of hybrids is Witkacy + Tymbcio (1932), customarily described as the Self-Portrait with a Scorpion's Tail. A realistic study of the head with grayish hair and eyes looking at the viewer is combined with a bright tail resembling the body of a snake, or possibly a scorpion. The serpent human-like creature appears in the centre of an oval, among balls of varying sizes. From the back and near the cheeks the head is protected by a darker shell. The decoratively bent tail easily hold up the disproportionately large and heavy head. Such beings are a recurrent element of drug-induced visions. On the left, there is a caricature of Tymbcio drawn in a different convention. He is dressed in a baggy hooded robe, under which a long nose, an eye resembling a bead, teeth and a short beard can be seen. The genuine inspiration for this figure was Witkiewicz's friend Edmund Strążyski.[18] Tymbcio like a fakir reaches out his hand with claw-like nails, enchants and bewitches the dance of the head placed at the end of the tail. The "Cobra" reacts to his gestures with anxiety and raises its right eyebrow.

Frequently, when assuming the role of a megalomaniac, a dilettante and a snob a painting requires the addition of text to a painting. Witkiewicz often directly expresses his excessive self esteem not only in literature. The commentaries of the artist on his paintings underline his supposed ease in creating portraits and craftsmanship; for example, the charcoal self-portrait for Anna Oderfeld (1912) was "made in an hour" and on the self-portrait with a samovar (1917) Witkacy noted "please, don't bother me with talent." It is likely that such notes are in irony and should be treated as more of a mockery, as in the case of the drawing Jas and Stas at Ineczka's where the work is complemented with the note: "drawn with heels."

We are presented with yet another such example, when we continue our analysis with the self-portrait dated July 7th 1930 dedicated to Janusz de Beaurain – a pilot, engineer and son of the psychologist Karol do Beaurain,

---

[18] T. Pawlak: Mahatma – Tymbcio. O korespondencji Witkacego z Marią i Edmundem Strążyskimi, a presentation given at the session: Witkacy: bliski czy daleki, from September 17th to 19th, 2009 organized by the Museum of the Middle Pomerania.

who was to be involved in psycholanalytical activity with the youthful Witkiewicz in 1912. The painting presents the torso of young Witkiewicz captured en trois quarts, partially hidden behind a zigzagged surface that is traditionally interpreted as a curtain. Here the subject is squinting and smiles almost sardonically. The portrait is a caricature due to the enlargement of the eyes, nose and forehead as well as the overtly triangular face. The artist made several comments on the painting: he noted that he had not been drinking for two months, 'porter + tea,' and also added a sentence written in white crayon: 'A false friend / is a luxury / that even I / cannot afford' drawn from Witkacy's aphorisms.[19] An elaborate signature in the top part of the painting contains a self-ironical dedication: "To the Honourable Sir / Colonel Janusz de Beaurain / instead of a wreath on the Beloved Master's grave / Grateful employees of The S. I. Witkiewicz Portrait Painting Firm!"[20]

Witkiewicz appears in the text as the author of maxims and as the owner of the "Company." The "maxim" is, in fact, a reference to Salomon's parable about a true friend. The construction of this maxim is based on a paradox which is, incidentally, characteristic of a dandy. In the first part of the sentence, instead of the glorification of a true friend, there is seeming praise of the opposite. The word "luxury" has an ambivalent meaning. On the one hand, it denotes a pleasure that one can rarely afford. On the other hand, it is something unnecessary and redundant. Witkacy expresses in a euphemistic way, the general truth that the costs of having a false friend are too high.

By writing such a maxim on the painting dedicated to Janusz de Beaurain, Witkacy makes an ironic allusion to their relationship that can be understood only by considering certain specific situations from the artist's biography. What is more, the exaggerated entitling of Janusz de Beaurain as "Honourable Sir" also adds to the ironic undertone of the work of art. It is of course, also possible that the painting and dedication were meant to be only a practical joke.

The name The S. I. Witkiewicz Portrait Painting Firm appears in the catalogue from the Garliński exhibition of April 1925 as the name of a one-man utility enterprise "manufacturing" portraits.[21] There were some legendary "ceremonies" connected with the existence of the Portrait Company. For example, the most notable of these include, the employment of imaginary co-workers for various positions as well as giving them diverse pseudonyms.

---

[19] Signature from the picture. Stanisław Ignacy Witkiewicz (1885–1939). Katalog dzieł malarskich, Warszawa 1990, p. 114.

[20] Ibidem.

[21] S. I. Witkiewicz: Regulamin Firmy Portretowej 'S. I. Witkiewicz', [in:] idem: O Czystej Formie i inne pisma o sztuce, ed. J. Degler, Warszawa 2003, p. 27.

In the S.I.W. Directorate "the Home Village of the Master and Our Beloved Director the people employed were as follows: Chief of Cabinet [...] Witkasiewicz, Cashier – Witkasiński, Secretary General – Witkaze and Courier – Witkasik or Witkasieńko. Furthermore the signatures of the company 'documents' are sometimes derived from the deceased co-workers of the Master."[22] Multiple characters created by Witkacy also appear when seeing clients out. Depending on the situation, Witkasik would fetch the coat, Witkasiński would open the door, Witkasiewicz would hand over the hat or present the portrait.[23]

The dedication which appears on the portrait sometimes creates a certain situation: the grateful employees of The S. I. Witkiewicz Portrait Painting Firm "instead of a wreath on the Beloved Master's grave" offered a portrait of their principal, to the colonel. Witkacy here mocks official conventions of commemorating the deceased during funerals. Even though the content of the inscription is a reflection of what is usually written on a wreath, leaving a painting on a grave would still be controversial. If we assume that the "Master" is the principal of the employees, it becomes clear that the reason for the employees to be grateful and to call him beloved is in fact his death. The meaning of the words in Witkacy's art, commonly bear no reflection of the visual message. This is most evident in the portrayal of the young man who, with a hint of a playful smile and dressed in an unbuttoned shirt, does not look at all like a "Master." This fact notwithstanding, by making himself a sepulchral portrait, Witkiewicz challenges the tradition of funereal portraiture.

A good example of the assumption of the role of a dilettante and a snob may be the self-caricature dated May 30th 1933 – Mahatma Witkac. My translation of the inscription is as follows: Mahatma Witkac invoked a Small Ghost from the Remote Past on a Piece of Ectoplasm. The scene is that of a spiritualistic séance, drawn "almost in the dark" and is formed as a linear composition. At the bottom, the background is unfinished and the signature is mixed together with the notes. This text is separated from the drawings by a wavy line, above which, among diagonal black lines, there are two figures. A fragment of Witkacy's torso, his head in the top right corner of the painting, is in the forefront. The nature of the drawing is very much that of a caricature. This is effected through the following means: strands of hair that stick out, a protruding eye, a disproportionately long, hooked, pointy nose, fish-like, pink lips with drooping corners, the pink blush on a sunken cheek,

---

[22] S. Okołowicz: Przeciw Nicości..., op. cit., p. 29.
[23] H. I. Krahelska: 'Ceremoniały' Witkacego, „Panorama" 1973, nr 1, p. 34–35.

the large ear, the neck with a protruding Adam's apple and an arm which is disproportionately small in comparison to the head. Mahatma presents the "small vision" invoked in front of himself – a torso and head of a young woman drawn in a realistic convention. The model has a slender face, a well-shaped small nose, pink lips, and big blue eyes looking at the viewer with kindness. Her beauty, the elegant clothing and the slight blush dismiss any interpretation that she is a ghost or a phantom.

The title Mahatma, meaning literally, a magnanimous man was reserved in India for distinguished ascetics, mystics and philosophers. Joanna Siedlecka mentions that Witkiewicz often referred to himself as Mahatma[24] and uses this word in his morning bathing songs.[25] In the letter to his wife Jadwiga from August, 1929, Witkiewicz signs himself as "Mahatma Witkacy from Równia Krupowa"[26] and writes that he had created a self-portrait "as Mahatma Witkac."[27] Edmund Strążyski in a peyote turban portrait from May, 1929 is called Mahatma Tymbcio. In The Only Way Out, the narrator presents a description of Marceli: "Wouldn't he paint it, if only instead of [...] using vodka and cocaine he had used his will, purity of life i.e. the so called 'mahatmizm' as the engine for this artistic machine."[28] A similar understanding of this word is presented in Witkacy's letters to his wife in which he claims: "I want to mahatmize completely" (July 23rd, 1930), "5 years of mahatma and then szlus = voilà mon idée" (July 24th, 1930), "I like less and less the mahatmising project, especially now when I see that Tymbcios are not happy at all" (July 26th, 1930).[29] An interesting point is that the analysed image was made by Witkiewicz without smoking or drinking.

Likewise, we must not forget the dilettantism demonstrated through the invoking of spirits. Witkiewicz was interested in spiritualism and took part in such sessions.[30] Mahatma invokes a "small vision" on a piece of ectoplasm

---

[24] J. Siedlecka: Mahatma Witkac, Warszawa 1992, p. 10.

[25] A. Micińska: Witkacy – poeta, [in:] eadem: Istnienie poszczególne: Stanisław Ignacy Witkiewicz, ed. J. Degler, Wrocław 2003, p. 257.

[26] S. I. Witkiewicz: Listy do żony 1928–1931, prepared to print by A. Micińska, edited and footnoted by J. Degler, Warszawa 2007, p. 129.

[27] S. Okołowicz: Portrety metafizyczne, „Konteksty" 2000, nr 1–4, p. 195.

[28] S. I. Witkiewicz: Jedyne wyjście, ed. A. Micińska, Warszawa 1993, p. 222.

[29] Idem: Listy do żony 1928–1931, op. cit., p. 197–199.

[30] In 1922 Witkacy wrote to Kazimiera Żuławska that he had attended three spirystystyczne séances with the medium Jan Guzik in Warsaw: "I saw the phantom of miss Janczewska and other wonders" (see: Żuławski: Z domu, Warszawa 1979, p. 235). Jadwiga Witkiewiczowa dates her husband's interests in spirituality to the years 1925–1927. In addition, she mentions the medium Modrzewski – alias Franek Kluski, whose séances Witkacy also attended. It is likely that the name of the dish written on Mahatma Witkac

– a substance that drools from the mouth of a medium during a hypnotic trance. A humorous effect is created by adding a unit of measurement used in reference to the solid matter, to the word "ectoplasm" while on the visual level ectoplasm is drawn in black lines.

Witkiewicz is consistent to the point of mockery in registering all of the stimulants that accompanied the process of painting. On the portrait of Mahatma, he wrote down all the medication that he had taken, together with a list of meals and beverages: "anti-cough pills + tea + noodles with gravy + Ems water + aspirin." Witkacy mocks his own system. His signature is his "formula for the work of art" in which the inspiration is reinforced by chemical substances, and which he here expresses the ironic distance of the artist towards his creation, drawings and himself.

On June 1st, 1933 Auto-Witkacy was created and complemented with a commentary saying: "Let the dilettante of life in itself standing over his grave die in peace." This self-portrait in which the artist calls himself the dilettante would seem to support the accuracy of the diagnosis of a self-discrediting strategy, in particular the role of a dilettante.

The pastel drawing shown here presents the upper body of Witkacy captured en trois quarts to the left, in a tight display frame. The face is evenly lit. On the forehead, nose and cheeks, the artist placed shades of white and red. The idealized features are brought out by a soft moulding. The "prettiness" is underlined by the smooth skin, the black triangle-shaped eyebrows, slicked back hair, the nose shorter than in reality, eyes with big green irises and full, dark, red lips. The effeminate lips are in contrast with the grim eyes glowering at the viewer from under bushy eyebrows. The head itself seems to be suspended in the air. Apart from the suggested collar of the shirt, the body has no distinct shape. The shoulder line is detached from the head. The background is filled with thick lines in cold hues that reflect the shape of the head. In the lower part of the painting there are inscriptions: the author notes, other than the dates and the usual markings of the amount of cigarettes smoked while painting, the drinking of two beers and the use of nasal drops.

---

is not accidental (noodles – pol. kluski). Witkacy "claimed that he had seen his dead fiancée quite clearly" (J. Witkiewiczowa: Wspomnienia o Stanisławie Ignacym Witkiewiczu, [in:] Spotkanie z Witkacym. Materiały sesji poświęconej twórczości Stanisława Ignacego Witkiewicza (Jelenia Góra, March 2nd–5th, 1978), ed. J. Degler, Jelenia Góra 1979, p. 88–89). A protokol from the session with Kluski from the year 1925 mentioned by Tadeusz Kłak (Witkiewicz na seansie spirytystycznym, „Akcent" 1985, nr 2–3 (20–21), p. 83–89) after the book by Norbert Okołowicz.

The word "dilettante" is usually used in reference to an artist, or someone involved in science, but also one who is amateurish and lackadaisical. The combination of the words "a dilettante of life," which proves to be a considerable phraseological invention of the author, brings out a self-satirical undertone, unless – like a dandy – one decides to treat life as art. In the article Demonism of Zakopane Witkiewicz claims that: "[...] life is transformed into art and accidents are collected in order to create complexes that are abstractly beautiful in character."[31] "Life in itself" can also be interpreted in the context suggested in Maciej Korbowa and Bellatrix as a synonym of physical love.[32] "A dilettante of life in itself" is "standing over his grave" (even though on the visual level it is not presented) and demands from everybody permission to "die in peace." Therefore, the question remains, as to whether it is another coquettish attempt to challenge preconceptions, or is it the self-assuring confession of a dandy haunted by sickness?[33] The anticipations and forecasts of a forthcoming death are inscribed in the same poetics as presented by offering a portrait instead of a wreath on the grave or The Last Cigarette (1922). Witkacy also refers to the topos of an artist appreciated postmortem. One cannot ignore the element of megalomania in such an attitude.

Finally, let us recall the words of Marceli from The Only Way Out, the last painter of the Pure Form who spoke about the "fictional prolongation of the personal lifeline of the author:"[34] "Oh! – Something howled quietly inside him in grief over the fact that one cannot live his life at least fifty times exploring each time a different side of his diverse nature."[35] Therefore, not one self-portrait but a collection of images of a dandy's face might, in a sense, manage to realize the dream of which Marceli spoke.

The self-portraits of Stanisław Ignacy Witkiewicz which I have chosen for the above discussion would, I submit, clearly prove the existence and operation of a self-discrediting strategy in Witkacy's life. More precisely, feminization or assumption of roles such as those of a megalomaniac, a snob or a dilettante gave rise to brilliant artistic realizations and are indeed not

---

[31] S. I. Witkiewicz: Demonizm Zakopanego, [in:] idem: Bez kompromisu, op. cit., p. 500.

[32] Idem: Maciej Korbowa i Bellatrix, [in:] idem: Dramaty I, ed. J. Degler, Warszawa 1996, p. 116.

[33] Witkiewicz at the time of creating the portrait suffered from an acute inflammation of sinuses. See: J. Proszyk: O przyjaźni Witkacego z Kazimierą i Stanisławem Alberti, a presentation given at the session: Witkacy: bliski czy daleki, organized in September 17th to 19th, 2009 by the Museum of the Middle Pomerania.

[34] S. I. Witkiewicz: Jedyne wyjście, op. cit., p. 145.

[35] Ibidem, p. 221–222.

a matter of marginal concern. Such inspirations, derived from dandyism, became an integral part of his life and oeuvre. Unusual distance towards himself together with a great deal of self-criticism is only one important element of his brilliant personality. Thanks to Witkacy, I should like to conclude that I hope it has been possible to illuminate here that laughter directed towards oneself is a fundamentally essential feature of human existence.

Abstract

Many researchers of Witkacy's oeuvre alert us to the strong presence of 'dandyism' both in his literary work and in his biography. The classification of 'dandyism' is significant, however, for his entire work including his art. It should be recalled that 'dandyism' is not only seen as an exaggerated concern with appearance but also an attitude expressed in a certain individuality of style, eccentricity, nonchalance and skepticism. This paper analyzes the self-discrediting strategy in Witkacy's work, first described by Grzegorz Grochowski. It draws attention to the way in which Witkacy assumes various roles that usually have controversial cultural connotations. These include feminine self-stylization, the role of megalomaniac, snob, or amateur. The intention of the contribution is to explore the ways in which this self-discrediting strategy has been articulated in self-portraits.

I would like to thank The National Museum in Warsaw and Agra-Art Auction House in Warsaw for the permission to print.

Dorota Niedziałkowska
Catholic University of Lublin

S. I. Witkiewicz: Self-Portrait as a Woman, October 11th, 1927
pastel/paper, 63 x 48 cm
personal property (sold at Agra-Art Auction House in 2006)

S. I. Witkiewicz: Witkacy + Tymbcio, January 1932, pastel/paper
lost drawing, illustration from:
A. Micińska: Witkacy. Life and Works, Warsaw 1991

S. I. Witkiewicz: Self-portrait Dedicated to Janusz de Beaurain, July 7th, 1930
pastel/paper, 64.2 x 48.5 cm, property J. Koprowski, Warsaw, illustration from:
Stanisław Ignacy Witkiewicz (1885–1939). Katalog dzieł malarskich, ed. I. Jakimowicz
in cooperation with A. Żakiewicz, Warszawa 1990

S. I. Witkiewicz: Mahatma Witkac, May 30th, 1933
charcoal, pastel/paper, 63 x 47.5 cm, property K. Wojakowa, Zakopane
illustration from: A. Micińska: Witkacy. Life and Works, Warsaw 1991

S. I. Witkiewicz: Auto-Witkacy, June 1st, 1933, pastel/paper, 68.8 x 49.1 cm
The National Museum in Warsaw

Witkacy: 21st Century Perspectives

Christine Kiebuzińska

Witkacy and Ghelderode: Goethe's Faust Transformed into a Grotesque Cabaret

The farce, realistic and surrealistic, trivial and yet transfigured, is an essential expression of Stanisław Ignacy Witkiewicz's (1885–1939) The Beelzebub Sonata[1] and Michel de Ghelderode's (1898–1962) The Death of Doctor Faust.[2] Damned or redeemed, tragical or travestied, noble, foolish, or darkly sinister, the figure of Faust has been the basis for endless representations ever since Johann Spies in Frankfurt am Main in 1587 compiled a chapbook Historia von Doktor Johann Fausten based on the puppet plays presented throughout Europe and England. Thus from its first beginnings the Faust myth became a rich intermedial source for puppet theaters and also Christopher Marlowe's The Tragical History of Doctor Faustus (1604), a play with grotesque renderings of hell as well as burlesque slapstick. But it was Johann Wolfgang von Goethe in 1806, more than any other writer, who was respon-

---

[1] S. I. Witkiewicz: The Beelzebub Sonata [in:] idem: Beelzebub Sonata: Plays Essays, and Documents, ed. and trans. D. Gerould and J. Kosicka, New York 1980, p. 21–65. Further references will appear within the text.

[2] M. de Ghelderode: The Death of Doctor Faust [in:] Michel de Ghelderode: Seven Plays, Volume 2, trans. G. Hauger, New York 1964, p. 95–150. Further references to the play will appear within the text.

sible for endowing Faust with human longing to penetrate the essence of being itself, and his poignant Gretchen episode soon became the source for many variations, among them Charles Gounod's popular opera (1859), whose plot reduced Faust's existential quest into a lyrical rendition of sentimental longing, seduction and abandonment. By the time of Witkacy's The Beelzebub Sonata and Michel de Ghelderode's The Death of Doctor Faust, both written in 1925, endless variations on the Faustian theme had proliferated in plays, novels, and operas.

What distinguishes Witkacy and Ghelderode's variations is that the Faust myth and the character's yearning to experience the joys and sorrows, "what to all mankind is apportioned"[3] had become trivialized, as if the possibility of "striving" is no longer possible in an age in which philosophy, art movements, as well as ideological "isms" serve as self-serving chatter to augment individual sophistication. Carl Schorske observes that the bourgeois transformed his "appropriated aesthetic culture inward to the cultivation of the self, of his personal uniqueness."[4] The inner world of an artist like Istvan is thwarted by convention, as Witkacy's precursor, Hugo von Hofmannstahl, expressed in A Letter to Lord Chandos, "The abstract terms of which the tongue must avail itself as a matter of course [...] these terms crumbled in my mouth like mouldy fungi."[5] Similarly, Istvan expresses the desire to transcend to capture "the absolute isolation of every single individual" in his compositions, but comes to the realization, "I write notes the same way I'd write figures in a ledger" (W 25). Both Ghelderode's and Witkacy's antiheroes reflect the tendency towards narcissism and a hypertrophy of feelings. Witkacy's Istvan fears squandering the preciousness of his "feelings" before the "diabolical rabble" (W 42) that wants to appropriate his genius. And Ghelderode's Faust while strutting about in various attitudes "like an actor" questions, "And why this desire for the absolute, this perpetual, sublime, and puerile drivel of the soul" (G 100).

It is evident from both Witkacy and Ghelderode's subtitles to their plays that theirs is a project of subversion, for Ghelderode's play is subtitled "A Tragedy for the Music Hall" and Witkacy's "What Really Happened in Mordovar." In their separate projects of deformation, the Faustian myth appears as old goods suitable for either a music hall or a grotesque rendering of the salon in Mordovar, Witkacy's jab at the "murderous" conditions

---

[3] J. W. Goethe: Faust A Tragedy, trans. W. Arndt and ed. C. Hamlin, New York 2001, p. 47.

[4] C. E. Schorske: Fin-De-Siecle Vienna: Politics and Culture, New York 1981, p. 9.

[5] H. von Hofmannstahl: The Letter of Lord Chandos, [in:] Hugo von Hofmannstahl: Selected Prose, New York 1952, 129–141, p. 133–134.

that consume Istvan's creativity. In Witkacy's play the Faust legend has deteriorated to the extent that its only remnants are the grandmother's tale of strange happenings at Mount Czikla where supposedly the entrance to hell is located and where a composer had once attempted to make a pact with the devil. Instead he came to a bad end and was found hanging outside the supposed entrance to hell, a plot that will be replicated within the play. As Daniel Gerould aptly observes, Istvan "is acting out a pseudo legendary drama in a world of sham and plagiarism."[6]

Though Ghelderode's plot and character are still somewhat related to Goethe's tragedy, in Ghelderode's burlesque Faust has become a bad actor stuck in the eternal replaying of his solipsistic role. Ghelderode introduces calculated incongruities of time and space that are immediately evident in the play's basic setting: "a city of the past and of the future in Flanders: in the sixteenth and twentieth centuries simultaneously" (G 98). With the aid of the Mephistophelean Diamatoruscant Faust replays the plot of seduction and abandonment of Marguerite. In addition to the mocking variation of Goethe's plot, Ghelderode's emptied out triad of characters are mirrored by bad actors enacting the same plot both on the stage of the music hall.

Witkacy's Istvan, a name out of a clichéd Hungarian operetta, is yet another variant from his entire oeuvre of frustrated "striving" artists attempting to create in the climate of the pretentious and murderous Mordovar circle with its contempt for originality, what Istvan calls "the howling dog reaction [...] whether you play him Beethoven or Richard Strauss – he howls because his feelings are stirred up by the sheer noise of the sounds" (W 42). Like so many of Witkacy's blocked wannabe artists, Istvan who feels within him "a spatial-auditory vision of sounds which [he] cannot capture in duration" (W 41), unless he is shocked into creation by Beelzebub. But even Beelzebub is plagued with the same desires as everyman, "who missed his calling in life" and dreams that someone else will incarnate his ideas – ones he doesn't know himself (W 26). Despite his lack of skills he "feels" a sonata inside himself "like a huge charge of explosives for which there is no fuse or match" (W 35), and he intends to harness Istvan's talent in order to realize hid ambition to become the pianist of his "Beelzebub Sonata."

In both plays the Mephistophelian character has been deprived of his most of his powers of negation. As Diamatoruscant in Ghelderode, though he retains some of Mephistopheles' hauteur in his red suit, he nevertheless makes an adjustment to middle class values and wears cuffs and a bowler hat. In fact he appears to be more of a theatrical "illusionist" in the style of

---

[6] D. Gerould: Witkacy: Stanisław Ignacy Witkiewicz as an Imaginative Writer, Seattle 1981, p. 260.

Goethe's Mephistopheles as a trickster in Auerbach's Tavern than a sinister devil. In Witkacy's derision of the diabolic he is a Brazilian planter with a lengthy quasi-aristocratic name, Baltazar de Campos de Baleastadar. He is also an impresario, who, in the mock fun-house hell decked up in black and red "demonic frippery" (W 38) suddenly acquires a tail, and to add to this "third-rate demonic effect" (W 40), he produces fake horns with a pump in his pocket. All these effects transform him into Beelzebub the master of the cabaret "fixed up as a comparatively fantastic hell" (W 38) where appropriate perverse examples of insatiability are, if not incarnated, then talked about a great deal. Not only do both playwrights undermine the potential of a twentieth-century Faust figure and its attendant Mephistophelean character, but they also mock Naturalism in the theater, and in Witkacy's play even the possibility of Pure Form.

Gerould comments that for Witkacy, "Pure Form was a theoretical gesticulation, a polemical stance,"[7] as can be determined from the model that Witkacy considers to be the essence of Pure Form begins with these words, "Three characters dressed in red who come on stage and bow to no one in particular [...]," and the assemblage of images he presented in this model led him to speculate that, "if the play is seriously written and appropriately produced, this method can create a work of unsuspected beauty [...] all in a uniform style and unlike anything which has previously existed."[8] Witkacy's attempt to create a new language for drama that dispensed with convention was an undertaking that could never be perfectly realized, for what he ultimately found that talking about it was not the same as creating it in words or stage images. It is no wonder that Witkacy mocks himself by putting the critique of Pure Form in the mouth of the Baroness, the most conventional of his characters: "[...] that insatiability for form: that constant acceleration of the fever of life! Even in total seclusion, even reading only the Bible and drinking milk, one cannot isolate oneself from the spirit of the times" (W 58). As Gerald Genette observes, "Self-pastiche as a genre can consist only of self-imitations," a practice that Witkacy extended into a mocking self-caricature.[9]

Thus, despite his desire for penetrating beyond the usual theatrical forms, Witkacy can only provide discourse about it, and consequently The Beelzebub Sonata is as much propelled by the twin engines of debate on the

---

[7] D. Gerould: Introduction: Witkacy and the Creative Life, [in:] The Witkiewicz Reader, ed. and trans. D. Gerould, Evanston 1992, 1–33, p. 4.

[8] S. I. Witkiewicz: Czysta Forma w Teatrze, ed. J. Degler, Warszawa 1977, p. 77–78.

[9] G. Genette: Palimpsests: Literature in the Second Degree, trans Ch. Newman and C. Doubinsky, Lincoln 1997, p. 125.

role of the artist in society, as it is by the somewhat deformed plot of a pseudo Faustian legend about a musician who wanted to create "the kind of sonata that Beelzebub himself might have written!" (W 31) All of Witkacy's characters are inauthentic, and the contrived Mordovar legend propels the happenstance of the appearance of Rio Bamba who announces the arrival of Baleastadar. From then all characters are doomed to act out "tangled web of a new ultrasurreal possibility." And even though the plot has been set into motion, the characters themselves question their role, as for example, when Baleastadar appears dressed in the frippery of the demonic of black cape and hat he protests, "I don't feel the slightest bit like Beelzebub" (W 39).

The action of Witkacy's play is symmetrically arranged with Act I taking place in the modestly furnished living room of Grandmother Julia located on the less fashionable shore of the lake. Act II enacts hell as cabaret already envisioned by the Grandmother's tale and located in the very same subterranean vault of Mount Czikla. Act III represents Witkacy's experimentation with the interpenetration of pluralities of existence, for he conceives a series of curtains that ultimately reveal the salon as hell. The action of the first layer is a narrow strip in the forefront in Baroness Jackals salon where she and Istvan's aunt are knitting by a fireplace and discussing that Baron Jackals might be arrested for having murdered Hilda; as a factor of simultaneity the parting curtain reveals Hilda in a black ball dress informs them that Beelzebub Sonata is already being talked about "perhaps even in Budapest" (W 60). At the utterance by Istvan's aunt that art doesn't need "perversionalism" (W 60) the curtain is drawn and the entire hell from Act II is visible lighted in deep red.

Intertextuality is the basis of Witkacy's fricassee of self referential topics and characters that pervades all of his plays, novels and theory of Pure Form; in The Beelzebub Sonata his familiar themes and recurring discussions on the conflict between creativity and the social constraints imposed by both the salon and the cabaret, insatiability, Hilda – the demonic woman, marriage and its deadening impact on the creative spirit, the mechanization of the creative force, its appropriation by performers, the possibility of achieving Pure Form, etc. are given a new airing, albeit in a more or less the same context of the philistine salon. Not that Istvan in his wavering between a conventional middle class life and a life devoted to art represents a strong counter voice, for though he wants to compose a sonata that may be transformed in a way no one has ever heard before, all he seems to accomplish is to "jot down notes on the staves the way a book-keeper jots down figures in his ledger" (W 31). Indeed it seems that Witkacy is mocking his own endeavors, for Istvan's realization that the experience of artists have been "transported into another dimension, and that's why their biographers are concerned with these details to a ridiculous extent" (W 30) seems to allude to the preoccupation of Witkacy's public more with his buffoonery than with his art.

There is no other recourse but to sell one's soul to a fake Beelzebub or to yet another red-haired demonic woman from Witkacy's stable, who just happens to be an opera singer from Budapest. But as is usually the case in Witkacy's oeuvre, Hilda the demonic woman is not as dangerous as the "cuttlefish" variety of seeming innocent pretty girls like Christina who shift their affections from one character to another all on the same page or wherever the "tremendous gale" casts them. For the moment she's switched from the snob Baron Jackals who's rejected her fearing a "misalliance," but suddenly it is discovered that Istvan in the arbitrary rise and fall of status in the salon has been elevated in rank to a count. Thereby, in "cuttlefish" fashion she entices Istvan to return, "Back there in our dear peaceful Mordovar – those peaceful evenings of ours" (W 49–50) when they played fourhanded piano. Istvan realizes that if he had married her he would never have been an artist. "For me you're only the theme for a macabre minuet which will be second part of my sonata" (W 50). Once both Jackals and Istvan become "corpsed," even though Jackals needs to be re-killed once he becomes a rather boring and nice corpse, and despite the fact that Christine has also been corpsed, she becomes Baleastadar's groupie accompanying him on his world wide tour as the "Paganini of the piano" performing Istvan's "Beelzebub Sonata." The legend that the grandmother recounted has been fulfilled; Istvan, a kaput little artist, is seen hanging by his suspenders from a pine tree with Mount Czikla in the background. Baleastadar's conclusion as he points to the heap of compositions Istvan left behind, "We won't squeeze anything more demonic out of them" (W 64).

The Beelzebub Sonata is infused by mental somersaults as Istvan, in a kind of Dionysian frenzy, attempts to compose music that will produce a metaphysical shudder. That Witkacy is serious about his project is evident in the epigraph to the play, a misquotation from Beethoven, "Musik ist höhere Offenbarung als jede Religion und Philosophie,"[10] misquoted once again in his novel Insatiability. Witkacy tellingly substitutes Beethoven's original "Weissheit "with "Religion," for part of Witkacy's esoteric quest is to recreate

---

[10] L. Beethoven: Letter to Bettina, 1810. "Musik ist höhere Offenbarung als alle Weissheit und Philosophie. Wem sich meine Musik auftut, der muss frei werden von all dem Elend, womit sich die anderen Menschen schleppen." Philos.-website.de/autoren.

the forgotten religious shock and wonder that Greeks must have felt when they first saw Dionysian spectacles. Rather than revelation through wisdom, Witkacy is more interested in the metaphysics of religion, for within the dialogue Istvan echoes Beethoven's epigraph, "Religion, just as much as philosophy, is an intellectually inspired working out of certain feelings which I call metaphysical" (W 30).

But what kind of composition is this "Beelzebub Sonata" described by Istvan as "the formal spatial conception in music" that he is in the process of composing at the end of Act II, a composition that even the rather philistine Baron Jackals is listening to "in a state of ecstasy," and one that propels Rio Bamba and the Grandmother to dance a fantastic dance at the first chords of the wild music. Of course they might just like to dance, for they also dance a fashionable shimmy, a dance that Baleastadar puts down as "so hopelessly night club-cabaret, so tasteless" (W 50).

Given Witkacy's epigraph from Beethoven and his mention in Pure Form in the Theater that Beethoven's musical expressiveness was quite likely considered dissonant by Haydn[11] that it might be Beethoven's Tempest Sonata in D Minor Op. 31 with its 2nd demonic movement, the very same sonata that Strindberg thought about in his The Ghost Sonata. It is possible that Witkacy may also be referring to Karol Szymanowski who corresponds to the erotically charged Putricidis Hardonne in Witkacy's Insatiability; Witkacy's description of Szymanowski's career seems to be a cynical projection of his own status: "The entire world of contemporary music had become bent on his destruction. He was barred from concerts, virtuosos were discouraged from performing his works by persons alluding to all sorts of imaginary difficulties."[12] While Gerould has proposed Schonberg's Second String Quartet, I'm in favor of Szymanowski's Second Piano Sonata Op. 21. This speculation is supported in Witkacy's Insatiability when he describes the effect of Szymanowski/Putricidis music, "This was art, not the sort of thumping performed by blasé prestidigators, or intellectual inventors of new sensual thrills for hysterical females [...] And so full was this music that it operated at first through the sensorium [...] in order to gain access to that secret underground where it abode in reality, inaccessible to cheap or sentimental breast-beaters."[13] In contrast, Baleastadar who played, "magnificently with gestures typical of a frenetic pianist" (W 64), may never gain access to interpret "that secret underground" of Istvan's Beelzebub Sonata.

---

[11] S. I. Witkiewicz: Czysta Forma w Teatrze, op. cit., p. 67.
[12] Idem: Insatiability, trans. L. Iribarne, Urbana 1977, p. 46.
[13] Ibidem, p. 161.

Ghelderode much like Witkacy had distinct opinions about music that he integrates into the very action of the play. While Witkacy appears to be more interested in a romantic and modernist musical composition to serve contextualize the Beelzebub Sonata, Ghelderode is more interested in contemporary music akin to that of the Les Six, a group of young French and Swiss composers (comprising Poulenc, Milhaud, Auric, Durey, Honegger and Tailleferre), who embraced melodies and sounds that were considered more appropriate for music halls than for concert halls: "I very much enjoy fairground cacophonies," Ghelderode comments, "orchestrations, street organs, mechanical pianos, not forgetting nostalgic accordions." The writing of The Death of Doctor Faust he explains was accompanied by a tune from the fair, "a sort of Renish dance that a Limonaire organ played doggedly not far from my window."[14] Consequently snippets of a sort of Brechtian Gebrauchsmusik pervade his play.

Both Witkacy and Ghelderode attempted to shatter all traces of illusion-creating drama in order to reveal the transparency of the theatrical world. While Witkacy's The Beelzebub Sonata represents the last stage of his twenty-two known plays, Ghelderode's The Death of Doctor Faust was one of his early plays, and the first one to be staged. Unlike Witkacy's extensive treatise on Pure Form, Ghelderode left few reflections on the formal properties of his over sixty plays, and only in his Ostend Interviews did he provide reflections on the sources of his art, among them his collection of marionettes and puppets: "All these effigies thrill me by the fact of heir somewhat magical nature, and even though flesh and blood actors can weary me and often disappoint me, marionettes, because of their natural reserve and silence, manage to console me."[15] He insists – akin to Heinrich von Kleist – that marionettes have the potential to reveal a theater in its pure and savage state. In addition, Ghelderode maintains that for him a theatrical work does not exist without the "sensuousness proper to the plastic arts," for like in his contemporary James Ensor 's paintings of low women, clowns, and crowds of sinister down – and outs, there is nothing glorious about Ghelderode's Faust, his devil Diamotoruscant, nor his servant-girl Marguerite.

What distinguishes Ghelderode's The Death of Doctor Faust are elements of grotesque burlesque in the construction of both characters and plot, for he simultaneously looks back to the tradition of the early comic puppet theatres and looks forward to a postmodern theater with looping interpolations of other media: film, popular music, ballet and the music hall. Ghelderode is

---

[14] M. de Ghelderode: The Ostend Interviews, [in:] idem: Michel de Ghelderode Seven Plays, Vol. 1., trans. G. Hauger, New York 1960, 1–26, p. 9–10.

[15] Ibidem, p. 23.

striving to create simultaneity of action, and to achieve his goals he assembles a number of "happenings", among them a scene of a Loudspeaker, which reports bizarre news, a Prophet who wanders about reporting the "End of the World" and crowds that cheer on or boo all events. Much like his contemporary Jean Cocteau who in his play Les Mariés de la tour Eiffel (1921) crosses the border between drama and ballet, with fantastic effects such as speaking Telegraphs and a Loudspeaker, Ghelderode too crosses intermedial borders with inclusion of a film projection, a radio announcer, and even ballet sequences. The different media depend on and refer to each other, both explicitly and implicitly; they interact as elements of Ghelderode's particular communicative strategies as constituents of a wider cultural environment. At the same time, all the elements provide an internal critique of media's power to over-stimulate and influence the public.

Though seduction and abandonment are part of the plot of Ghelderode's The Death of Doctor Faust, the subtitle, "A Tragedy for a Music Hall" hints at an intermedial clash, for the music hall does not lend itself to Gounod-like lyrical expressions of either tragedy or sentimental longing. In his "remake" of the bare bones of Goethe's Gretchen tragedy Ghelderode's Faust is transformed into a clown stuck in the eternal replaying of his greatly reduced role. His Faust no longer strives for the absolute; instead he struggles to find himself, a self that is curiously at odds with the traditional self-aware Faustian personality. Indeed Ghelderode's character wallows in a middle class version of an identity crisis as he moans and yawns, "Weariness, weariness [...] a whole century of songs. It is dark, dirty and vulgar!" (G 100) Unlike Istvan, he is not pondering the big questions about metaphysics or choices between life and art. Instead he is imprisoned into a role from literature, for according to him, "Humanity is dying from literature" (G 100). The tawdry stage where even the "darkness is faked" and a cacophony of sounds and flashing neon intrude on his dusty sixteenth century study decked out with the "appurtenances of bygone scientific sentimentality," of the endless representations of the same into which he's been immured. As he comes to the conclusion that whoever scripted him, made him "incomplete, unfinished" (G 100), he breaks out of the sixteenth century tawdry theatrical world, and the next time we see him he has entered the twentieth century "Tavern of the Four Seasons" at carnival time wearing his centuries old costume. He is greeted by Diamotoruscant: "So you are Faust! Who would not know you? You have been put in novels, in plays in operas" (G 112).

In Ghelderode's mise en abyme structure, the Gretchen tragedy is simultaneously enacted on the stage of the music hall by bad actors, and this mock-Pirandellian setting allows for dialogue between characters and actors. In fact, the stage actors playing Faust and Marguerite are nameless and replicate the plot, for they too, inspired by the roles they're playing are having a love affair. In fact they believe that their acting is more authentic than reality. For example, the actor playing the devil mocks Diamotoruscant as a "music-hall artiste," for though he's a "fake devil" he takes his art seriously. "Watch me," he exhorts Diamotoruscant with gestures-poses-blazing eyes with tremolos, "How dark it is! – as in a criminal's soul!" "Not bad!" Diamotoruscant comments cynically, "What captivating acting." And while Diamotoruscant cheers the actor on to even greater histrionic excesses, the crowd having had enough of the fake devil's overacting demands, "Slaughter him! Curtain! Boo! Boo!" (G 119–121)

What disappears in Ghelderode's farce is Goethe's Gretchen's moving plight, for she is transformed into "a little servant girl" who on her afternoon off hopes to hook up with someone "interesting" at the music hall. Indeed she's soon set up by Diamotoruscant to meet the venerable scholar Faust who has wandered out from the sixteenth century, and who, as is scripted, takes the girl to a cheap hotel. With a perverse interest in the goings on in the hotel, Diamatoruscant chats up the Barker of the cinema across from the hotel. The Barker 's spiel exhorts the passersby to experience the melodramatic romance of everlasting illusion in the cinema, "A tragic love story where fate plays a part beyond words. Pathetic. Moving. Boxes five franks. Virtue punished and vice rewarded! A family show! Highly educational!" (G 123) Even Diamatoruscant is seduced into entering the cinema and emerges "weeping bitterly," and despite the Barker's assurance, "Calm yourself […] it's not real," the poor devil succumbs to "the power of imitation" (G 126).

The seeming tawdry plot that appears in cinematic representation connects to Faust's clumsy seduction of Marguerite in the cheap hotel across the square. And while the Barker keeps up his spiel announcing, "Throbbing drama of sin and remorse" (G 124), Faust, once he's had the girl, wants nothing more to do with her. Despite Faust's pleas to respect his status as a scholar, the hysterical girl cries out of the window to the boohooing crowd spilling out of the cinema that she's been violated, "I'll shout if I want! You're a swine, in spite of your theatrical costume and fine airs! You lied to me! You talked to me about springtime and your joyless soul! You talked so well that I believed you! And you showed me a horrible, painful thing, me a young girl" (G 127). When the over stimulated crowd spilling out of the cinema hears about the innocent girl's "violation" it rushes to kill Faust. Fortunately he is saved by the wit of Diamotoruscant who deludes the crowd into thinking that what they assumed was reality is actually a clever ploy to advertise the production of "Faust" to be performed that night and every night in the local tavern.

In his treatment of the bare bones of Goethe's by now over-familiar plot Ghelderode has a great deal of freedom to create an intermedial spectacle. For example, when Marguerite in despair has thrown herself under a tram, Ghelderode pulls out all sorts of stage effects, a newsreel presenting all twenty three pieces of her body being pulled out, newsboys rushing about announcing the very same news, and an almost instant court trial that condemns Faust. Immediately in balletic style the hunt for Faust is conducted by a patrol of gendarmes with huge bearskins and wooden sabers. They proceed in balletic movements to take three steps forward and two back, "making headway in this manner" as they halt, mark time, turn about and go off in another direction" (G 137).

At the same time, Ghelderode uses frequent interruptions of stage actions with magnesium flashes, the appearing and disappearing spoke of a merry-go-round, an electric sign that flashes, UNIVERSE FOR SALE OR TO RENT, searchlights, lightning, fireworks, cinema placards and flashing screen images. Musical fragments also intrude into the action as ironic comments on the action. For example, an orchestra plays in four-part harmony an old tune in a minor key to accompany Marguerite's entrance into the tavern; when Faust appears on the scene, it breaks off suddenly. The aural world of the play is quite noisy with sounds of a hurdy-gurdy from the town fair, the Loud-Speaker blaring sensational news, loud banging from the mise-en--scene being constructed for the performance of the bare bones production of Faust on the music hall stage, the Barker's spiel for the love story unfolding in the cinema, newspaper boys hawking the latest scandals such as the abandonment of Marguerite by the dirty Doctor Faust, the instant replay by newsreel announcements of the crime and its trial, and the crowd cheering and egging on whatever version of the same plot that appears on the movie screen. Strokes of gongs, drums, and booms from airplanes add to the cacophony of intruding sounds of the fairground carrousel. Some of the dialogue is amplified to sound as if the words come from the deep well of history by way of phonograph recordings. When we come to the conclusion of the play we recognize that Ghelderode has totally undermined any vestige of poignancy, for when the "authentic" Faust has shot himself at play's end, the orchestra plays a funeral march "in a rapid, nay frenzied rhythm, in the style of Offenbach" (G 150).

In addition to introducing dazzling sound effects and choreographed sequences, Ghelderode, like Witkacy, also pays a great deal of attention to the visual world of his play, and though not a painter himself, he draws simultaneously from the visual and grotesque Flemish tradition of painting from Hieronymus Bosch and his contemporary Ostender James Ensor, and many of Ensor's paintings of crowds in grotesque masks costumed like clowns reappear in Ghelderode's play as rather ghoulish representations. The visual intertextuality between Ghelderode's drama and Ensor's paintings is evident from the his notation in the opening prologue that his Faust "is to appear to the spectator as a clown to whom a tragedian's role has been entrusted" (G 99). In the First Episode taking place in the Tavern of the Four Seasons, the customers appear with "painted faces, like dummies, in traditional attitudes," and like automatons, they all get up together, "make disjointed gestures, stagger" (G 104). Intruding randomly on the scene Three Maskers appear, "one in a yellow peplum and with black plumes on his head, the second clad in a silver shroud and wearing a crown of sham jewels, and the last all pink, smug, and bloated;" Ghelderode's notation for staging reads (Copy James Ensor's maskers) (G 109). Once Marguerite turns up in the Tavern they surround her with threatening gestures. However, unlike Ensor's paintings, none of Ghelderode's invasions are static representations, for these images are constantly in motion, for example "a stream of ugly-faced people come out of the cinema" (G 129), and "maskers, peaceful or boisterous cross the scene," while passers-by "with various gaits, a phantom cab, everyday supers- -seamen, black coated workers, lonely men, prostitutes, etc." (G 122) provide a visual spectacle. In fact the scenes are so busy with the simultaneity of happenings that the intentionally banal dialogue becomes only one aspect bridging traditional drama and Ghelderode's spectacular world.

Ghelderode's solution to the problem of simultaneity of imagery and dramatic text is to write many scenes on two columns on one page, at times concurrent dialogue between the putatively real characters and those rehearsing their scene on the tavern stage, at other times juxtaposing pantomime scenes to the melodramatic dialogue in the opposite column. For example, on one side of the page the actress Marguerite, the actor playing the devil and the actor Faust flee from the crowd pursuing them speak their lines fraught with suitably frantic desperation amplified by "phonograph voices." Juxtaposed on the same page a corresponding movement occurs, for a crowd enters "with balletic movement," among them the cinema Barker reading a newspaper with a question mark bigger than himself, three judges with convict's faces, a medical expert with a giant syringe, and an executioner with a huge ax accompanied by strong men and quacks from the fair, profligates and women with expressive and variously colored countenances. In the meantime above their heads the cinema reports the sensational and gory news that Marguerite was pulled out from underneath the tram in twenty-three pieces, while simultaneously the judges in court take out those very same pieces, "head, arms, heart, hands, etc. thighs are taken out! Admiration by the men, who try to touch!" (G 140) The body is carted out, and the screen lights up again to show confusion in the court. When this scene empties out a solitary image of Death, "skipping, with a huge scythe listens at Faust's door, then "goes off like a ballet dancer" (G 148) is added to the assemblage of Ghelderode's Bosch-like grotesquerie. It is no wonder that the actor playing Faust responds to these threats and suddenly leaps onto the other column of the page wherein he's done in by the crowd, "Kill him! Monster" (G 146). The executioner waves his ax, and the actor is borne away. Only a solitary newsboy gallops past, shouting the latest news presumably the latest account of Faust's capture and death, but he cannot be heard.

It is inevitable that the supposedly authentic Faust and the actor Faust must collide. Ghelderode, however, is not interested in presenting a Pirandellian philosophical debate between reality and theater, but more in producing the effect of a slapstick puppet play that totally undermines the "tragic death" aspect of Ghelderode's title. Unlike in the medieval puppet plays or Marlowe's tragedy no hell opens up to swallow Faust, for instead of a moral, we are left with a musical joke, a galloping funeral march in the style of Offenbach. His is not a theater of ideas, but of images, for as Ghelderode insisted, "I've never written a piece a these and I never will. The theatre is an art of instinct and not of reason. The playwright must live only by vision and divination, relegating reason to an auxiliary position. Any topical idea or fad is slavery. [...] Art cannot be subjugated to any system of ideas." He cautions against a theater wherein poetry is "announced by placards," for without "its obsessional or possessional power, its marvels" the theater disintegrates and "crumbles away."[16]

While Witkacy's attempts to undermine the political and social metanarratives taking place in Poland within his plays diverge from Ghelderode's metatheatrical approach, both playwrights are very much united in their theoretical quest for something akin to Pure Form in the theater. What both Witkacy and Ghelderode created in their plays is the attenuation of what Walter Benjamin refers to as the "aura" of a work of art, for both have detached the Faust myth from the domain of traditional interpretation. Presumably, to paraphrase Benjamin, both playwrights without necessarily intending it, "issued an invitation of far-reaching liquidation "[17] of vestiges of the unity and coherence of Naturalism in the theater.

---

[16] Ibidem, p. 11.

[17] W. Benjamin: The Work of Art in Mechanical Reproduction, [in:] idem: Illuminations, trans. H. Zohn, New York 1969, 217–251, p. 221.

Abstract

The farce, realistic and surrealistic, trivial and yet transfigured, is an essential expression of both Stanisław Ignacy Witkiewicz's The Beelzebub Sonata and Michel de Ghelderode's The Tragic Death of Doctor Faustus. Both plays were written in 1925, and the subtitle of each play informs that we are at a great distance from Goethe's transcendent drama, for Ghelderode's play is subtitled "A Tragedy for the Music Hall" and Witkacy's "What Really Happened in Mordovar." This paper explores the deformation of any traces of Goethe's tragic Faust, as each playwright situates his play in a grotesque cabaret. In both plays the Mephistophelian character has been deprived of his powers of negation, and instead as Diamotoruscant in Ghelderode's version produces cheap tricks akin to those of Goethe's "Witches Kitchen" in the music hall. Not only do both playwrights ridicule the potential of a twentieth-century Faust figure, but they also mock Naturalism in the theater and in Witkacy's play even the possibility of a Theatre of Pure Form.

Prof. Christine Kiebuzińska
University of Virginia

Marta A. Skwara

What is still not Known about Witkacy's Intertextuality? An Analysis of Witkacy and Słowacki

It may seem surprising that the relationship between Słowacki and Witkacy has never been explored within Polish literary studies. It becomes even more surprising when we go over the following basic facts concerning both writers. Firstly, both Słowacki, a romantic, and Witkacy, a modernist artist have become titanic figures of Polish theatre much beyond their own epochs. Secondly, Słowacki's dramatic works were highly esteemed by Witkacy and, moreover, both artists belonged to the same tradition of "artistic theatre" (teatr artystyczny) according to Witkacy's words. The author of the theory of Pure Form in theatre put it this way: "Mówię [...] o teatrze artystycznym, który u nas zapoczątkował Słowacki, a którego w artystycznej interpretacji filarem był Wyspiański i mógłby być Miciński [...]" ("I am speaking [...] about the artistic theatre, which Słowacki began in Poland: Wyspiański was a pillar of its artistic interpretation, and Miciński could have been another one...")[1] Witkacy placed himself at the end of this long line of tradition

---

[1] S. I. Witkiewicz: Teatr i inne pisma o teatrze, ed. by J. Degler, PIW, Warszawa 1995, p. 370.

being, in his own opinion, one of the Polish theatre artists who explored the idea of theatre as a means of experiencing the Mystery of Existence (przeżywanie Tajemnicy Istnienia).

However what exact role Słowacki played in this tradition has to be reconstructed. Witkacy did not devote any text to Słowacki's theatrical achievements, contrary to his explicit appreciation of Wyspiański's theatre.[2] Still there are various remarks on Słowacki in Witkacy's essays on the aesthetics of theatre which can shed some light on the issue. Contrary to the rich intertextuality connecting his plays – especially Nowe Wyzwolenie (The New Deliverance, 1920) and Szewcy (Shoemakers, 1927–1934) – with Wyspiański's works there are very few explicit intertextual devices (such as quotations, paraphrases or direct metatextual allusions) employed by Witkacy in relation to Słowacki's works. It is no wonder that it was Wyspiański who has attracted the attention of Witkacy scholars. In an excellent and still standard monograph on Witkacy published by Daniel Gerould in 1981, Słowacki is not even mentioned while Wyspiański is not only mentioned many times in the context of Witkacy, but also his dramas, especially Wyzwolenie (The Deliverance), are analyzed as subjects of Witkacy's intertextual plays.[3] In another, more recent, monograph by Jan Błoński, Słowacki appears incidentally and still much less frequently than Wyspiański. Once, Słowacki even seems to appear simply by mistake.[4] Yet it is Błoński's recognition which places Słowacki's artistic world in the context of Witkacy's theatre, even though it is mostly in the form of perceptive hints.[5] If we were to make an attempt to search for the presence of Słowacki in the most recent Polish publication on Witkacy (i.e. in a rich chapter devoted to Witkacy in Michał P. Markowski's book) we would find only a single reference. Namely, a remark on the sense of boredom felt by Słowacki in Paris in the 1830s. with regard to Witkacy's sense of spleen.[6]

The above examples might convince us that there is little to explore. Moreover, modern Polish and non-Polish readers may well be convinced that there is no connection between Słowacki and Witkacy at all. Not only does some distinctive line of tradition seem to get lost in this way, but also

---

[2] Ibidem, p. 361–367.

[3] D. Gerould: Stanisław Ignacy Witkiewicz as an Imaginative Writer, University of London Press, Seattle and London 1981, p. 109–110.

[4] J. Błoński: Witkacy. Sztukmistrz, filozof, estetyk, Wydawnictwo Literackie, Kraków 2000, p. 184.

[5] Ibidem, p. 144.

[6] M. P. Markowski: Polska literatura nowoczesna. Leśmian, Schulz, Witkacy, Universitas, Kraków 2007, p. 299.

simple awareness of the fact that the world famous Witkacy[7] whose plays regularly appear both on world and Polish stages, has something in common with the hermetic Słowacki, a mystic Polish artist from the past, whose highly complicated symbolic dramas are hardly ever staged in the world. The whole heritage of Polish theatre tradition is misunderstood in this way, together with the manner in which we perceive Polish romantic literature as such and its importance for modernity and "postmodernity." I should claim that it was Witkacy, perhaps as one of the first theoreticians and practitioners of the theatre, who put Słowacki's dramas in a unique perspective, beyond national tradition yet not outside it. Thus I would like to touch upon two basic matters here: how the importance of Słowacki for Witkacy can be explored and how Witkacy's connections with Słowacki shed light onto the meaning of both Słowacki's and Witkacy's heritage today.

Let me start at the very beginning with the role Słowacki may have played in Witkacy's education. Since this was not a formal education, not counting the external exams that Witkacy took at Habsburg gymnasiums where Słowacki's works were not on reading lists, home education was especially important. Some unique evidence of Witkacy's upbringing survived, the letters which his father, himself an artist, would write to his son in the years 1903–1913. The presence of Słowacki in the correspondence is quite characteristic and typical of the role which Stanisław Witkiewicz played in the life of his son. First of all Słowacki, together with other romantic Polish writers, creates the language of the correspondence to some extent since his texts are paraphrased and quoted. Moral values derived from the quotations are the most visible modes of referring to Słowacki by Witkacy's father. Sometimes, quite characteristically, his interpretation concerns the value of art.[8] It is also worth mentioning in these preparatory remarks that some particular stage performances were evoked in the letters, especially in the context of Helena Modrzejewska, Witkacy's godmother, who used to star in Słowacki's dramas.[9] Considering that theatre was a way of experiencing the world both for father and son, one can assume that Słowacki's art must have been in the very centre of that experience.

---

[7] Thanks to translations into English by Daniel Gerould and others and thanks to connections with the theatre of absurd pointed out by Martin Esslin, Witkacy made his impact on the world stage.

[8] S. Witkiewicz: Listy do syna, ed. by B. Wojnowska, A. Micińska, Państwowy Instytut Wydawniczy, Warszawa 1969, p. 221. (When it is not specified otherwise, translations are mine.)

[9] Ibidem, p. 83.

If we proceed now to the opinions voiced by Witkacy himself, as a mature artist and theoretician, we can find many remarks about Słowacki which circle around the same notion: Słowacki is always referred to as the creator of the "artistic theatre," a theatre in which the representation of reality is the least important factor. In the main theoretical work on theatre published by Witkacy in 1923 (Teatr) Słowacki is described as one of "the great masters of the stage" whose works possess pure formal values to the highest degree (czysto formalne wartości w najwyższym stopniu)[10] similarly to the work of Shakespeare. Słowacki's theatre – together with that of Shakespeare and Wyspiański – is often seen as an example of an excellent formal construction which enables the audience to experience the strangeness of existence in the theatre.[11] We are also told that the work of Słowacki (and of Wyspiański, the two artists are always mentioned in chronological order) is an example of Pure Form created without any particular life deformations: "dzieła Słowackiego lub Wyspiańskiego uznaję za Czystą Formę osiągniętą bez daleko idących deformacji życiowych" ("I regard works by Słowacki or Wyspiański as Pure Form achieved without far-fetched life deformations").[12] Yet, according to Witkacy, both artists of the past: Słowacki and Wyspiański (as with Shakespeare and Molier) achieved pure formal values in their theatre works only to some limited extent. Having appreciated their achievements, Witkacy saw himself as the artist who must go beyond anything they had ever done.

Some elementary assumptions on which Witkacy based his idea of theatre should be recollected here, since without them Witkacy's remarks on Słowacki, as general as they were, would seem too vague. First of all, it was essential for Witkacy to see theatre as a complex art which originally stemmed from religious ritual. Formerly, in ancient Greece, the essence of the performance was linked with a myth so that a performance could easily evoke "metaphysical feelings" (uczucia metafizyczne). Because religion and art have long since become separate and do not coexist in such a symbiosis any more, theatre artists have to seek their own ways of evoking "metaphysical feelings." According to Witkacy, the aim of any theatre has never been a simple representation of life, and nothing is more wrong than a realistic or naturalistic performance. It does not mean that theatre is a place for nonsense, which Witkacy would emphasize in many different ways,[13] but it is not a place for "life veracity" either. What is fundamental both for Witkacy's

---

[10] S. I. Witkiewicz: Teatr i inne pisma o teatrze, op. cit., p. 93.
[11] Ibidem, p. 154–155.
[12] Ibidem, p. 194–195.
[13] Ibidem, p. 36, 39, 46.

theory and practice is the deep conviction concerning the artists' freedom of creation: there should be no limit to artistic imagination. However, such freedom of creation should not lead to chaos but to artistic unity, to the inner, pure construction – Pure Form (Czysta Forma). The most strongly emphasized need of modern theatre was "fantastic psychology" of characters, which was the sole way of relieving the theatre of the burden of reality and logic of life. Only the logic of fantastic characters and their actions can create "the stage form of becoming" (sceniczna forma stawania się).[14] In theatre, Witkacy claims, we want to be in an absolutely different world.[15] Having left it, we should feel like we have awoken from a strange dream, in which even the simplest things were marked by some bizarre, inscrutable charm characteristic of night dreams that cannot be compared to anything else.[16] In such a performance, a special role is ascribed to poetry or artistic prose, since the language of the performance is an essential factor of "the stage form of becoming" and should coincide with the actions of characters. The unity of action, language, visual effects and music aims to create absolute beauty and absolute truth of a strange-as-a-dream theatre in which one is able to experience The Eternal Mystery of Existence (Wieczna Tajemnica Istnienia).[17] Formal beauty is relative though. There are no objective criteria to measure it as "life usefulness" (użyteczność życiowa) does not apply to it. Yet the beauty of performance can be felt by the audience. Thus the only measure of the value of theatre is such an artistic creation that enables the audience to enter the world of fantasy and to experience the Mystery, even though Pure Form is never fully achieved being an unattainable artistic ideal.[18] In light of such views, it does not seem accidental that Słowacki with his admirable scenic imagination, poetic language and, as Calude Backvis put it "amazing literary cocktails"[19] appears to be the first Polish Pure Form artist.

However, when we read or watch Witkacy's plays they seem anything but Słowacki-like dramas. Direct allusions to Słowacki can even enforce such an impression. Jan Maciej Karol Wścieklica (John Matthew Charles the Furious), the title character of a "three-act drama without corpses" completed in 1922, wishes that he could talk like Słowacki, or at least like Słonimski but he can only "throw up every word in disgust, as if they were pieces of undi-

---

[14] Ibidem, p. 39.
[15] Ibidem, p. 40.
[16] Ibidem.
[17] Ibidem, p. 76.
[18] Ibidem, p. 127–128.
[19] Quoted in Cz. Miłosz: The History of Polish Literature, The Macmillan Company, London 1969, p. 233.

gested rutabaga" ("Teraz chciałbym mówić jak Słowacki, albo niechby choć jak Słonimski, a wyrzyguję każde słowo ze wstrętem, jak kawałki nie strawionej brukwi").[20] Nevertheless, this remark has more serious consequences for the whole drama than it may seem. To my mind, particular elements evoke Słowacki's world, namely one of his best known dramatic works Kordian (Kordian) (1833), usually placed among our "national" dramas. Czesław Miłosz believed that Kordian "exemplifies that type of Romantic drama which is most specifically Polish, dealing as it does with history in the making."[21] Moreover, it could be added that this Polish Romantic drama also deals with the hero and with his role "in the making of society."

When we see the character of Kordian on the stage for the first time, he relates the story of his life underneath a big linden tree (lipa) in front of a country house. Wścieklica is also put under a linden tree at the beginning of the first act of Witkacy's play. The scene was often connected with the famous symbol of the linden tree that was established by Jan Kochanowski in Renaissance Polish poetry, and interpreted simply as a parody of a traditional peaceful manor estate atmosphere.[22] I would insist that it is important to connect the symbol with Słowacki's drama, as it may be the first meaningful indication of Witkacy's intertextual plays. Both heroes – an adult (Wscieklica is 39), and a youth (Kordian is 15) – begin their monologues underneath a traditional Polish tree with reflections on their useless and broken lives. They both complain about lack of will:

Kordian: Jam bezsilny! (I am helpless!)[23]
Wścieklica: Ja swej woli ni mam. (I have no will)[24]

And they both come to helpless conclusions:

Kordian: Nie wyjdę z tego... Mogłem być czymś... będę niczym... (I won't come out of this...I could have been something... I will be nothing...)[25]

Wścieklica: Jestem tu jak lalka gumowa, z której wypuszczono powietrze... (I am like a rubber doll from which the air was let out...)[26]

---

[20] S. I. Witkiewicz: Dramaty, vol. III, ed. by J. Degler, PIW, Warszawa 2004, p. 13.
[21] Cz. Miłosz: The History of Polish Literature, op. cit., p. 234.
[22] J. Błoński: Witkacy. Sztukmistrz, filozof, estetyk, op. cit., p. 316.
[23] J. Słowacki: Kordian, [in:] idem: Dramaty, vol. III, ed. by E. Sawrymowicz, Zakład Narodowy Imienia Ossolińskich, Wrocław 1987, p. 113.
[24] S. I. Witkiewicz: Dramaty, vol. III, op. cit., p. 12.
[25] J. Słowacki: Kordian, op. cit., p. 114.
[26] S. I. Witkiewicz: Dramaty, vol. III, op. cit., p. 17.

The difference lies not only in the tone of their monologues – while Wścieklica says: "Popsuło mi się we łbie" ("I've lost my mind"), Kordian declares: "Otom ja sam jak drzewo zwarzone od kiści, / sto we mnie żądz, sto uczuć, sto uwiędłych liści" ("Here I am alone as a tree deteriorated to the roots, a hundred cravings in me, a hundred feelings, a hundred withered leaves") – but also in their situations, ironically inverted. The young hero begins his adult life (while there is autumn outside), the adult hero ends his life-career (while there is spring outside). It does not seem to be just a matter of chance that Wścieklica used to pasture pigs till he was 15 ("do piętnastego roku życia gonił za świniami po polach")[27] and points to that age as the turning point in his life, while Kordian is 15 when Słowacki's drama begins. Both heroes search for great ideals, Kordian tries to find the answer to a question somehow resembling the famous Hamletian dilemma: "żyć? alboli nie żyć?" ("to live or not to live?")[28] Wścieklica has to find an answer to a more pragmatic question: to be or not to be... the president of the republic. They both find themselves on a symbolic "pass of life" (przełęcz życia), and the expression denotes commonplace repertoire of both artists. Witkacy alludes to a romantic monologue based on a passage taken from Shakespaeare's King Lear, a text read by Kordian on a white cliff in Dover; this reading ends with Kordian's gesture of resignation in confrontation with reality. Wścieklica's monologue, mimetically follows the romantic language but paradoxically ends with a declaration of action, which proves to be a fake one in the end.

> Kordian: ...Zakręci się w głowie, / Gdy rzucisz wzrok w przepaści ubiegłe spod nogi... / [...] O! nie patrzę dłużej, / Bo myśl skręcona głową w otchłań mnie zanurzy... (You'll feel dizzy / when looking down into the precipice running out from below your feet / [...] Oh! I don't look anymore / as my thoughts twisted with head push me into the abyss...)[29]

> Wścieklica: Ale dziś stoję na przełęczy życia i to jest to, co lubię tak bardzo: nieodgadniona przyszłość piętrzy się przede mną, jak tajemnicza forteca, którą muszę zdobyć. (But today I stand on the pass of life and this is what I like so much: the inscrutable future piles up in front of me as a mysterious fortress which I must conquer.)[30]

---

[27] Ibidem, p. 14.
[28] J. Słowacki: Kordian, op. cit., p. 113.
[29] Ibidem, p. 124–125.
[30] S. I. Witkiewicz: Dramaty, vol. III, op. cit., p. 29.

In another scene Witkacy's character wants to reconcile himself with God and write a testament which is meant to be a confession by "the most contradictory spirit which has ever existed in the world" to future generations. Yet he cannot produce a word. Since Wścieklica's testament may be interpreted as an allusion to Słowacki's famous poem Testament Mój both romantic language and poetic rituals are put into an ironic context. Wścieklica's visit to a cloister and his temporary joining of an order enforce the impression of the evocation of widely recognized romantic rites. The role of two women in each hero's biography might be pointed out as one more allusive device. Laura, the object of Kordian's romantic love is transformed into Rozalia, Wścieklica's wife. Both female characters cannot understand the heroes' inner suffering and they manifest their lack of understanding in much the same way, though in a different tone.

> Laura to Kordian: Źle, jeśli się pan będzie marzeniem zapalał. (It will be bad, if you fire up with a dream, Sir.)[31]

> Rozalia to Wścieklica: Ty chyba masz gorączkę. (You must have a fever.)[32]

The second pair of women: Wioletta and Wanda represent carnal love in each text respectively. In view of the fact that the first pair of lovers (Kordian – Wioletta) are supposed to be Romantic and the second (Wścieklica – Wanda) just grotesque, one is struck to observe how similarly the lovers speak to each other:

> Kordian: moja droga. Ty mię kochasz... (my dear. You love me...)
> Wioletta: Nad życie! (More than life!)[33]

> Wścieklica: Czy kochasz mnie? (Do you love me?)
> Wanda: Tak. Bardzo... (Yes, very much...)[34]

Evidently, the language of both scenes mimetically follows a hackneyed language of a romance and both heroines have their very own pragmatic aims: they endeavor to manipulate the hero in order to bring him down to earth. Yet it is not in the plot where we find the most striking and meaningful

---

[31] J. Słowacki: Kordian, op. cit., p. 119.
[32] S. I. Witkiewicz: Dramaty, vol. III, op. cit., p. 14.
[33] J. Słowacki: Kordian, op. cit., p. 126.
[34] S. I. Witkiewicz: Dramaty, vol. III, op. cit., p. 29.

intertextual plays but it is in the language which sometimes can be provocatively different in tone, but can become mimetically similar, and may even denote seemingly similar situations which nonetheless result in totally different denouements. Let us examine the most crucial example. Towards the end of the unproductive period of our heroes' lives, which was similarly filled with doubts and marked by the impossibility of commissioning any important undertaking, Słowacki's hero says: "w powietrza błękicie skąpałem się... i ożyłem..." ("I bathed in the blue of the sky'... and I came alive...")[35] Witkacy's hero seems to echo: "Płynę spokojnie na falach niewiadomego. Odpoczywam" ("I am calmly swimming on the waves of the unknown. I am resting.")[36] Their floating state leads to understanding and recognition of their faith, both heroes feel unbound and capable of achieving any imaginable great aim. Yet Kordian's famous utterance was changed significantly in Wikacy's play. While Słowacki's hero declares on the top of Mont Blanc: "Jam jest posąg człowieka na posągu świata" ("I am a statue of a man on a statue of the world"),[37] Wścieklica announces in his room: "Patrzę na siebie jak na obraz w muzeum" ("I look at myself like at a picture in a museum").[38] The romantic monumental sublimation is replaced with the grotesque objectification. The titanic omnipotent romantic figure set in nature is turned into an object set in an artificial space: in a museum where art objects or just relicts of the past are kept.

The irony lies in the fact that, contrary to romantic heroes, Witkacy's character is a life success. All Wścieklica's ambitions have been fulfilled and he has possessed power over the world which his romantic predecessor could not achieve. At the end of the play Wścieklica does become the President but paradoxically this makes him suffer since his "psychological core" is broken. His inability to renew heroic rites corresponds with the lost beauty of the play. Its "grotesque macabre style," described in the author's stage notes, culminates at the end in the roars of the crowds which enthusiastically greet "a flabby hero" (sflaczałego bohatera) who is literarily "dragged out of his house" by his political allies.[39] The scene can be interpreted as the last inverted allusion to the romantic hero who – as the Polish audience of all generations must remember due to school readings – was carried away by a cloud while crying out the name of his compatriots: Polacy!!! (Poles!!!). The romantic hero goes up, the grotesque character goes down, Poles are the

---

[35] J. Słowacki: Kordian, op. cit., p. 133.
[36] S. I. Witkiewicz: Dramaty, vol. III, op. cit., p. 48.
[37] J. Słowacki: Kordian, op. cit., p. 132.
[38] S. I. Witkiewicz: Dramaty, vol. III, op. cit., p. 49.
[39] Ibidem, p. 59.

objects of their undertakings. In the romantic drama we cannot see them – Poles are the romantic hero's idealized construction. In the grotesque play they do appear on the stage, yet as "crowds," which is significant. Wścieklica's inability to speak like Słowacki and to write a poetic testament to future generations marks the failure of art which is not needed any more; crowds are happy with the "flabby hero" they are delivered. We should not forget here that Witkacy's struggle for Pure Form in theatre was the last attempt to renew art before it disappeared forever. His dark philosophy of history, according to which humanity, after a series of bloody revolutions, will come to apathy and prosperity with no metaphysical needs whatsoever, stood in sharp contrast with the romantic vision of history and art. According to Słowacki's Testament Mój, let us recollect another famous quotation – that art was believed to change ordinary human beings into angels: "zostanie po mnie ta siła fatalna [...] aż was, zjadacze chleba – w aniołów przerobi" ("And yet, what will remain after me is this powerful destiny [...] until it will transform you – bread-eaters – into angels"). Romantic heroes would lose their struggle for power over reality, yet would achieve individuality and beauty – the third act of Słowacki's drama develops this idea – art was saved. Witkacy's hero possesses all the needed political power, yet loses beauty and individuality. Art is lost and the epoch of grayness is approaching.

Witkacy's language sardonically emphasizes the modern shift in the meaning of individuality and sense of art. The only piece of poetry we find in the play reads:

> Witaj nam prezydencie. Masz
> godne siebie zajecie. Królujże
> nam wśród chwały, Złącz, co
> porwane w kawały [...]

> President, we welcome you
> And the noble deeds you do.
> Be our king in glory,
> Unite this for what we are sorry [...][40]

The crisis of artistic language is experienced and commented on by most of Witkacy's heroes. Sajetan, the character from Witkacy's last play Szewcy (Shoemakers, 1934) should also be recollected in the context of the character's relationship with Słowacki's tradition. At some point of his absurd activities, he announces proudly: "Jak Wernyhora jaki będę gadał jeszcze

---

[40] Ibidem, p. 58.

długo dość" ("As some Wernyhora I will speak for quite a long time");[41] only in order to correct himself: "Ale gdzie ta" ("But what"). His words follow a statement by another character (Puczymorda) on "reality in prophetic dimensions" which comes "after Wyspiański" and which is manipulated in reality and in art alike.[42] The character lies bare both the workshop of Pure Form in theatre (constructed out of pieces of other literary works) and the contemporary misuses of the romantic tradition. Wernyhora, a folk Ukrainian prophet, would significantly appear in Polish romantic art, also in Słowacki's drama Sen srebrny Salomei (Salomea's Silver Dream), which makes Witkacy's audience evoke the literary tradition "before Wyspiański." For Witkacy any (mis)interpretation of literature, especially high patriotic literature based on romantic patterns, is valuable only when it becomes an element of artistic construction. It was not in prophesizing (always mentioned in ironic quotes: "wieszczenie") that Witkacy saw the crucial value of Polish romantic literature and its meaning for modernity, but in fantasy bordering on surrealism. This is where Witkacy found his inspiration. That is where I see his point of departure, the basis of his own artistic construction built up – amongst others – on components of Słowacki's artistic imagination. In the second part of my paper I should like to demonstrate how Witkacy exploits and transforms Słowacki's plot and stage effects. Thus we leave the world of Witkacy's inter-textual relationships with Słowacki's dramas and enter the world of "artistic theatre" they both share.

Scenes of violence seem to connect the two artists in a unique way. Let us recollect how violence is presented by Słowacki in Sen srebrny Salomei, the only one of Słowacki's dramas which Witkacy recalls in his theatre polemics[43] in connection with a controversial performance by Teofil Trzciński, the same director who also staged Witkacy's play Tumor Mózgowicz (1923). In Słowacki's drama, the bloody crime committed on Gruszczyński's family, whose members were slaughtered without mercy (bez litości w pień wymordowana), is depicted in vivid pictures based on contrasts. For instance, there is the fairytale-like "quiet and pious house" ("cichy i pobożny domek")[44] of the good family which is turned into a massacre scene: everything inside it is splattered with blood and everybody there is dead. Corpses are left naked on the floor and beds, kids are "chopped severely" ("porąbane srodze") like objects. Their dead mother still clings to their bodies which are

---

[41] Ibidem, p. 390.
[42] Ibidem.
[43] Idem: Teatr i inne pisma o teatrze, op. cit., p. 408.
[44] J. Słowacki: Sen srebrny Salomei, [in:] Dramaty, vol. V, ed. by E. Sawrymowicz, Zakład Narodowy Imienia Ossolińskich, Wrocław 1987, p. 140.

beheaded and green-legged. Her own body has been cut with knives and her bosom has been turned into "a dog's grave" ("psia mogiła").[45] The dehumanization of human beings could not go further it seems. Yet that inhuman massacre acquires its symbolic meaning in the course of the play. It is put into the historical and mythical sphere where the bloodiest crimes – not shown on the stage like in ancient dramas – may serve future generations. Eventually, the crime brings about the self-understanding of the heroes and leads to rebirth.

Witkacy's bloody crimes should not seem shocking in comparison to the slaughter described by Sawa, Słowacki's character. However, Witkacy makes us see them on stage and confronts us with them repeatedly, as if the surrealistic potential of disintegrated body parts is an aim in itself, not a means by which understanding can be acquired. The manner in which he creates massacres of all sorts is not any more appalling than Słowacki's descriptions. I would even say that Słowacki is his unattainable Master in this respect, but Witkacy makes the scenes of bloody violence more surrealistic. They are not incorporated into meaningful wholes, disintegrated human body parts mark disintegration of art and of life. Let us look closer at a group of 12 characters called Bojarzy (Boyars) from a play entitled Janulka córka Fizdejki (Janulka, daughter of Fizdejko, 1923). They are portrayed as wild peasants (dzikie chłopstwo w kożuchach i czapkach) and their description, typical of Witkacy's syncretic intertextuality which often simultaneously alludes to many works, ironically evokes another Polish romantic text, namely one of Mickiewicz's well-known ballads.[46] Yet what Witkacy's Boyars do is exactly what Słowacki's peasants do in Sen srebrny Salomei - they perform a wild thoughtless slaughter, multiplied in a grotesque vein. First, following the order of their Master, they form a line and chop each other up: the first one hacks to death the second one, the third one, the fourth and so on. Next, another shorter line is formed and the first Boyar chops away the third, etc. The last two fight a duel but when the winner attempts to seize power he is shot to death by the Master. However, the Boyars come back to life (and to the stage) in the fourth act, as the two main characters, Fizdejko and his wife Elza, are enjoying their perfect lives in their little house (mały domek). It should be noted that the description of the house has a lot in common with the idyllic Polish manor estate (dworek), as well as with particular realizations of the motif of "dworek," e. g. Gruszczyński's house in Słowacki's drama. As soon as Fizdejko declares his happiness due to the fact that the awful

---

[45] Ibidem, p. 141.
[46] S. I. Witkiewicz: Dramaty, vol. III, op. cit., p. 97.

Boyars have been "rubbed out utterly" ("doszczętnie ukatrupieni"), they pop up like puppets and begin another slaughter. This time everybody, except the new ruler, are hacked to death and the blood floods the scene while the heroes of the future Joël Kranz and Amalia look at the slaughter "with a smile." There is no rebirth, except a grotesque one (represented by the Boyars' return to life), and there is no profound understanding. We should not be deluged by the cabaret language of the scenes, since the language has lost its connection with art irreversibly as we have observed above. By repeating political bloody crimes, committed by "wild peasants" known from Słowacki's drama but devoid of the meaning Słowacki ascribed to them, Witkacy deconstructs national myths and pushes romantic imagination to the limits. It was not by chance that Wernyhora was evoked as a figure of the past by Witkacy – the prophecy of rebirth simply cannot be uttered any more.

In the surrealistic disintegration of human bodies and human rites, theatrical endeavors around a dead body play a special role and they can also be seen as an amplification of Słowacki's stage effects. The scene from Słowacki drama in which the corpse of Gruszczyński is put in a chair by Regimentarz who asks the dead for forgiveness, does not exceed a realistic convention, though it is experienced as strange by witnesses in the play and most probably by the audience as well. The corpse is removed from the stage as soon as the forgiveness is given. The potential surrealistic effect of the corpse put on display and spoken to was used by Witkacy in two of his dramas Sonata Belzebuba (The Belzebub Sonata, 1925) and Matka (The Mother, 1924). While in the former corpses put in chairs symbolize the dark faith of the main hero (Istvan, an artist) who becomes a mannequin, a doll in the devil's hand, a modern Faust, in the latter the scene is handled more surrealistically. Leon, the hero of Witkacy's play, is – just like Słowacki's Leon from Sen srebrny Salomei – a bad immoral son who undergoes a spiritual change (yet it would be counterproductive to point out more similarities between the two characters). He places his mother's corpse on a pedestal and speaks to it. In the meantime, a younger version of his mother appears and talks to Leon. Moreover, she calls the corpse a "humbug" and dissects it into pieces: a wooden head, old clothes and the straw with which "the mother" was stuffed are scattered all over the stage. Leon loses the only sense of his life, and soon he himself is dissected by workers. The dead body and the live character become one and the same and then disappear. No forgiveness is granted to anybody. Once again we are confronted with emptiness; the empty black stage emphasizes the symbolic emptiness of the world.

One more motif – which can be seen as common to Słowacki and Witkacy, and pushed to the limits by the latter – is the dream understood both as a prophetic state and as a fantastic world of its own; a dream in which everything can happen. Such dreams are characteristic of Słowacki's Salomea. In one of them she can see "a red stain," the symbol of a bloody crime (reminiscent of Lady Macbeth's famous vision) which acquires a deeper meaning in the play. The dreams of Witkacy's characters, often called "bad dreams" are deprived of symbolic explanations and are repeated time after time, bearing more and more absurd meanings. Such are the dreams of Elza and of Fizdejko. Perhaps just one scene, in which a ghost kills another ghost with "a real Winchester," can render a sense of overwhelming absurdity. Especially since this scene is followed by "a strange coincidence:" the meeting of four identical dreams sometimes called "a miracle."[47] The "miracle" was built up on a long theatre tradition, in which Shakespeare, Calderon de la Barca and Słowacki, who rendered one of Calderon's dramas into Polish, play eminent roles; Witkacy's version of la vida es sueno lays the motif bare for the audience and once again opens the scene for the absurd.

Witkacy's multiplied fantasy, based on well-known motifs which connect him not only with Słowacki, but often, through Słowacki, with broader theatre tradition, especially with Shakespeare, is not aimed at ridiculing the tradition of fantasy in the theatre. Jan Błoński poses the following question with regard to the surrealistic devices in Witkacy's play Nowe Wyzwolenie: "What is the difference between a cloud which speaks with a human voice in Słowacki's Kordian and Richard the third (English king and Shakespeare's hero and Witkacy's hero) put together with an soldering iron in a salon of an oldish tigress?"[48] To answer this question, I would say that the difference does not lie in the presence of fantastic devices themselves, but in the frequency with which they are applied and in their emphasized surrealism. The more their meaning becomes vague and bitterly ironic, the wider a scene opens up for the absurd. Since the time when human life was embedded in myth and history has inevitably passed, which paradoxically only a madman – such as Walpurg – can see clearly nowadays:

> Dawniej nie było [...] perwersji w sztuce. A życie nie było bezcelowym poruszaniem się bezdusznych automatów. Społeczeństwo jako maszyna nie istniało. (Before, art wasn't perverted [...] Life wasn't the aimless movement of soulless automatons. Society was not a machine.[49]

---

[47] Ibidem, p. 166.
[48] J. Błoński: Witkacy. Sztukmistrz, filozof, estetyk, op. cit., p. 144.
[49] S. I. Witkiewicz: Dramaty, vol. III, op. cit., p. 68.

Witkacy's nostalgia for the art of the past and his irony towards modernity is expressed, among other means, by his evoking of Słowacki, both in the theory of Pure Form and in his plays. It is through intertextual relationships and by developing the world of fantasy and multiplying the world of grotesque characters – for whom Ślaz, a figure from one more Słowacki's symbolic drama Lilla Weneda, or Grabiec, a character from his fairy-tale like drama Balladyna, could be perfect prototypes – that Witkacy creates a theatre which becomes not only fantastic but also grotesquely surrealistic. Martin Esslin was right when he said that Witkacy "takes up and continues the vein of dream and grotesque fantasy."[50] Yet with Strindberg and Wedekind on the one side and Artaud, Beckett, Ionesco, Genet on the other, Słowacki should also be remembered. In particular, when we bear in mind that Witkacy's Polish predecessor took up and masterly continued Shakespeare's motif of the "play within a play," playing "theatre" with his audience. It was Słowacki who made his characters speak with other literary texts and who began to use the words "theatre" and "wings," or expressions such as "to go behind the scenes" and "to play comedy" in their double meaning, especially in his late drama Fantazy (1844). Such a play on words and on conventions might have been one more attraction for Witkacy who liked nothing more than playing with his audience, of which his drama Szalona lokomotywa (The Crazy Locomotive, 1923) is perhaps the best example. While Słowacki's character comments on all too romantic a behavior of a young hero: "Ot i teatry!" ("Just theatres!")[51] Witkacy makes the character of his Szalona lokomotywa shout angrily: "To nie jest przedstawienie w teatrze!" ("This is not a theatre performance!")[52] Thus it could be said that both Słowacki and Witkacy have opened the door of the theatre to postmodernity. Undoubtedly, the latter without the former cannot be profoundly understood.[53]

Abstract

The author addresses the extent to which Witkacy's work should be seen in relation to Romantic playwright Juliusz Słowacki who began the Artistic Theater in Poland according to Witkacy's own words. While subsequent creators of Artistic Theatre, especially Sta-

---

[50] M. Esslin: Introduction, op. cit., p. 4.

[51] J. Słowacki, Juliusz: Fantazy (Nowa Dejanira), [in:] idem: Dramaty, vol. IV, ed. by E. Sawrymowicz, Zakład Narodowy Imienia Ossolinskich, Wrocław 1987, p. 431.

[52] S. I. Witkiewicz: Dramaty, vol. III, op. cit., p. 586.

[53] For more detailed analysis of this topic, please see my monograph: Wśród Witkacoidów: W świecie tekstów, w świecie mitów, Wydawnictwo Uniwersytetu Wrocławskiego, Wrocław 2012.

nisław Wyspiański, the author of symbolic national dramas, attracted much attention among Witkacy scholars, Słowacki has been barely mentioned in the context of Witkacy theatre. The author compares Słowacki's Kordian with Witkacy's John Mathew Charles the Furious and concludes that both the protagonists' dilemmas and their self-referential statements are profoundly connected. In addition, the author presents an analysis of both Słowacki's and Witkacy's treatment of the motifs of 'Violence' 'A Corpse' 'A Dream' and 'A Ghost.' It is argued that Witkacy deconstructs national myths and pushes romantic imagination to the limits, developing elements of romantic fantasy bordering on surrealism typical of Słowacki into modern surrealistic theatre.

Prof. Marta Skwara
University of Szczecin

J. Greg Perkins

Eluding the Void: Art and Humor as Anodynes for Witkiewicz, Beckett, and Faulkner

Stanisław Ignacy Witkiewicz (or Witkacy) was educated by his renowned artist father to be what has been described as a "Nietzschean genius."[1] As a consequence of the father's tutelage, the son became a polymath, and evolved into a consummate creative artist and philosopher. So engaged, Witkacy was a painter, aesthetician, playwright, and novelist, and evolved into the "most remarkable and versatile personality active in Poland during the first half of the twentieth century."[2]

Neither the Irish writer Samuel Beckett nor the American William Faulkner, born 21 and 12 years respectively after Witkacy, can come close to laying claim to such a background with respect to paternal lineage or tutelage. Beckett's father, William, was a successful businessman who was described as, "Easy-going, fun-loving and jovial; his was a secular outlook, rejoicing in the world as he was given it, greeting it with enthusiasm and shrewdly ac-

---

[1] D. Gerould: Witkacy: Stanisław Ignacy Witkiewicz as Imaginative Writer, University of Washington Press, 1981, p. 5.
[2] Ibidem, p. IX.

cepting its values."³ Father and son developed a closeness, as evidenced by the two often going on walks together. This activity is often reflected in Beckett's writing.⁴

Faulkner's father, Murry, by contrast, was a stalwart upholder of the family tradition of paternal alcoholism (one that was passed down to his famous progeny) . Essentially drifting within a succession of jobs, Murry was typed as a "mean drunk" who would have to be rescued from an assortment of freezing alleyways by wife and son.⁵ Any closeness of the two was greatly hampered by the father referring to the son as "Snake Lips."⁶

As regards education, there is also a pronounced disparity between Witkacy being groomed by his father, and the schooling received by Beckett and Faulkner. The former thrived in academic settings, including those at the university level;⁷ the latter started being truant from elementary school in the sixth grade, and dropped out of high school in his sophomore year. Faulkner would briefly attend Ole Miss as a special student.⁸

Notwithstanding differences in background, the three men possessed a distinct predilection for solitude. A friend who knew Witkacy for twelve years characterized him in these terms: "Childlikeness, based on a nonacceptance of reality – hence the necessity of existing in a fictional reality (art, drugs). The need of friendship and the need of solitariness."⁹

Being alone or seeking solitude was also an oft cited desire of Beckett. As stated in one of his biographies: "When he was very young, Sam, blond and pretty, was not considered exceptionally bright (also an opinion held of Faulkner), but he learned to read very quickly and was a thoughtful child. He was very fond of being alone, at his happiest when he could curl up by himself with, at first, a picture book or, later, a proper book to read."¹⁰

Faulkner's penchant for solitude, aloofness and privacy was legendary. Self acknowledged as, "The cat who walks alone," and devoting countless hours to sailing by himself on his boat on Lake Sardis, he was liked by most of his schoolmates, but intimate with none. To many people of Oxford, his

---

[3] A. Cronin: Samuel Beckett: the Last Modernist, Harper Collins, 1997, p. 13.

[4] Ibidem, p. 26.

[5] J. Sensibar: Faulkner and Love, Yale University Press, 2009, p. 29.

[6] Ibidem, p. 176.

[7] J. Knowlson: Damned to Fame: The Life of Samuel Beckett, Simon and Schuster, 1996, p. 81.

[8] J. Parini: One Matchless Time: A Life of William Faulkner, Harper Collins, 2004, p. 49.

[9] D. Gerould, op. cit., p. 18.

[10] J. Knowlson, op. cit., p. 44.

costumes and behavior later in life made him a joke to a point at which they referred to him as "Count-no account."[11]

Witkacy, Beckett, and Faulkner were solitary genius-creators. A Schopenhauerean common denominator exists in the creative outputs of all three men, and frequently translates to a sullen pessimism which suffuses their works. Serving as its backdrop, is the concept of the void, or as Brecht so aptly stated, "[We] happen to be on a small knob of stone twisting endlessly through the void round a second-rate star, just one among myriads."[12]

To the outside world as much as it paid attention to a young Witkacy, the painter-writer-philosopher became that "madman Witkacy" – a sex fiend, drug addict, and demented dilettante whose plays seemed like the wildest nonsense,"[13] reminiscent of Jarry who succumbed to overindulgence at the age of 34, and author of a series of plays categorized as, "The Triumph of Nothingness."[14]

In Esslin's The Theatre of the Absurd, he was described as one of the most brilliant figures of the European avant-garde of his time, whose importance [in 1973] was [then] being discovered outside his native Poland."[15] In a quote ascribed to Witold Gombrowicz, "There were three of us; Witkiewicz, Bruno Schultz and myself- the three Polish avant-garde between the wars. Only Witkiewicz remains to be discovered."[16] Philosophically, Witkacy was described as an existentialist many years before the movement appeared in France and championed by Camus and Sartre.[17]

The major theme in all of Witkacy's work was captured in a 1979 review of Insatiability, one of his two dystopian novels.[18] As expressed therein, the theme is, "the growing mechanization of life, understood not as dehumanizing technology, but rather as social and psychic regimentation. In dozens of plays and three large novels, Witkacy portrays the threatened extinction of

---

[11] B. Wasson: Count no 'Count: Flashbacks to Faulkner, University Press of Mississippi, 1983, p. 19–20.

[12] J. Rohn: Silencing the Music of the Spheres. Galileo by Bertold Brecht, November 12, 2006, http://www.lablit.com/article/172.

[13] D. Gerould, op. cit., p. 3.

[14] Ibidem, p. 207.

[15] M. Esslin: The Theatre of the Absurd: Revised Updated Edition, The Overlook Press, 1973, p. 343.

[16] S. I. Witkiewicz: Insatiability, trans. by L. Iribarne, Northwestern University Press, 1996, quote on dust jacket.

[17] The Madman and the Nun and Other Plays, eds. D. Gerould, C. S. Durer, University of Washington Press, 1968, p. XLVIII.

[18] Books in Review: Science Fiction Studies, 19, Vol. 6, November 1979, http://www.depauw.edu/sfs/birs/bir19.htm.

a decadent individualism. The degenerate remnants of a once creative mankind will be replaced by a new race of invading levelers who will establish the reign of mass conformity modeled on the beehive and anthill by what Orwell calls insect-men," or Vonnegut has Diana Moon Glaumpers enforce with her double-barreled ten-gauge shot gun.[19]

Brecht's "small knot of stone twisting endlessly through the void" was described by Beckett in Waiting for Godot as, This bitch of an earth.[20] From the same play he has Pozzo speak the hauntingly sombre lines referring to mothers, "They give birth astride of a grave. The light gleams for an instant, and then it's night once more."[21] In reference to the existence of a beneficent deity answering Clov's prayer in Endgame, Hamm truculently interjects, "The bastard, he doesn't exist."[22] From Malone Dies, Beckett borrows from the atomistic philosophy of Democritus when the main protagonist asserts, "Nothing is more real than nothing."[23] Only a few other writers, such as Kafka, have given voice to essential questions without the need for the sustaining illusion of meaning and values."[24]

One of Faulkner's best allusions to such a world appeared in Go Down Moses, in which it is referred to as the "worthless, tideless rock cooling in the last crimson evening."[25] There is another toward the end of The Mansion, his next to last novel, where there is an exchange between Gavin Stevens and his friend, V. K. Ratliff, as they set out to deliver the escape money Linda has left for Mink.

> So maybe there's a moral in it somewhere, if you jest knowed where to look.
> There aren't any morals, Stevens said, People just do the best they can.
> The pore sons of bitches, Ratliff said.
> The pore sons of bitches, Stevens said. Drive on. Pick it up.[26]

In his work, Faulkner constantly experimented, questing throughout for the perfect form, "a vase," like the one an old Roman so loved that "he wore

---

[19] K. Vonnegut, Jr.: Harrison Bergeron, [in:] idem: Welcome to the Monkey House, Delacorte Press, 1968.

[20] S. Beckett: Waiting for Godot, Faber and Faber Limited, 1956, p. 37.

[21] Ibidem, p. 89.

[22] Idem: Endgame, Faber and Faber, 1958, p. 38.

[23] Idem: Malone Dies, Grove Press, 1956, p. 16.

[24] D. S. Burt: The Literary 100, The Revised Edition, Checkmark Books, p. 178.

[25] W. Faulkner: Go Down Moses, Random House, 1942, p. 284.

[26] Idem: The Mansion, Random House, 1959, p. 429.

slowly [the rim] away with kissing it."²⁷ The implement by which he did so was language which he described as, "That Meager and fragile thread – by which the little surface corners and edges of men's secret and solitary lives may be joined for an instant now and then before sinking back into the darkness where the spirit cried for the first time and was not heard and will cry for the last time and will not be heard then either."²⁸ "Gazing unflinchingly into the abyss we all hope isn't there,"²⁹ Faulkner has been grouped with Kafka, Sartre, Camus and Beckett whose work is unsettling precisely because it ruthlessly invades our inner privacy and inexorably lays bare man's fears and anxieties, his bestiality and his loneliness."³⁰

Art, as defined as the creative outputs of Witkacy, Beckett, and Faulkner, was a primary raison d'être for each throughout their lives. As voiced by Boy-Żeliński, a critic-friend in the interwar years, "Witkiewicz is by birth, by race, to the very marrow of his bones an artist; he lives exclusively by art and for art. And his relationship to art is profoundly dramatic; he is one of those tormented spirits who in art seek the solution not to art, not to the problem of success, but to the problem of their own being."³¹ "I live constantly on the edge of the abyss, he confessed, constructing new selves out of nothingness."³²

In 1944, Faulkner wrote, "I'm telling the same story over and over which is myself and the world. That's all a writer does, he tells his own biography in a thousand different terms."³³ He also remarked in statements reminiscent of what was said about Witkacy, that the individual so engaged pursues his or her lofty objectives with the sole purpose of creating in order to, "[Scribble] 'Kilroy was here,' on the wall of the final and irrevocable oblivion through which he must someday pass."³⁴ Beckett described the process as a

---

[27] Faulkner and the Craft of Fiction, eds. D. Fowler and A. J. Abadie, 1987, Faulkner and Yoknapatawpha Conference, University Press of Mississippi, 1989, p. IX.

[28] D. Kartiganer: The Fragile Thread, The University of Massachusetts Press, 1979, Faulkner quote from Absalom, Absalom (Vintage Corrected Text, p. 202), cited as epigraph.

[29] Observation made by Dr. Ch. Peek at the 2008 Faulkner and Yoknapatawpha Conference: Faulkner: the Returns of the Text.

[30] M. Friedman: To Deny Our Nothingnes: Contemporary Images of Man, Delacorte Press, 1967, p. 20.

[31] The Witkiewicz Reader, ed. D. Gerould, Northwestern University Press, 1992, p. 1.

[32] Ibidem, p. 2.

[33] M. Cowley: The Faulkner-Cowley File: Letters and Memories 1944–1962, The Viking Press, 1966, p. 14.

[34] J. B. Meriwether, M. Millgate: Lion in the Garden: Interviews with William Faulkner 1926–1962, Random House, 1968, p. 253.

truly ontological quest.[35] Both men believed the artist must work with ignorance and impotence.[36]

The paths traveled by each man to arrive at such a station were about as disparate as could be imagined. Prodded on by his father and reinforced by a musician mother in a European culture that attached value to individuals so occupied, Witkacy's journey started with his debut as playwright at the age of 8 and spanned almost half a century. Described as an incessant Nietzschean quest to explain his own presence on earth, Witkacy's creative efforts reflected his attempts to justify his existence, to place himself, his art, his entire life and work within the critical framework of a theory that could explicate his being.[37]

This theory was "Pure Form," which for Witkacy was an expression of the modernist ideal of an autonomous art freed of referentiality; an epiphany transcending everydayness and putting one in direct contact with the structure of the universe.[38] He did not feel himself to be part of any of the radical artistic movements of his time, and was regarded as a total outsider, as well as the deplorably eccentric son of a revered father.[39]

Acknowledged as one of the greatest modernists, Faulkner grew up in the American south where artistic expression was viewed as effeminate. Being raised in Oxford, Mississippi, Faulkner has been described as, "Going off into the woods [alone] with his tablet and pencil.[40] He would often project himself as a dandy to unsympathetic, less than understanding townspeople.[41] Sherwood Anderson provided the role model and advice that only an established writer could offer.[42]

In his second novel, Mosquitoes, Faulkner described the creative process or art as, "Hackneyed accidents which make up this world- love and life and death and sex and sorrow brought together by chance in perfect proportions and [taking] on a kind of splendid and timeless beauty."[43] For him, the act of writing was, "Sacrificial and mediatory, a gradual sacrificing of the self in an attempt to attain immortality through the mediation of language."[44]

---

[35] J. Calder: The Philosophy of Samuel Beckett, Calder Publications, 2001, p. 76.
[36] A Walk With Faulkner, "New York Times Book Review", Jan. 30, 1955, p. 4; M. Robinson: The Long Sonata of the Dead: A Study of Samuel Beckett, Grove Press, 1969, p. 33.
[37] D. Gerould: The Witkiewicz Reader, op. cit., p. 2.
[38] Ibidem, p. 3.
[39] Ibidem, p. 4–5.
[40] J. Sensibar, op. cit., p. 47.
[41] J. Parini: One Matcless Time, op. cit., p. 23.
[42] Ibidem, p. 69.
[43] W. Faulkner: Mosquitoes, Boni and Liveright, 1927, p. 39.
[44] J. T. Irwin: Doubling and Incest: Repetition and Revenge, The Johns Hopkins University Press, 1977, p. 159.

The shape of ideas mattered to Beckett even if he didn't believe in them.[45] At least on the surface, his evolution as a modernist writer appeared to be much more conventional than either Witkacy's or Faulkner's, with neither parent having an interest in literature.[46] Remembered by a life-long friend as having developed an interest in poetry at boarding school, he was educated to play a traditional role in the Anglo-Anglican community and excelled in athletics.[47] It wasn't until he was 22 that he met James Joyce, and became a frequent visitor in his home.[48]

Humor was pervasive throughout the works of each. Witkacy's writing has been described as parody and political satire not unlike Brecht and Mayakovsky,[49] and ahead of his time awaiting Ionesco and Beckett.[50] His theatre was appreciated by only the most intelligent critics, and described as, "Metaphysical buffoonery and supercaberet, presenting the sadness, boredom and despair of modern civilization with a spasmodic laugh,"[51] and further it was depicted as a "comedy of corpses, a mocking irreverent humor and grotesque style built on parody and irony."[52]

Beckett has been described as one of the funniest writers of the age, whose induced laughter often dies aborning, and is brought about by Chaplin-like characters who are clowns however dimly or acutely aware of the void and all its terrors.[53] For him, humor was the key to the buzzing confusion, an approach that gave meaning to "the mess" where no religious or philosophical system was capable of doing so.[54]

"Laughter is presented by Beckett, as by Schopenhauer, as the only bearable reaction to the misery of the human condition."[55] As described in the novel Watt by Arsene who has been described as a "specialist in laughing matters,[56] a laugh can be categorized as follows: "The bitter, the hollow and –

---

[45] S. Beckett, quoted by H. Hobsen: Samuel Beckett: Dramatist of the Year, "International Theatre Annual" London 1956, No. 1, p. 153.

[46] A. Cronin, op. cit., p. 37.

[47] Ibidem, p. 47.

[48] K. and A. Hamilton: Condemned to Life; the World of Samuel Beckett, W. B. Eerdmans Publishing Company, 1976, p. 19.

[49] Twentieth Century Polish Avant-Garde Drama: Plays, Scenarios, Critical Documents, ed. D. Gerould, Cornell University Press, 1977, p. 33.

[50] D. Gerould and C. S. Durer, The Madman and the Nun, p. XXXVII.

[51] Ibidem.

[52] Ibidem, p. XXIII.

[53] Samuel Beckett: I Can't Go On, I'll Go On, ed. R. W. Seaver, Grove Press, 1976, p. IX.

[54] K. and A. Hamilton, op. cit., p. 59.

[55] Ibidem.

[56] R. Cohn: Samuel Beckett: the Comic Gamut, Rutgers University Press, 1962, p. 286.

Haw! Haw! – the mirthless. The bitter laugh laughs at that which is not good, it is the ethical laugh. The hollow laugh laughs at that which is not true, it is the intellectual laugh. Not good! Not True! Well well. But the mirthless laugh is the dianoetic laugh, down in the snout – Haw! – so. It is the laugh of laughs, the risus purus, the laugh laughing at the laugh, the beholding, the saluting of the highest joke, in a word the laugh that laughs – silence please – at that which is unhappy."[57]

Faulkner was the master of convoluted, complex verbosity within which his humor is multidimensional. He was acknowledged by a prominent critic as a writer of comedy whose only possible peer in the United States was Mark Twain.[58] More recently, his legacy in this regard has been tapped by Hollywood's Coen brothers whose subtle allusions from his novels and outright modeling of a character upon him are easily recognizable.[59]

Interspersed among works which were unrivalled in analyzing solitude's desolation with a more refined cruelty,[60] this pervasiveness of humor seen in Faulkner is needed since, "Pure tragedy is not finally appropriate to [his] vision of the absurd. He saw an absurd universe peopled by absurd men whose reaction to absurdity must be automatically ironic."[61] His vast array of humor is offered as counterpoise to a vision in which, in his own words, "It is what we (groundlings, dwellers in and backbone of a small town interchangeable with and duplicate of ten thousand little dead clottings of human life about the land) saw, refined, and classified as the expert, the man who had himself seen his own and scudding shadow upon the face of a puny and remote earth."[62]

Providing comic relief to the black or comedy of savage extremity found in novels such as Sanctuary and Pylon,[63] and derived from a cosmic pessimism,[64] it is what has been described by Campbell and Foster as Southern frontier humor[65] which assumed a greater importance as he grew older.

---

[57] K. and A. Hamilton, op. cit., p. 60.

[58] Observation made by J. B. Carothers at the 36th Faulkner and Yoknapatawpha Conference, Faulkner and Mystery.

[59] William Faulkner: the Perfect Coen Brothers Hero, http://www.moreintelligentlife.com/story/William-faulkner-perfect-coen-brothers-hero.

[60] A. Rousseaux: Le Litteraire, October 19, 1946.

[61] R. B. Hauck: A Cheerful Nihilism: Confidence and the Absurd in American Humerous Fiction, Indiana University Press, 1991, p. 175.

[62] J. Blotner: Faulkner, a Biography, Random House, 1974, p. 862.

[63] J. L. Langley, Jr.: The Tragic Mask: A Study of Faulkner's Heroes, The University of North Carolina Press, 1963, p. 102.

[64] H. M. Campbell and E. F. Ruel: William Faulkner: a Critical Appraisal, University of Oklahoma Press, 1951, p. 139.

[65] Ibidem, p. 102.

Examples of this genre include the tall tale, dialectal variations, hyperbole, understatement, obscenity, Aesopian animal humor, trick situations, Negro humor, and so on.

Establishing a case for art and humor as anodynes or ameliorative for Witkacy, Beckett and Faulkner is speculative at best. Given the commonality of their respective visions, the rather trite "tormented genius" moniker definitely seems to apply to all three. Even so, overt manifestations of "tormented" was manifested under different guises.

Considerable controversy exists among Beckett's biographers as to exactly how he projected himself to the outside world. The spectrum ranges from, "Surprisingly the most balanced and serene of men" and "Thoroughly charming and witty," to, "A ghostly specter of a man," "Gloomy and depressed – an eccentric controlled by an inner torment," and "[Someone who] spent long periods of time curled upon the bed in a fetal position, searching for the happiness, perfection, and immobility he remembered from the womb." Weighing in on the side of the more positive attributes, Gordon collated details from a wide assemblage of Beckett scholarship and proposed that Beckett, "Was a gentle but heroic man with a reservoir of toughness and strength that enabled him to pursue both an altruistic bent and the need for artistic fulfillment." She concludes by asserting that his life was inspiring.[66]

An element that appears to be an undercurrent for the duration of Beckett's creative life was that of control. Although he periodically discussed suicide with his friends throughout his adult life, this was done in the context of an abstraction, and ultimately his life span underscores his view that, "Existence, to which we are condemned without our permission, was something to be endured."[67] Similarly, his history of heavy drinking was done after 5:00 pm, and was marked by behavior which, "Was never boisterous or over talkative, if anything, more remote."[68] His one period of psychoanalysis occurred relatively early in his life.[69]

Resilience, courage, and the need to endure also come to mind with Faulkner, particularly in the sense that he was able to provide support to what amounted to an extended family and eventually become the largest landowner in Oxford.[70] On the other hand, the element of control observed

---

[66] L. Gordon: The World of Samuel Beckett: 1906–1946, Yale University Press, 1996, p. 2–3.

[67] A. Cronin: op. cit., p. 58.

[68] Ibidem, p. 517.

[69] L. Gordon, op. cit., p. 113.

[70] F. R. Karl: William Faulkner; American Writer, Weidenfeld and Nicoson, 1989, p. 584–585.

with Beckett is already seen slipping with behavior wherein he, "Sought hopelessly and ritualistically to drink himself into oblivion."[71] Such behavior was taken to such extremes that one biographer of note observed that it, coupled with other self destructive behavior, ultimately led to his "breaking of the pencil" and a passive sort of suicide which led to his sudden and unexpected death when taken to Byhalia to "dry out" after his last alcoholic binge close to his 65th birthday.[72]

Faulkner was a profoundly unhappy man as attested to by such an adroit observer of human nature, as Tennessee Williams who received a glimpse into the Faulknerian soul in 1955. After a chance encounter with the Nobel laureate, the playwright remarked to Hemingway that, "Faulkner's terrible distraught eyes had moved him to tears."[73] A biographer who also happened to be a personal friend remarked, "He didn't have a happy day in his life."[74]

He also was described as a man, "Beset by demons [whose] commerce with the past (and the tumult within) was something fierce and unhinging, so powerful that the only two ways it could be withstood was via writing and drink."[75] He underwent electroshock therapy and psychotherapy relatively late in his life in the early 1950s.[76]

Perhaps it was Faulkner himself who provided the greatest insight into his inner most thoughts when he penned the following: "All of a sudden it's over and all you have left is a block of stone with scratches on it provided there was someone to remember to have the marble scratched and set up or had time to, and it rains on it and the sun shines on it and after awhile they don't even remember the name and what the scratches were trying to tell and it doesn't matter."[77]

And, finally, we are left with the Cassandra-like "Nietzschean genius" whose much deserved recognition is the subject of this publication. Witkacy's world was a tragedy acted out as farce, a cosmic amusement park, designed by Dali and Magritte, where Strindberg sells peanuts and popcorn, while Spengler performs a cooch dance, Heidegger and Sartre turn somer-

---

[71] P. Weinstein: The Land's Turn, [in:] Faulkner and The Ecology of the South, eds. J. R. Urgo and A. J. Abadie, University Press of Mississippi, 2005, p. 27.

[72] F. R. Karl, op. cit., p. 995, 1038.

[73] S. B. Oates: William Faulkner: the Man and the Artist, Harper and Row, 1987, p. 287.

[74] Observation made by Dr. D. Kartiganer in reference to J. Blotner at the 35th Faulkner and Yoknapatawpha Conference, The Returns of the Text.

[75] A. Weinstein: Recovering Your Story: Proust, Joyce, Woolf, Faulkner, Morrison, Random House, 2006, p. 406.

[76] P. Weinstein: Becoming Faulkner: the Art and Life of William Faulkner, Oxford University Press, 2010, p. 218.

[77] W. Faulkner: Absalom, Absalom, Random House, 1936, p. 131.

saults, Dostoevsky and Nietzsche sling custard pies at one another,[78] and, at the risk of sounding presumptuous, Beckett and Faulkner alternate in shooting one another out of a cannon.

Little about how he comported himself throughout his life connoted "control." The aforementioned quote attributed to him about living on the abyss, certainly bears this out, as does a quote cited by Professor Gerould, "Better to end in beautiful madness than in gray, boring banality and stagnation."[79] Often walking through streets, as a harlequin, Witkacy enjoyed provocation every bit as much as Oscar Wilde.[80] Then there was his practice of experimenting with alcohol, and a variety of other drugs with such regularity that he authored a book about the experience.[81] It was another facet of Witkacy's make-up, however, that provided the greatest insight as to his emotional lability – his chronic fixation on suicide, contrasted with either Beckett or Faulkner.

"From an early age, he experienced a curious detachment toward himself and regarded his own life and especially his inevitable death as an object of endless study as though his existence and ultimate extinction were a work of art to be savored."[82] As a theme, suicide was mentioned throughout his work, and actually represents the driving force of his art as exemplified by the last group of his surviving plays written between 1922–1925. These were prophetic in a sense of what was to come in 1939 in that they are concerned with the cost of the artist and creative personality of achieving his goals and realizing his calling.[83]

For the man who was a consummate artist and well ahead of his time in so many ways, this entailed a series of "preliminary suicides," warm-ups if you will, in which self-destruction was necessary in order to create in the modern world. In other words, "mastery means shattering the very matrix of creation." "Such artists-creators achieve recognition only after they have destroyed themselves, and success comes when it is too late to be anything but pure mockery."[84]

---

[78] B. Dukore: Who Was Witkacy, "Theatre Quarterly" 1975–1976, nr 5–6, p. 65.

[79] Czysta Forma w teatrze, ed. J. Degler, Wydawnictwa Artystyczne i Filmowe, 1977, p. 91, The date of the compostion is 1919.

[80] D. Gerould and C. S. Durer, op. cit., p. IX.

[81] Cz. Miłosz: Emperor of the Earth: Modes of Eccentric Vision, University of California Press, 1977, p. 34.

[82] D. Gerould, Witkacy, op. cit. p. 4.

[83] Ibidem, p. 207.

[84] Ibidem, p. 208–209.

It has been said that, "Until the outbreak of the Second World War, [Witkiewicz] was understood only by a few- maybe because [everyone] was all still before, while he was already after."[85] At the onset of the Second World War when Poland was caught between the Scylla and Charybdis of invading armies, Witkacy, "Took sleeping pills in a forest, woke up and cut his wrists with a razor, against a magnificent natural background as in Farewell to Autumn."[86]

His last words, spoken to a woman who was with him at the end were in Russian, "I won't go on living as less than myself."[87] He could no longer cope. Art and humor had run their respective courses and had been exhausted to a point where they provided fuel to his desire for self destruction and annihilation. At that instant the world lost a truly unique and amazingly talented individual. For him this would have been a richly deserved accolade.

Abstract

The author considers the extent to which the literary work of these writers was driven by a response to the apparent vacuousness of existence. A brief overview of their lives traces the interplay of eschatological questions and the forces of creativity. Impressions gleaned from such varied backgrounds were often interwoven into their creative outputs which often share a Schopenhauerean common denominator. This often translates to a sullen pessimism which suffuses their respective works and emanates from the concept of the void. Establishing a case for the degree to which art and humor acted as anodynes is speculative; there is no question concerning the importance of both in their lives. Art, or engagement in the creative process, occupied the mainstay of their intellectual lives. Moreover, humor, particularly of the black or mordant variety, is a hallmark of the trio's entire oeuvre.

Dr. Greg Perkins
Former Pharmaceutical Industry Senior Executive

---

[85] D. Gerould and C. S. Durer, op. cit., p. XVII.
[86] Cz. Miłosz, op. cit., p. 153.
[87] D. Gerould and C. S. Durer, op. cit., p. LI.

Annex:
Witkacy's Portraits and the Słupsk Collection

Portrait of Michał Białynicki-Birula, 27 XII 1930
pastel, paper; 65 x 48 cm; inv. no. MPŚ-M/43

Joint Portrait of Helena and Teodor Białyniccy-Birula, 24 II 1930
pastel, paper; 47 x 63 cm; inv. no. MPŚ-M/123

Portrait of Józef Jan Głogowski – Il pensieroso, 1934
pastel, paper; 65 x 50 cm; inv. no. MPŚ-M/628

Portrait of Włodzimierz Nawrocki, XI 1926
pastel, paper; 70 x 50 cm; inv. no. MPŚ-M/689

Jan Leszczyński as Robespierre, IX 1931
pastel, charcoal, paper; 65 x 52 cm; inv. no. MPŚ-M/1294

Portrait of Nena Stachurska, 12 X 1929
pastel, paper; 65 x 50 cm; inv. no. MPŚ-M/131

Portrait of Nena Stachurska, 10 IX 1929
pastel, paper; 66 x 51 cm; inv. no. MPŚ-M/47

Portrait of Nena Stachurska, 8 IV 1930
pastel, paper; 64 x 49 cm; inv. no. MPŚ-M/104

Italian Landscape, 1904
oil, canvas; 32 x 48 cm; inv. no. MPŚ-M/1223

Portrait of Jadwiga Netzel, 15 VIII 1939
pastel, paper; 65 x 50 cm; inv. no. MPŚ-M/538

Self-Portrait from a Mirrored Reflection, 1906
oil, plywood; 21 x 16 cm; inv. no. MPŚ-M/135

Composition (with a Dancer), 1916
pastel, paper; 47 x 63 cm; inv. no. MPŚ-M/1198

Jupiter Transforming Himself into a Bull, 1921
oil, canvas; 77 x 91 cm; inv. no. MPŚ-M/684

Portrait of Maria Nawrocka, VII 1925 pastel,
paper; 115 x 99 cm; inv. no. MPŚ-M/682

Portrait of Anna Nawrocka, 1925
pastel, paper; 62 x 47 cm; inv. no. MPŚ-M/694

Portrait of Maria Nawrocka, 19 IV 1929 pastel,
paper; 63 x 38 cm; inv. no. MPŚ-M/712

Portrait of Helena Białynicka-Birula, IV 1927
pastel, paper; 64 x 48 cm; inv. no. MPŚ-M/33

Portrait of Teodor Białynicki-Birula, II 1928
pastel, paper; 65 x 48 cm; inv. no. MPŚ-M/28

Portrait of Zofia Schroeder, 1 III 1931
pastel, paper; 64 x 48 cm; inv. no. MPŚ-M/1147

Portrait of Izabela Zborowska, IV 1934 pastel,
paper; 65 x 50 cm; inv. no. MPŚ-M/1169

Portrait of Irena Krzywicka, 17 XI 1928 pastel, paper; 64 x 48 cm; inv. no. MPŚ-M/882

Portrait of Michał Choromański, III 1930 pastel, paper; 63 x 48 cm; inv. no. MPŚ-M/31

Portrait of Kazimiera Żuławska, 3 VII 1926
pastel, paper; 57 x 43 cm; inv. no. MPŚ-M/1293

Portrait of Rafał Malczewski, 28 III 1930
pastel, paper; 65 x 51 cm; inv. no. MPŚ-M/98

Portrait of Tadeusz Boy-Żeleński, XI 1928
pastel, paper; 61 x 47 cm; inv. no. MPŚ-M/879

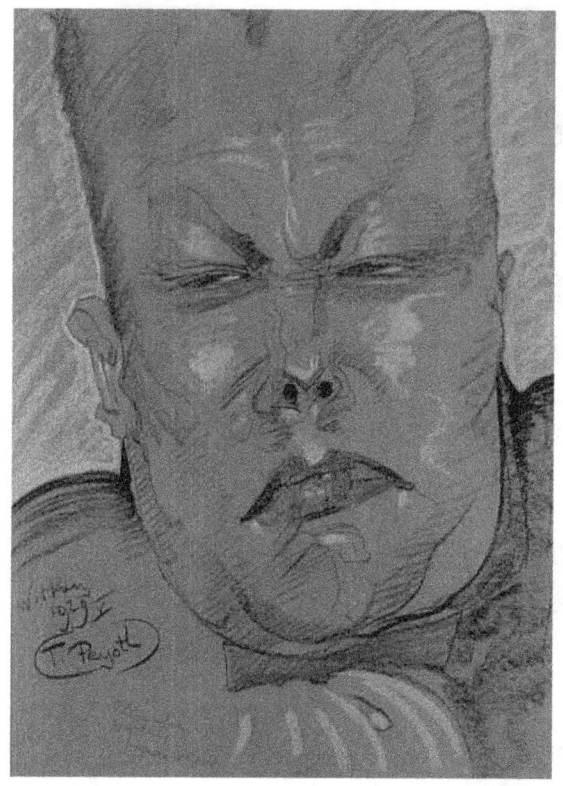

Portrait of Janusz de Beaurain, V 1929 pastel,
paper; 67 x 49 cm; inv. no. MPŚ-M/119

Portrait of Kazimierz Sosnkowski, III 1930
pastel, paper; 65 x 50 cm; inv. no. MPŚ-M/66

Portrait of Ludwik de Laveaux, I 1929 pastel,
paper; 67 x 49 cm; inv. no. MPŚ-M/53

Portrait of Jan Humpola, I 1928
pastel, paper; 67 x 49 cm; inv. no. MPŚ-M/1230

A Monk Battling with Insanity, 18 I 1924 pencil,
paper; 20,7 x 15,5 cm; inv. no. MPŚ-M/638

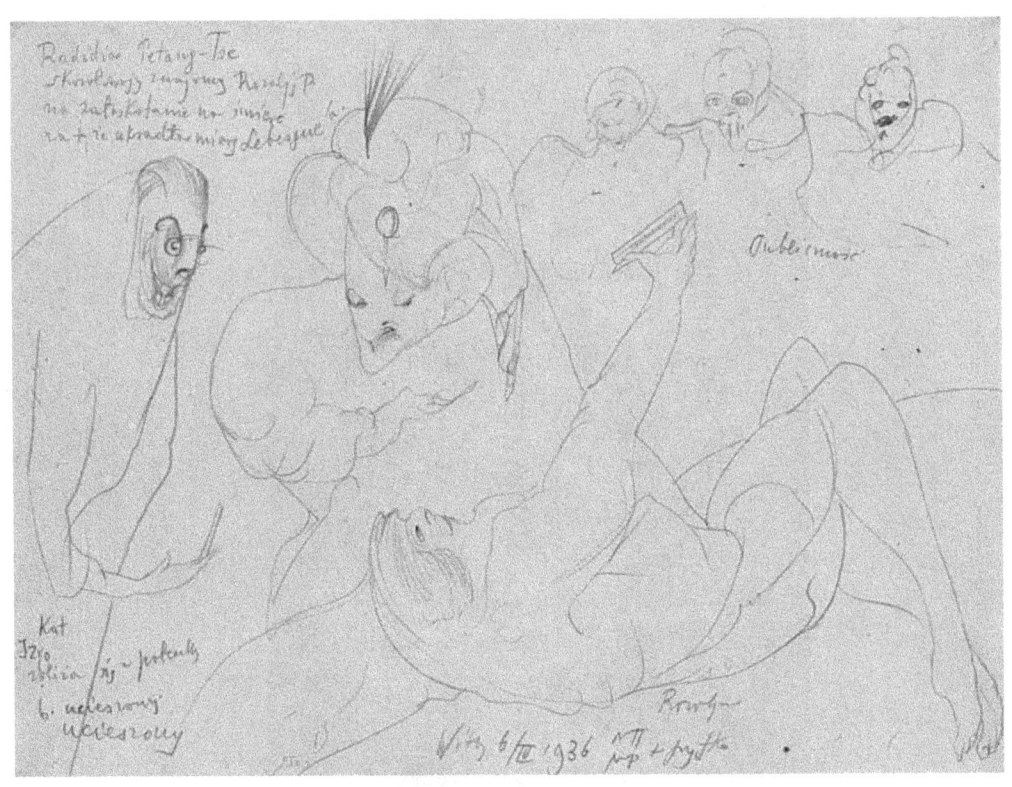

Rajah Petang-Tse..., 6 III 1936
pencil, paper; 23 x 29 cm; inv. no. MPŚ-M/632

Portrait of Irena Solska with a Man, 1910 charcoal,
paper; 46 x 62 cm; inv. no. MPŚ-M/1182

Fictional Portrait, 12 X 1931
pastel, paper; 65 x 50 cm; inv. no. MPŚ-M/105

Winter Landscape II, 1912
oil, canvas; 59 x 70 cm; inv. no. MPŚ-M/1299

Composition – Lady Macbeth, 7 I 1933
pastel, paper; 70 x 100 cm; inv. no. MPŚ-M/106

Australian Landscape, 1918
pastel, paper; 49 x 63 cm; inv. no. MPŚ-M/1115

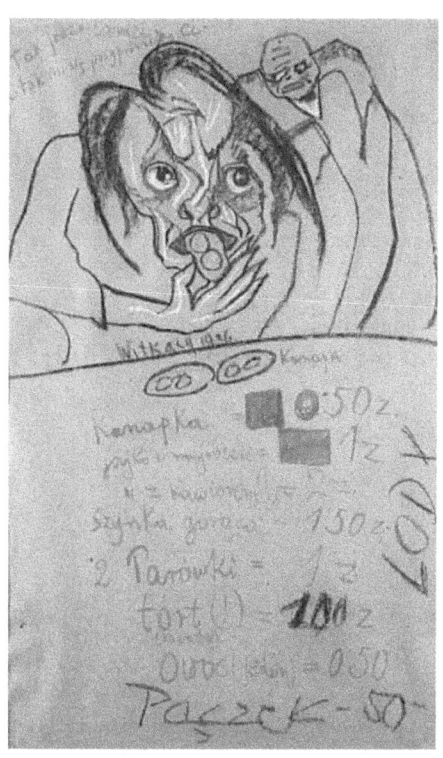

Menu: "That's How They Eat...", 1926
pastel, ink, paper; 91 x 56 cm; inv. no. MPŚ-M/716

Menu: "This is How a Woman Drinks...", 1926
pastel, ink, paper; 90 x 55 cm; inv. no. MPŚ-M/718

About the Contributors

Kevin Anthony Hayes is an actor, director and Polish theatre specialist with around twenty five years involvement in Polish culture. He had the pleasure of living behind the 'Wall' for almost three years from October 1986, as a Polish Government and British Council Scholar. He then worked as a theatre director at Kraków's famous Stary Theatre, alongside such luminaries as Andrzej Wajda, Krystian Lupa and Jerzy Jarocki. As the first Englishman to direct at the Stary he was responsible for a very successful revival of 'THE IMPORTANCE...' which ran for well over a hundred performances through the whole transitional period in Poland. All in all he has directed and produced quite a number of plays in Poland. The emphasis has always been on confronting relevant social and political realities with the mystique of artistic and literary subtlety.

In 2000 he was awarded an 'Uprawnienia' or Diploma, in Theatre Directing by the Polish Association of Theatrical Artists (Z.A.S.P.). He spent a season at the prestigious Contemporary Theatre in Wrocław acting in Polish in Waldemar Krzystek's production of 'THE LOW MEADOWS' based on the bestseller of the same name by Piotr Siemion. He has worked as a Senior Lecturer in Practical Phonetics at Warsaw University's Institute of Applied Linguistics. Whilst he does not claim to be an academic his controversial paper on 'The Vision of Homo Sovieticus as it appears in the Dramas of Stanisław Ignacy Witkiewicz' was banned from publication in Russia following the author's presentation of it at 'The First International Conference devoted to Stanisław Ignacy Witkiewicz' at The Actors Centre St. Petersburg in 1993. He has worked for Polish Radio and Television, presenting and making programmes at The National News Service in Warsaw. This included a very popular cycle of Comic Weather Forecasts on TELEEXPRESS. He has appeared in a number of Polish feature films. He has translated classic Polish work for the film director Jerzy Skolimowski, has interviewed leading Polish film directors such as Filip Bajon, Agnieszka Holland and Krzysztof Zanussi, in English for Polish television. In 2007 he was awarded a 'Green Card' on the basis of being considered 'An Alien of Extraordinary Ability' in the realm of Polish Theatre.

Prof. Lech Sokół, Historian of Drama and Theatre, is the former Director of Institute of Arts History of Polish Academy of Sciences, Warsaw (1999–2007). At present, he is the Head of the Department of Theatre History and

Theory, and specialises in Comparative History of Drama and Theatre. He also holds the following titles and positions: professor of Scandinavian and Comparative Literature, Chair of Scandinavian, Warsaw School of Social Sciences and Humanities, professor of Modern and Comparative Drama at the Warsaw Drama Academy. He is the Co-editor, with professor Witold Maciejewski, of the yearbook "Acta Sueco-Polonica."

Professor Sokół has authored numerous publications on Polish, Scandinavian and French Drama and Literature in a variety of languages, including Polish, English, French, Swedish, and Norwegian. His book publications include but are not limited to: (in Polish) The Grotesque in the Drama of Stanislaw Ignacy Witkiewicz (1973), August Strindberg (1981), Witkacy and Strindberg: Distant and Close (1995), Faces of Modernism: Baudelaire – Ibsen – Strindberg – Wyspiański – Witkacy (In preparation).

Anna Brochocka graduated in 2004 from the Adam Mickiewicz University in Poznań with an MA in History of Art (thesis: Pagan influences in early Byzantine Icons). Since 2005 she has been working for the Museum of the Middle Pomerania in Słupsk (Muzeum Pomorza Środkowego w Słupsku) in The History of Art Department and as an Assistant Curator of the Witkacy Collection. Her primary research interests include the history of culture and religion and the history of Pomerania. Her publications focus mainly on; Pomeranian history, traditions, art and funereal art in particular.

John D. Barlow is Professor Emeritus of English and German, Dean Emeritus of the School of Liberal Arts, and Senior Fellow at the Institute for American Thought at Indiana University (Indianapolis). He was Visiting Professor of English at Middlebury College in 2004. His areas of interest have been German literature, comparative literature, film studies, and music. Principal publications: German Expressionist Film, Boston, 1982; "Alexander Zemlinsky" in The American Scholar, Autumn 1992; "Visual Literacy and the Holocaust" in Remembering for the Future, Oxford, 1989; and translations of Jean Améry (On Aging, Bloomington, 1994 and On Suicide, Bloomington, 1999) and Martin Heidegger ("Plato's Doctrine of Truth" in Twentieth Century Philosophy, New York, 1962). He presented papers on Witkiewicz and music at the Witkacy 2009 conference in London and the Witkacy 2010 conference in Washington.

Daniel Gerould held the Lucille Lortel Distinguished Professor of Theatre and Comparative Literature at the Graduate Center, City University of New York, and director of publications at the Martin E. Segal Theatre Center. He edited 'Slavic and East European Performance' and of the twelve-volume Routledge/Harwood Polish and Eastern European Theatre Archive. He translated the plays of Witkiewicz and wrote extensively about twentieth-century avant-garde drama and theatre. His books include Witkacy: A Study of Stanisław Ignacy Witkiewicz as an Imaginative Writer, The Witkiewicz Reader, and The Guillotine: Its Legend and Lore. He also edited Theatre/Theory/Theatre: The Major Critical Texts from Aristotle and Zeami to Soyinka and Havel and several anthologies, including American Melodrama and Symbolist Drama. His play Candaules Commissioner has been performed in France, Germany, and America.

Michael Goddard is a Lecturer in Media Studies at the University of Salford. He has published widely on Polish and international cinema and visual culture as well as cultural theory. He recently completed a book on the cinema of Raul Ruiz. Most recently, his research focuses on contemporary Polish visual and popular culture, as well as on subversive media and popular practices in both Eastern and Western Europe, particularly in the 1970s.

Christine Kiebuzińska, has PhD in Comparative Literature from the University of Maryland (1984) and is a Professor at Virginia Tech. She teaches modern drama, film and comp lit courses. She has published a number of articles on Witkacy, including chapters in her Revolutionaries in the Theater: Meyerhold, Brecht and Witkiewicz (1988) and Intertextual Loops in Modern Drama (2001); Artaud and Witkiewicz: A Relationship based on the Mystery of Existence [in:] Antonin Artaud and the Modern Theater (1994); Witkacy: The Metaphysical Theater of Pure Form (1989); Witkacy's Theory of Pure Form: Change, Dissolution, and Uncertainty (1993). In addition she has written on Brecht, Brecht and the Problem of Influence [in:] A Bertolt Brecht Reference Companion (2001). She has recently focused on Elfriede Jelinek: Elfriede Jelinek: Staging a Heideggerian Postmodern Debate in Totenauberg [in:] Postmodern Stages and Beyond (2008); Historicizing Austria in Elfriede Jelinek's Burgtheater and Totenauberg [in:] Fünfzig Jahre Staatsvertrag (2009); Postmemory in Austrian Post-Holocaust Literature: Elfriede Jelinek's Totenauberg and Thomas Bernhard's Heldenplatz [in:] Trajectories of Memory: Representations of the Holocaust (2009); Violence and Pornography in Elfriede Jelinek's Princess Plays [in:] Gender and Trauma: Interdisciplinary Dialogues (2012). She is currently working on variations of the Faust myth in modern drama.

Bryce Lease joined the Drama Department at University of Exeter (UK) in 2010, having lectured previously at the University of Bristol. He is currently completing a monograph, We don't want to talk about Communism: The New Political Theatre in Poland, and working on the research project, "A Queer Nation? Public Space, Citizenship & Alternative Sexuality in South Africa," which investigates the intersections between non-normative sexual identities, minority rights, and public space in South Africa. His research interests include contemporary European theatre, national identity, gender, sexuality & politics, and queer studies.

Agnieszka Marczyk received a Ph.D. in Intellectual History from the University of Pennsylvania. Her research primarily focuses on relations between culture and politics, intercultural transfer and exchange, literary modernism, and history of the self. Her dissertation examined aesthetic innovation in interwar Poland, focusing on the innovators' relationship to Polish cultural traditions and to Europe. Her work has been supported by the Fulbright-Hays Dissertation Fellowship, the ACLS East European Studies Dissertation Fellowship, as well as several fellowships from the University of Pennsylvania. She has also taught as a lecturer at Collegium Civitas in Warsaw and currently works as a freelance translator.

Dorota Niedziałkowska graduated in the History of Art (MA thesis explored Stanisław Ignacy Witkiewicz's self-portraits in 2005) and Polish philology (in 2007) at the Catholic University of Lublin John Paul II. Currently, she is preparing her doctoral dissertation in modern Polish literature. She works as a publisher in Catholic University Publishing House and as an academic instructor at the university. She has also participated in Witkacy's conferences in Zakopane, Słupsk (2009), and Washington DC (2010). She is interested in most of Witkacy's paintings, especially analysing self-portraits in the aspect of dandyism.

Greg Perkins Scientist by training (Ph.D in Biochemistry; postdoctoral training in Neurochemistry) who has made a lifelong avocation of literature. Currently retired. Highlights of professional career have been as a senior executive in four multinational pharmaceutical companies, and, more recently, the Biotech realm, which includes a brief stint as CEO for a fledgling startup company in Oxford, Mississippi (Faulkner's hometown). Career has spanned approximately thirty seven years and involved managing large functional areas of Clinical Research, Drug Safety, Medical Affairs, Compliance, and Quality Control/Compliance. Involved in international Research and Development at the highest levels. Participated in the development of the first two commercially available drugs for AIDS. Designed and executed novel clinical trial programs, one of the first OTC conversions of a prescription drug, and generation of data used in support of television advertising. Derived models for the hypothetical modes of actions of various pharmacological agents. Expert witness in two therapeutic areas. Presented at multiple conferences. Accomplished author in the drug development arena with numerous successful New Drug Applications, Investigational New Drug Applications, twenty four published scientific papers, a forward to a book entitled International Drug Regulatory Mechanisms, and book (Pharmaceutical Marketing: Principles, Environment, and Practice) which has been translated into Japanese and Russian. Former Senior Editor of the Haworth Series in Drug Discovery.

Interest in literature involves both a long history of writing (publication not actively pursued), study, voluminous reading, and collecting antiquarian books with a concentration on 20th century literature. Active participation to date has been confined to attendance at twelve Yoknapatawpha (Faulkner) conferences. Focuses of interest include absurdist and Modernist literatures, as well as the inadequacy of language as a means of expression and depiction of what could be viewed as extreme human events. First encounter with Witkacy was a serendipitous purchase of The Madman and the Nun and Other Plays more than thirty years ago. Exposure to Beckett in a meaningful way occurred about the same time, and almost total immersion in Faulkner has been a more recent undertaking. Two original works resonating with Witkacy's writing are a play of the absurd, The Carrot: an Ontological Farce; and a novel entitled The Cosmic Idiot depicting the end of the world. Balance of oeuvre consists of a collection of early poems, epigrams, and essays (Inhaling the Nothingness), and fifteen books which are fictive constructs and representations mounted upon multiple scaffolding of tragic facts. The single literary publication is: J. Greg Perkins, Ph.D; Thwarted Legacies: Four and a Half Underappreciated American Authors; The Journal, Book Club of Washington; Spring 2012; pages 10-17.

Paweł Polit is an art critic and curator. Education: MA in Philosophy at the University of Warsaw (1990) and MA in Curating and Commissioning Contemporary Art at the Royal College of Art, London (1997). He curated exhibtions at the Centre for Contemporary Art Ujazdowski Castle, Warsaw, among others: Peter Downsbrough (1994); Conceptual Reflection in Polish Art 1965–1975 (1999), Stanisław Ignacy Witkiewicz (2004), Martin Creed (2004), Bruce Nauman (2009). Published widely on contemporary art in exhibition catalogues and art periodicals. Since 1997 Paweł Polit has been curator of Auditorium Programme at the CCA Ujazdowski Castle. Since 2001 he has taught American art at the American Studies Centre, University of Warsaw.

Gordon Ramsay lectures in drama, performance and creative writing at the University of Nottingham, U.K. As a playwright, he received a Fulbright Award to attend the University of Iowa Playwrights Workshop and has had professional readings, workshops and performances of a number of plays, including Pas De Deux (White Bear, London), The Woman Who Turned Into A Clock (The Gate, London) and 1X/X1 (Lion and Unicorn,

London). Most recently, following work with a director and actors from Nottingham Playhouse, he has developed a play based on material from the Milton Rokeach archive (Michigan State University), due for performance in 2013. He has published articles on Italian Futurist performance and is currently working on a collection of newly translated Futurist short plays (sintesi), a number of which received performances in Loughborough and Nottingham in 2009. He was awarded a National Teaching Fellowship in 2011 and is a member of the Ages and Stages Advisory Panel, an interdisciplinary project investigating the Place of Theatre in Representations and Recollections of Ageing (2009–2012).

Mark Rudnicki is a Term Assistant Professor of English at George Mason University, where he teaches courses in composition, research methods, philosophy, and world literatures. Previously, he taught at University of Warsaw, Jagiellonian University, and George Washington University. He is the recipient of two Kościuszko Foundation Research Fellowships and has spoken at various conferences primarily on the intersection of philosophy and literature in the works of Witkacy, Gombrowicz, and Schulz. He received a Ph.D. in comparative literature from the State University of New York at Buffalo.

Marta A. Skwara, dr. hab., a professor of Polish and Comparative literature at the University of Szczecin, the editor-in-chief of the comparative magazine "Rocznik Komparatystyczny" (Comparative Yearbook) published by the University of Szczecin in co-operation with the Universities of Warsaw, Brussels (ULB) and Greifswald. She received her Ph.D. and absolved her habilitation (in both cases, in Polish and comparative literature) at the University of Wrocław in 1995 and in 2005 respectively. She is one of the founders of the Transatlantic Walt Whitman Association (Paris 2007), and a beneficiary of the Kościuszko Foundation scholarship (2009) and the Polish-American Fulbright Commission scholarship (2011) spent at the University of Iowa and the University of Nebraska-Lincoln. Her publications comprise seven monographs, of which two are co-authored, two edited volumes, an extensive chapter in an academic handbook on comparative literature, and 55 articles. In 2007 and 2010 she won two Polish Academy grants, one for the book on Walt Whitman's tradition in Polish literature and culture and one for the book on series of translations that she is currently working on. Recently she published the book on "Polish Whitman" (2010) and a monograph on Witkacy's characters Wśród Witkacoidów. W świecie tekstów, w świecie mitów [Among Witkacoids. In the World of Texts, in the World of Myths], Wrocław: Wydawnictwo Uniwersytetu Wrocławskiego 2012.

Malgorzata Vražić received an MA and Ph.D. from Warsaw University, Institute of Polish Literature, Department of the Literature of Positivism and the Young Poland Period. Her dissertation was entitled Stanisław Witkiewicz and Witkacy – two paradigms of art, two visions of culture. She has been a lecturer at University of Warsaw and SWPS in Warsaw and is a member of Jury of Polish Language and Literature "Olympic" contest. She is a member of Laboratory of Modernism Literature of Central and Eastern Europe (Warsaw University) and cooperates with scientific and artistic magazine "Literacje." She has numerous publications including: "The reality, imagination and art – about Charles Baudelaire esthetics" (Warsaw 2004); "Narkotyki. Niemyte dusze – strange Witkacy's guide" (Warsaw 2004); "Witkiewicz – between ethics and esthetics problems" (Warsaw 2006); "Poetics of criminal novels by Marek Krajewski" (2006); "The faces of Thanatos in Witkacy's novels and art creativity"(Łódź 2007), "Illusions of narcissism. Cultural assertions by Witkacy" (Kraków 2010); "The acts of sins and regions of utopia – an essay about The story of a Sin by Stefan Żeromski" (Warsaw 2011); She is co-author of several scientific books: "Young Poland Period" (Kraków 2006); "Modernism: meetings. An anthology of texts"(Warsaw 2008); "Rewriting XIXth century"(Warsaw 2011).

Ewa Wąchocka, Professor, the Director of the Department of Theatre Studies at the University of Silesia (Katowice, Poland). She is occupied in the 20th century drama and theatre as well as theory of drama, she also practises as a theatre critic. Her publications include the following books: Między sztuką a filozofią. O teorii krytyki artystycznej Stanisława Ignacego Witkiewicza 1992 (Between Art and Philosophy. On Stanisław Ignacy Witkiewicz's Theory of Art Criticism), Od symbolizmu do post-teatru 1996 (From Symbolism to Post-Theatre), Autor i dramat 1999 (Author and Drama), Współczesne metody badań teatralnych 2003 (Modern Methodology of Theatre Research), and Milczenie w dwudziestowiecznym dramacie 2005 (Silence in the Twentieth century Drama) as well as articles in many collective works. She is the editor of Pohledy II – Punkty widzenia II 2004, Teatr – media – kultura 2006 (Theatre – Media – Culture) and Przestrzenie we współczesnym teatrze i dramacie 2009 (Spaces in the Contemporary Theatre and Drama), and she co-operates with Polish and German journals among others "Dialog," "Pamiętnik Literacki" and "Balagan. Slavisches Drama, Theater und Kino".

Anna Żakiewicz, PhD, Art Historian, Head of the Contemporary Prints and Drawings Department at the National Museum in Warsaw, Poland (which holds 123 works by Witkacy). She is the author of over 80 publications, mainly on Witkacy's paintings and their connections with his dramas and novels. She is the curator of 13 exhibitions (among others:

five shows of Witkacy's works) and participated in over 20 conferences (among others in Chicago and St Petersburg, delivering papers mainly on Witkacy; last year alone she presented the following papers: Reading Stevenson. Duality of Personality in Witkacy's Early Portraiture at the conference Rethinking Polish Modernism, Birbeck College, London, 12–13 June; and Witkacy's Painting as a Frozen Drama at the conference Witkacy as a Social and Political Visionary, the University of Westminster, London, 17–18 September. She is co-author and editor of the following websites: www.witkacy.hg.pl and www.mnw.art.pl. She is preparing a book The Small Boy's Youth on Witkacy's early works (executed before 1914) for publication in 2010. Presently, she is interested in the problem of hypertext and its role in contemporary literature and visual arts.

Beata Zgodzińska – Art Historian. She graduated from the Adam Mickiewicz University in Poznań in 1987 with an MA in history of art; she is the curator at the Museum of the Middle Pomerania in Słupsk and the head of History & Art Department; she is also responsible for the Museum's Witkacy collection; she has organised over 25 temporary exhibitions; and she has authored over 60 publications on nineteenth and twentieth-century art, culture and history, including nearly 20 studies on Witkacy.